Plastic Bodies:
Rebuilding Sensation After Phenomenology

New Metaphysics

Series Editors: Graham Harman and Bruno Latour

The world is due for a resurgence of original speculative metaphysics. The New Metaphysics series aims to provide a safe house for such thinking amidst the demoralizing caution and prudence of professional academic philosophy. We do not aim to bridge the analytic-continental divide, since we are equally impatient with nail-filing analytic critique and the continental reverence for dusty textual monuments. We favor instead the spirit of the intellectual gambler, and wish to discover and promote authors who meet this description. Like an emergent recording company, what we seek are traces of a new metaphysical 'sound' from any nation of the world. The editors are open to translations of neglected metaphysical classics, and will consider secondary works of especial force and daring. But our main interest is to stimulate the birth of disturbing masterpieces of twenty-first century philosophy.

Tom Sparrow
Plastic Bodies:
Rebuilding Sensation After Phenomenology

O
OPEN HUMANITIES PRESS
London 2015

First edition published by Open Humanities Press 2015
Freely available online at http://openhumanitiespress.org

Copyright © 2015 Tom Sparrow, Foreword copyright © 2015 Catharine Malabou

This is an open access book, licensed under a Creative Commons By Attribution Share Alike license. Under this license, authors allow anyone to download, reuse, reprint, modify, distribute, and/or copy this book so long as the authors and source are cited and resulting derivative works are licensed under the same or similar license. No permission is required from the authors or the publisher. Statutory fair use and other rights are in no way affected by the above. Read more about the license at creativecommons.org/licenses/by-sa/4.0

Design by Katherine Gillieson
Cover Illustration by Tammy Lu

The cover illustration is copyright Tammy Lu 2015, used under a
Creative Commons By Attribution license (CC-BY).

ISBN-13 978-1-78542-001-6

OPEN HUMANITIES PRESS

Open Humanities Press is an international, scholar-led open access publishing collective whose mission is to make leading works of contemporary critical thought freely available worldwide. More at http://openhumanitiespress.org

Contents

Acknowledgments   9

Abbreviations   11

Foreword: After the Flesh *by Catherine Malabou*   13

Introduction   21
1. Post-Dualist Embodiment, with Some Theses on Sensation   25
2. Synchronic Bodies and Environmental Orientation   67
3. Perception, Sensation, and the Problem of Violence   111
4. Sensibility, Susceptibility, and the Genesis of Individuals   144
5. On Aesthetic Plasticity   177

Conclusion: Plasticity and Power   219

Notes   237

Works Cited   274

For Fred Evans, tireless activist, teacher, and friend

Acknowledgments

This project was born at Duquesne University in Pittsburgh, Pennsylvania. During my time there I forged many friendships with faculty, staff, and students. Among those relationships several require recognition for the traces they have left on this book. Fred Evans not only taught me how to read Merleau-Ponty, he graciously and patiently helped me refine my central argument through its several iterations. I cannot imagine a more dedicated mentor or companion. Without Dan Selcer I would never have come to see the importance of philosophical method and I would have a much more routine grasp of the history of philosophy. George Yancy offered nothing but encouraging words and careful attention, even when I contacted him without warning at home. His encouragement will never cease. I am indebted to Silvia Benso of the Rochester Institute of Technology for agreeing to review my work on Levinas; her remarks on the text, even when critical, were always enthusiastic.

Among my other friends from Duquesne I must single out Pat Craig, John Fritz, Jacob Graham, Adam Hutchinson, Keith Martel, and Ryan Pfahl, all of whom contributed insight into my project and helped me think through its problems. Jim Swindal always was, and always will be, a vigilant advocate for me and the philosophical community at Duquesne. The directors of the Simon Silverman Phenomenology Center, first Dan Martino and now Jeff McCurry, always supported my work and accommodated me at the Center. Graham Harman has played a significant role in the formation of my own philosophical position, and his generous email correspondence from Cairo during the writing of my first draft was much appreciated. Now I thank him for allowing my book to find a home in his and Bruno Latour's "New Metaphysics" series. With the help of liaison Jon Cogburn, Mark Allan Ohm and Joel Andrepont readily accepted the task of translating Catherine Malabou's foreword. They did so with much-appreciated swiftness and skill. Finally, I am grateful to the two anonymous reviewers for Open Humanities Press who kindly asked me to craft portions of my text with more care and precision. Thanks to all of you.

Abbreviations

Texts by Levinas

EE	*Existence and Existents*
OB	*Otherwise than Being*
TI	*Totality and Infinity*
TO	*Time and the Other*

Texts by Merleau-Ponty

Child	"The Child's Relations with Others"
CD	"Cézanne's Doubt"
EM	"Eye and Mind"
ILVS	"Indirect Language and the Voices of Silence"
Nature	*Nature*
PP	*Phenomenology of Perception*
PrP	"The Primacy of Perception"
Shadow	"The Philosopher and His Shadow"
VI	*The Visible and the Invisible*

Foreword

After the Flesh

by Catherine Malabou

Translated by Mark Allan Ohm and Joel Andrepont

The body becomes worthy of philosophical examination when it is no longer a question of *the* body but of *my* body. Husserl introduces a fundamental distinction between *Körper*, the objective, anatomico-physiological body, and *Leib*, one's own body [*le corps propre*], the living body, the place of sensations and emotions, the "flesh." This distinction marks a decisive development in his thinking and saves the body from being merely an object of conceptual devaluation. By rejecting the methods of descriptive psychology in order to establish a transcendental phenomenology, Husserl grants a constitutive role to the "flesh" as lived body. *My* body must be considered in its individuality, its *incarnation* or *embodiment* (*Verleiblichung*), which amounts to considering the living corporeal body [*le vécu corporel*] in the purity of its manifestation. My body is a token of my own immediate worldly presence; it presents to the mind what Husserl calls *hyletic data* (the body's perceptual, sensory content, like touch, look, voice, kinaesthesia). In this way, the body becomes the worldly presence of an intentional subject's mental life.

The phenomenological body stands in the sphere of immanence (the sensation that I have of my body's immediate presence in the world), a sphere which, after the *epoché*, is reduced to the presence of the thing itself.

Sensation means that the thing reveals itself in the flesh and stands there before our eyes as something given to itself and in actuality.

The Husserlian analyses of the living corporeal body once again mark a major advancement in the history of philosophy. As a result of these analyses, the body, quite simply, acquires a value equal to that of the mind. The mind is no longer separable from the flesh that it animates and which gives it corporeal spatiality.

We can therefore ask whether it is possible to go further in this recognition of the essential status of the incarnate body than phenomenology does. It seems not. Even researchers in the cognitive sciences and the philosophy of mind still draw from Husserl: Francisco Varela, Alva Noë, Evan Thompson, and Shaun Gallagher, to name but a few, situate their work within his direct lineage. Is the phenomenological approach to the body impossible to overcome?

In an incredibly daring gesture, Tom Sparrow responds in the negative, and attempts to clear the way for nothing less than a *post-phenomenological* approach to the body.

Sparrow is clearly well aware of the considerable debt that continental philosophy owes to phenomenology. Phenomenology made possible several claims about the body: that it is not the case that the body is the tomb of the soul, as Plato claimed; that it is not the case that the body is a neutral extension caught in the movement which animates it, as Descartes showed; and that the body is much more than the place of sensibility, as Kant defined it. In fact, the senses always grasp things as they are for the consciousness that perceives them. It is in this way that corporeal space acquires its identity within the general realm of extension [*l'étendue générale*]. Thus there is no *a priori* spatial body. Despite all of this, Sparrow writes: "I attempt to build a theory of embodiment that could only come *after* phenomenology."

Why must we distance ourselves from the phenomenological approach to the body? Isn't the notion of embodiment essential? Hasn't it been used since in all the human sciences? Nonetheless, Sparrow maintains that we now need a "post-phenomenological perspective." "By this," he writes, "I mean a perspective which is not simply anti-phenomenological, but one which has gone through phenomenology and retained its kernel of truth, even if this kernel proves to be non-phenomenological in nature."

The problem is the following: I just said that the phenomenological conception of the *Leib* made possible the de-objectification of the body. But this necessary de-objectification has been clearly accompanied by a *de-materialization*. If the flesh was essential as the future of the physical body, now we need to question the future of the flesh. For this reason, the *materiality of the body* must be rethought. Sparrow argues that the phenomenological flesh in fact lacks matter. We need to reconceptualize matter. How can we avoid lapsing into both the naturalization and neutrality of the body? How can we conceive of matter without reverting to mechanism? In order to properly distinguish matter from mechanism, we will call this post-phenomenological materiality *plasticity*. Plasticity is thus defined as that which comes after the flesh.

The task is therefore to rethink the union between the material and the meaningful, which "does not necessarily entail the reduction of the mind to the brain, or consciousness to synaptic/neural activity." Nevertheless, it involves a rematerialization; sensation is the key to the process and will aid us in our understanding.

But first let us insist on an intermediary path. In order to examine the insufficiencies of the phenomenological concept of the flesh, Sparrow begins by pluralizing the theories of embodiment. In an entirely unexpected manner, he confronts the two extremes of the phenomenological specter: Merleau-Ponty and Levinas. They also criticized Husserl in their own way in the name of a certain materiality: "I see the aesthetics of Levinas and Merleau-Ponty as indispensable for reconciling a pluralistic conception of embodiment, even if ultimately the two thinkers hold incompatible metaphysical positions." Comparing these two philosophers allows us to understand what their critiques of classical phenomenology fail to do in order to become a *materialist phenomenology*, a philosophical undertaking Sparrow proposes to provide the grounds for: "My own view of the body as plastic emerges through an exploration of the phenomenologies of Merleau-Ponty and Levinas, with whom I travel up to the point at which they no longer pursue the questions that I would like answered by a theory of embodiment."

Merleau-Ponty and "Reversible Bodies"

Husserl insisted that the models of Euclidean geometry were incompatible with the perception of the reality of one's own body insofar as things are only represented in perception in the context of a geometry of surfaces. We can perceive neither the six faces of a cube nor the totality of our own body. Husserl argues that human perception includes the supplementary dimension of the infinite, including time in the perception of space (Riemannian space). In this way, the dynamics of a spatial body is integrated into perception itself. Thus, there is a perceptual creation of a dynamic image of the body, adding kinesthetic variations of the body of the thing to the dynamic image of our own movement in the spatial encounter. For example, if I walk toward a tree which is in my spatial field, the tree moves toward me just as much as I move toward it. We can therefore contrast this phenomenon, called a Riemannian image, with Euclidean perception.

For Merleau-Ponty, however, Husserl does not go far enough in grasping the interaction between body and world. Merleau-Ponty believes that his conception of the corporeal schema makes up for this lacuna. In the *Phenomenology of Perception* in particular, Merleau-Ponty himself makes use of the notion of plasticity. Plasticity is directly linked to being-in-the-world and to how the body develops its mediating role in the world. "[T]he … subject penetrates into the object by perception, assimilating its structure into his substance, and through this body the object directly regulates his movements."[1] Composed of habits, circuits, and sensorimotor schemata organized through sensory and comportmental experience, the corporeal schema already materializes the living body inasmuch as the latter can no longer distinguish its own flesh from that of the world.

The "reversible body" is both touching and touched, and the limit that separates a body from the world as well as from other bodies is, precisely, a plastic limit, that is, a malleable and pliable limit. Sparrow reminds us that: "By 'reversible' Merleau-Ponty means that at any moment the one who sees can become the one seen, or the one who touches can become the touched." Merleau-Ponty completes the material liberation of the concept of intersubjectivity, which Husserl still considers in relation to one's own selfhood [*égoïté*].

Despite all this, Sparrow argues that the corporeal schema still remains too personal [*individuel*], too anchored in an identity which can evolve, but which nevertheless remains what it is. In both Merleau-Ponty and Husserl, the integrity of one's own body in a sense resists its transformation through the materiality of the world. Examples from pathology demonstrate this resistance. For Merleau-Ponty, illness engenders a loss of identity, that is, a loss rather than a transformation of plasticity: "In the patient the perceptual field has lost this plasticity. ... The world in its entirety no longer suggests any meaning to him and conversely the meanings which occur to him are not embodied any longer in the given world."[2] The loss of plasticity entails a modification of the corporeal schema, this "system of equivalents ... whereby the different motor tasks are instantaneously transferable."[3] Of course, this loss is at least partially compensated for in the illness. But, for Merleau-Ponty, it is clear that compensating plasticity is not as strong as the primary formative plasticity of being-in-the-world. The meaning that it confers is an accidental meaning, without autonomy, which effectively initiates no new modality of being-in-the-world. "Illness," writes Merleau-Ponty,

> is a complete form of existence and the procedures which it employs to replace normal functions which have been destroyed are equally pathological phenomena. It is impossible to deduce the normal from the pathological, deficiencies from the substitute functions, by a mere change of the sign. We must take substitutions as substitutions, as allusions to some fundamental function that they are striving to make good, and the direct image of which they fail to furnish.[4]

Plasticity can thus be lost, and with it the integrity of the schema.

Levinas and "Susceptible Bodies"

Perhaps it is necessary to think that I am not in my body. Perhaps my body does not first say I, but you. Perhaps it characterizes itself in the first place by an absolute passivity through which the alterity of the flesh manifests itself to itself. Levinas maintains that "the subject cannot stay identical to itself."

Let us begin from Levinas's critique of Husserl. Sparrow writes that "Levinas's objection to phenomenological method is straightforward: if the objectifying acts of theoretical consciousness, what Husserl calls meaning-giving (*Sinngebung*) acts, are our primary mode of access to things, then those things can only appear to us as representations whose content is predetermined by the representing subject. In short, phenomenology becomes a modified transcendental idealism."

It is therefore a matter of breaking with representation. For Levinas, the distinction between the body and objects of the world tends to blur, but also opens up a material dimension to sensation. For him, there is no corporeal schema strictly speaking, but a *dwelling* in others. In my home, I am in the home of another. My furniture is hers. I am nourished by her presence, which is simultaneously inexhaustible. Passive joy [*la jouissance de la passivité*] is established on the horizon of desire. We could not know how to praise the striking beauty of the analysis of everydayness in *Totality and Infinity*, where nourishment, dwelling, and ornaments are described with as much ethical care and attention as are individuals. Everything is infinitely *susceptible*, and consequently, there is no *totality* [*tout*] but an infinity of encounters.

Nonetheless, Levinas rejects the concept of plasticity. The other, he writes, is never what "appear[s] in plastic form as an image, a portrait." Its beauty is this "supreme presence ... breaking through its plastic form with youth,"[5] which is why the other resists. Plasticity remains confined to the sculptural domain, bound to its function of embodiment or figuration in general, an enduring [*attardée*] function, always older than the face. The face, precisely, is not plastic; on the contrary, it can only "break through its own plastic image,"[6] "break up form."[7] It stands beyond form. It is a pure trace: "This existence abandoned by all and by itself, a trace of itself, imposed on *me*, assigns me in my last refuge with an incomparable force of assignation, inconvertible into forms [which] would give me at once a countenance."[8]

While the appearance of the face, its "epiphany" always provokes an emotional and sensible overturning (for another as well as for me), this overturning is not based on a transformation but on an abrupt break [*écart brusque*] without material or physiological genesis: "The face of the Other at each moment destroys and overflows the plastic image it leaves me...."[9] And this destruction is unimpeded [*sans procès*]: "The absolute experience is not disclosure but revelation: a coinciding of the expressed with him who expresses, which is the privileged manifestation of the Other, the manifestation of a face over and beyond form. Form— incessantly betraying its own manifestation, congealing into a plastic form, for it is adequate to the same—alienates the exteriority of the other."[10]

Is not this denial of plasticity Levinas's admission of resistance to the materiality that he continually celebrates elsewhere? Behind this denial isn't there the reaffirmation of the *fleshly* [*charnel*] character of the face, in the phenomenological sense of the term, with all the authenticity, spirituality, and invariability that this fleshly character entails?

Plasticity as the Future of the Flesh

Sparrow claims that "what is missing in [these views] is the practical or embodied dimension of sensation, or affirmation that it is sensation that delivers the materiality of the world to sensibility." And later he writes that "instead of reversibility and susceptibility, my view features the *plasticity* of the body and argues that the dynamism of plasticity is more true to the aesthetic dimension of existence as well as the transactional nature of intercorporeal encounters."

How can we understand this new plasticity? How can we simultaneously understand this new "aesthetics," which is presented here as both a theory of sensation and a theory of beauty?

In order to understand plasticity, we must begin from the *plastic material*, since it is plasticity which first necessitated its name. For Merleau-Ponty, the reversibility of touching-touched alludes to elasticity more than plasticity. "Plastic" refers to a material that cannot retrieve its original form once sculpted or molded. The plastic material retains the trace of its deformation. In this sense, plasticity inhibits reversibility. It also inhibits Levinasian *susceptibility* in the sense that the plastic is also an explosive material, which suspends the face-to-face encounter and assures its destructive violence of all alterity.

Of course, the flesh of the body and the flesh of the world are one. Nevertheless, this unity owes as much to the matter of things of the world as to the intentionality of the animate or incarnate body. Matter is also what destroys. Matter is also what has no body. Matter is also what forms the body precisely by contrasting the body with its objectality. Sparrow's analyses of the body-matter couple are extraordinary in their beauty, evocative power, and precision.

A case in point is his analysis of architecture. Sparrow draws from Juhani Pallasmaa's work, according to which "bodies adopt the structures of buildings in their skeletal structure and bodily sensations." Another astonishing passage draws from Yukio Mishima, who described his experience of bodybuilding in *Sun and Steel*: "His body lives from, metabolizes the steel no less than the sun. His body engages organic and inorganic matter and, enacting an unnatural participation, converts both into muscle. ... The idea that Mishima metabolizes sun and steel is more than metaphor. His body is sculpted and polished by repetitive exposure to metal and solar energy. Sun and steel territorialize his body and augment his vitality."

By taking up Merleau-Ponty's notion of habit, staying in tune with Levinas's hospitality, and recalling Husserl's fascinating pages in *Ideen* II, Sparrow clears his own path, which consists in inserting mechanical parts, shards of metal, stones, and machines into the body of phenomenology. Its plasticity delineates the space of a sensation and a sensibility that objectivizes the world by constructing it as one creates a work of art, a performance, an installation, or as one takes flight. Halfway between Husserl and Simondon, Merleau-Ponty and James, Levinas, Deleuze, and Dewey, Sparrow invites us to question this new dimension where the body is no longer the flesh. Plastic disembodiment is presented as a new economy of the sensible.

Here is not just another rehashing of the traditional division between the integrity of the phenomenological body, on the one hand, and its deconstruction, on the other. The incorporeal materials are neither signs nor symptoms nor immaterial things. We are beyond the difference between presence and the critique of metaphysics. It is no longer a matter of deciding between autoaffected and deterritorialized bodies.

The materialist phenomenology presented here is a rupture. A conservative rupture, of course, but a rupture nonetheless. A *rupture in formation*, like our bodies are.

Introduction

This is a book about embodiment, one of the cardinal themes of contemporary philosophy. This is also a book about phenomenology, which has done more than any other school to bring the body to the center of philosophical analysis. But this is not a book *of* phenomenology. While it draws liberally from the resources of phenomenology, the idea of embodiment assembled in its pages is quite often at odds with the first-person orientation of the phenomenological method. It is therefore as much about the limits of phenomenology as it is about the limits of the body. In the last analysis it is really about how we might rebuild the somewhat unfashionable concept of sensation following the rescue attempts made by Maurice Merleau-Ponty and Emmanuel Levinas.

Phenomenology is a natural place to begin this project, but not the right place to end it. This is because sensation, as I understand it here, is unsuitable for proper phenomenological investigation. It does not present itself phenomenally as an object of consciousness, or as what Husserl calls an intentional object. Sensation is something that happens *below* the phenomenal level, so at best it is a mediated datum of consciousness. Both Merleau-Ponty and Levinas recognized this. How, then, can we speak of this non-phenomenal sensation? My contention is that we experience it primarily through its *effects* and can thereby think it on the basis of these effects. Perception, passion, cognition, consciousness, identity, and freedom are some of these effects. These are indeed accessed phenomenally, but as *products* of sensation. This is not to say that sensation is their efficient cause, however. It is to say that sensation is their necessary condition. Sensation is thus an object as well-suited for speculation as it is for empirical analysis. Both Merleau-Ponty and Levinas explicitly opposed the latter, naturalistic, approach to sensation from the perspective of the former, and it is their perspective that I try to radicalize in this book.

To be clear: I am not attempting a phenomenology of sensation, and neither were Merleau-Ponty and Levinas. What I do is to take up their speculative remarks about sensation and develop these into a novel theory of embodiment, but one markedly more speculative than phenomenological. If I had to give a name to this project, I would call it a *speculative aesthetics*, although it certainly falls short of a comprehensive treatise. If its speculative dimension seems too programmatic, consider it a promise of future work. As it stands, it provides a constructive reading of the phenomenology of the body, but in the service of a non-phenomenological metaphysics.

Sensation is thus approached from two perspectives, the phenomenological and the speculative. A simple twofold argument is presented: *sensation is the basic material of subjectivity; as such, sensation is responsible in a non-trivial way for the subject's power to exist.* In question throughout the text is the function and constitution of the aesthetic dimension of embodiment, specifically the autonomous reality of sensation (*aisthesis*) and the materiality of aesthetics. Insofar as this materiality operates on the body below the level of conscious reflection, which is to say, imperceptibly, it resists phenomenological analysis. Phenomenology indeed has much to teach us about what it is like to live through sensations, but a hybrid method that draws upon phenomenology while simultaneously exceeding it is required to circumscribe the concept of sensation. Methodologically speaking, I approach phenomenology historically, not as a practitioner. I do not proceed from the *epoché* or phenomenological reduction, nor do I adhere to any specific phenomenological principles or its correlationism. It seems to me that if one claims to be doing phenomenology, then there must be at least some principles (the reductions, eidetic variation, for instance) guiding one's investigation. Otherwise, in what sense is it a method? As I have not identified and implemented any specific phenomenological principles, I cannot say that my view is the product of the phenomenological method. Instead, phenomenology appears here as an object of historical investigation and a tool for conceptual engineering.

Since I am primarily interested in how phenomenology fits into the history of embodiment, I do not conduct an exhaustive reading of the oeuvres of Merleau-Ponty and Levinas, nor do I perform a reconstruction of what their philosophies really strive to accomplish. The texts of phenomenology are taken up with the express aim of developing a theory of embodiment which takes sensation as its leading concept, something that cannot be done without looking carefully at the aesthetics of phenomenology. This entails an ambivalent reading of Merleau-Ponty. On the one hand, I draw liberally from his phenomenology of perception and the immense contribution he makes to the philosophy of embodiment and aesthetic theory. On the other hand, I insist on the basic immaterialism and anthropocentrism of his philosophy, which I attribute to his allegiance to phenomenology and non-Cartesian dualist ontology. As for Levinas, I admittedly read his work heretically. This simply means that I downplay his ethical program—which is, for many Levinasians, the essence of his philosophy—and emphasize instead his contribution to the metaphysics of embodiment, which is often overshadowed in the literature. Merleau-Ponty and Levinas set the stage for this book precisely because they inaugurate a renewal of the concept of sensation. But this renewal is not just the work of phenomenology; or, it cannot be completed by phenomenology. Both thinkers are also metaphysicians, and it is necessary to see how their respective (and in many ways univocal) responses to the history of philosophy square with what comes before and after them. My justification for calling them metaphysicians derives from the fact that they often make speculative claims that lack phenomenological evidence. Instead of seeing these claims simply as a breach of method, I take them as gestures toward an emergent philosophy of the body.

Naturally, it will be asked why I bother working through phenomenology at all. The reason is again historical. It is certainly true that the presuppositions—or purported lack thereof—of phenomenology and the other currents of twentieth-century philosophy diverge significantly. There are, however, more points of contact between phenomenology and, say, Deleuze and Spinoza, than usually acknowledged by partisan readings of the history of twentieth-century French philosophy. While I do think that readers must at the end of the day make some decisions about the relative merits of Merleau-Ponty and Foucault, or Levinas and Deleuze, to see their respective projects as mutually exclusive is to ignore the common history of their inquiries and to simplify a complex relationship.

The kind of philosophy undertaken here could not have occurred before phenomenology turned to the body. Philosophers were thinking about and analyzing bodies before the twentieth century, of course, but their concerns were often quite different from those debated in the last century. For instance, where early modern philosophers like Leibniz and Spinoza were eager to determine the metaphysical constitution of individual bodies and, indeed, ask whether or not individuals actually exist, contemporary thinkers of embodiment are primarily concerned with how the body informs knowledge acquisition, gender and racial identity, or intersubjectivity. Embodiment is now thoroughly incorporated into almost all the human sciences and phenomenology has been integral to this incorporation. It has even gained ground with analytic philosophers. What is called for now, however, is a *post*-phenomenological perspective. By this I mean a perspective which is not simply anti-phenomenological, but one which has gone through phenomenology and retained its kernel of truth, even if this kernel proves to be non-phenomenological in nature. For me, this is the truth of *plasticity*.

Therefore, I attempt to build a theory of embodiment that could only come *after* phenomenology. But I also retrieve a pre-phenomenological, occasionally pre-critical perspective, one which draws liberally from the materialist and empiricist traditions to see what effects they can produce today. In this respect this book is a work of metaphysics. It does not claim to have invented a brand new theory of the body, but to have mobilized several philosophical traditions and rebuilt the body using a diverse team of thinkers.

Chapter 1

Post-Dualist Embodiment, with Some Theses on Sensation

> Like a clever thief hidden inside a house, breathing quietly, waiting until everyone's asleep. I have looked deep inside myself, trying to detect something that might be there. But just as our consciousness is a maze, so too is our body. Everywhere you turn there's darkness, and a blind spot. Everywhere you find silent hints, everywhere a surprise is waiting for you.
>
> Murakami, *What I Talk About When I Talk About Running*

Problem and Method

Most of us experience our bodies daily as supported and resisted by the features of our environment—the solid earth, the smooth surfaces of our homes, the climate controlled rooms we work and play in. A wooden chair supports my weight as I type, a woolen duvet insulates me while I sleep. This point can be put in grander terms, as Glen Mazis has: "On an immediate level, we feel as though the earth is still. On a deeper level, we feel held by an embracing earth. It actively holds onto us, giving us the weight to walk, work, and love. The earth is not just inert, but a protector actively engaged with us."[11] Occasionally we are given over to the realization that the spaces we move through possess the power to overwhelm or destroy us.

The violence may surface from within as an untamed passion, or as a chance affliction or retraction of the environment's material support. César Aira's *An Episode in the Life of a Landscape Painter* allegorizes the possibility in this description of a lightning strike:

> What happened next bypassed his senses and went straight into his nervous system. In other words, it was over very quickly; it was pure action, a wild concatenation of events. The storm broke suddenly with a spectacular lightning bolt that traced a zig-zag arc clear across the sky. … The thunder crashing down impossibly enveloped him in millions of vibrations. The horse began to turn beneath him. It was still turning when a lightning bolt struck him on the head. Like a nickel statue, man and beast were lit up with electricity. For one horrific moment, regrettably to be repeated, Rugendas witnessed the spectacle of his body shining.[12]

Certain bodily transformations never present themselves phenomenally. Or they do, but only after they have happened, like an afterimage whose original image is forever lost. They affect us unwittingly, spontaneously causing a malfunction or disablement of the body that consciousness never directly witnesses. Common among these events is death, which, as Epicurus teaches, "is nothing to us, for that which is dissolved is *without sensation*; and that which lacks sensation is nothing to us."[13] Epicurus may be right about our experience of death, but I hope to show that he is wrong about corpses. Sensation, I will claim, is something undergone by animate and inanimate bodies alike, but it is undergone in such a way that we tend to forget it ever happened or that it is happening at every moment. Death, too, is happening at this very moment—for most of us, so imperceptibly that we only regard ourselves as *living* bodies.

No one will deny that environments impact identities. Home, school, work, and travel accumulate in us. The familiar, the public, the common become us. That we are where we come from is a truth readily affirmed by everyone. How does this happen? The present book provides a response to this question by investigating the promises and limits of phenomenology for conceptualizing the nature of bodies and their relation to the environment. Principally it asks: *What individuates a body? What constitutes its structural integrity? Of what is the body capable?* These questions are answered both indirectly and directly through collaborative and critical engagements with Merleau-Ponty and Levinas, both of whom offer in their analyses of sensation and sensibility directives rooted in, and gesturing beyond, the subjectivity of the "lived body." Since sensation is not often featured in phenomenological discussions, and because sensation, I contend, is necessary for conceiving both the activity and passivity of the body, its legitimacy as a philosophical concept is also defended. The turn to sensation in Merleau-Ponty and Levinas marks a significant departure from the residual idealism of Husserlian phenomenology—indeed, from the history of philosophy after Kant. In a sense, then, what I attempt here is a rescue of sensation from its devastation at the hands of the Critical philosophy. Phenomenology, I try to demonstrate, gets this rescue off the ground.

Sensation's revitalization has ontological and practical consequences that are nascent in phenomenology, but which cannot be fully captured by phenomenological analyses beholden to constructivist epistemology and aligned with anti-realist metaphysics. Therefore, I will eventually break with Merleau-Ponty and Levinas to deploy a realist metaphysics of sensation, one which thinks the body as a shining spectacle charged with forces uncontrived by eye or mind.

The movement beyond phenomenology raises ethical and political questions about how we should and should not comport our bodies toward others; it also poses questions about how we impact and structure our environments. But these derive from the more fundamental question of bodily relations. The problem of how we as individuals actually relate to other individuals, or how it is possible for one person to interact with, act upon, or know another individual must be addressed before we can draw up prescriptions. The relation question is epistemological and ontological; traditionally it has manifested as the problem of other minds or, more recently, the problem of intersubjectivity. These problems underlie the ongoing discussion of corporeal difference and its ethico-political consequences in contemporary continental philosophy. The saliency of these specific problems, however, only makes obvious sense in a dualist's metaphysical framework. It is of course possible to see the ethical and ontological as articulated or collapsed into each other, as in the monism of Spinoza. One of the principal challenges for post-dualist philosophy, Spinozist or other, is how to come to terms with this collapse.

Non-dualists like Spinoza must first explain how individuals emerge as individuals. Only then can they trouble themselves with how individuals can and should interact. The problem of individuation fascinated early modern philosophers as much as it is resurgent in contemporary thinkers like Simondon, Deleuze, DeLanda, Badiou and others. The dualist's problem of how I come to know the mind of another person, when all I perceive is the behavior of that person, only arises if he actually encounters another as an individual and believes that beyond his or her body there lies an ontologically unique thing called a mind. This is of course the ontology of Descartes, but it is also the ontology of Kant, who sees personhood as constituted by the hybrid of extended human body/non-extended, rational, and self-legislating ego.

From a practical viewpoint dualist ontology is a brilliant way to safeguard the freedom and, consequently, responsibility of the individual, because dualism acknowledges the body's subjection to causal laws while at the same time placing the mind/soul/ego/person at an infinite remove from the causal sphere. That is, outside the genesis of history. So, for instance, Kant's *Critique of Pure Reason*, which is not primarily a work in practical philosophy, makes the point of specifying the dual nature of the self in order to protect the freedom of the will from the determinations of causality.[14] The body suffers in the empirical world while the ego enjoys its isolation in the transcendental sphere; the *integrity* (moral and structural) of the person transcends, and in a sense structures, the corporeal world. Some consequences entailed in this distinction permit Kant to refer his ethical and political philosophy back to his epistemological, ontological, and aesthetic philosophies. These provide a strategic ontological foundation for his critique of practical reason and metaphysics of morals.[15] By entwining, without collapsing, the practical and ontological in the transcendental sphere, Kant can then assert in the *Critique of Judgment* that it is possible for aesthetic judgment of the dynamically sublime to "consider nature as a might that has no dominance over us" and, consequently, to awaken "in our power of reason, a different and nonsensible standard" derived from "the superiority [of the mind] over nature itself in its immensity."[16] Since the

Kantian subject sits outside of natural events, it is able to feel pleasure in the face of terrifying spectacles like natural disasters, and even exploit such events to reassert its intellectual power over, and freedom from, the material effects of nature.[17] Ironically, the feeling of powerlessness generated in the subject in the face of the sublime gets translated into a moral sentiment that then triggers the supersensible moral command which, as Kant phrases it, "obligates absolutely"[18] and evinces the moral superiority of humans over nature. As Paul Guyer puts it, "[the spectacle of the dynamical sublime] gives us the courage to measure ourselves against the physical power of nature and, in so doing, reveals the imperviousness of our purely moral character to threats from nature."[19] The systematic link between aesthetics and morality is possible, for Kant, because the subject is essentially conceived as an intellectual being with "unlimited freedom,"[20] not a corporeal being susceptible to the directives of the natural world.

The remarkable strength of the dualist position on subjectivity rests on how it logically reinforces the metaphysical with the practical, and vice versa, while leaving the intellectual or interior world uncontaminated by concrete events. Moreover, it opens an ethical space in which the sensible is subject to the judgments of the supersensible, while the sensible as such is afforded no inherent practical value. The capability and freedom of the individual are effectively immunized from the corporeality of other individuals as well the influences of the material world.

The embodied view of subjectivity that I will draw out of Merleau-Ponty and Levinas, among others, contests the dualist dichotomy along with its ethical and political implications. It not only assigns itself the task of accounting for the emergence of the subject, it also raises the difficulty of deriving a non-formal ethical imperative from the sensible realm without committing the naturalistic fallacy.[21] My conclusion argues that the formality of Kant's practical philosophy neglects the aesthetics of embodiment we find in Merleau-Ponty and Levinas, and that this neglect results from a difference of ontology. From the perspective of embodied subjectivity, we cannot maintain a basic distinction between our aesthetic and moral sensibilities, as though they belong to two distinct capacities or "faculties." We cannot concur with Kant that our moral sensibility operates in a space that cannot be traversed by the directives of corporeal life, or rather, that ultimately our affective life is at best the servant of our intellectual judgment. Instead, the material form of our moral sensibility and its ethical imperatives must be submitted as a replacement for the Kantian model.

Of course, the monist and materialist traditions, from Democritus to Hobbes, Spinoza, Marx and beyond have always contested the dualist's ontology and resolved the intersubjective problem in various ways. But, at least since Hegel, the dualist framework has been under attack from a perspective that can generally be called non-dualism or, perhaps, post-dualism. Hegel responds to Kant's partitioning of the world into noumenal and phenomenal regions by insisting on the superfluity of the noumenal. The *Phenomenology of Spirit* effectively demonstrates that the noumenal realm is unnecessary for explaining the movement of thought or history, and cannot be legitimately garnered from the Kantian critical project. Yet it would seem odd to apply the monist label to Hegel's philosophy. Likewise, it is not necessarily a materialism because it allows for the existence of forces (Spirit, Concept) that are neither physical in nature nor subject to causal laws. Bergson's *élan vital* would be an analogous force, one which shifts his non-dualist philosophy away from materialism and into vitalism. Nietzsche, too, could also be considered a non-dualist, yet non-materialist, philosopher. Nietzsche is too much of a psychoanalyst to be an eliminativist, and his philosophy of the body displays a complex understanding of both the quantitative and qualitative, physical and cosmological, as well as the aleatory dimensions of experience. And yet, he is more than willing to (almost) reduce consciousness to a dynamism of forces.[22]

What is the metaphysical status of these immaterial concepts or their counterparts in the phenomenological tradition, which worries more about overcoming dualism than it does about fending off charges of monism? If they are neither physical nor spiritual, where do we situate Hegel's Spirit, Nietzsche's force, or Bergson's *élan*? A central challenge for post-dualism is to overcome dualism without arresting motion, that is, without reducing animation to mechanism. The attempt at a non-reductive post-dualist ontology is alive in both Merleau-Ponty and Levinas. This is one of their primary attractions.

I acknowledge that it is problematic to place phenomenologists like Merleau-Ponty and Levinas into classical categories. But why, for instance, does Merleau-Ponty's late notion of "the flesh" (*la chair*) not result in a monist ontology, a monism of the flesh? Or, why does the identification of the self with the body not admit of a monism, as is sometimes contended?[23] Commentators prefer to cast what would otherwise be his monism as Merleau-Ponty's "philosophy of immanence," but it remains necessary to understand why this distinction is not merely nominal. The primacy of perception thesis—that is, the thesis that the world of perception is borne of perception—paradoxically holds that bodies and things are individuated prior to my perception *and* that subject and object are internally related and originate in perception. This avoids the standard version of dualism, but it also implies a contradiction. The apparent contradiction dissolves when we see that *from the perspective of perception* subject and object emerge together (idealism), but *from the ontological perspective* objects exist independently of the human perceiver (realism). Nevertheless, both subject and object belong to a single flesh, the sensible as such, whose purpose as a concept is to deflate the quarrel between idealism and realism about subjects and objects. Still, there is a pervasive conceptual dualism in Merleau-Ponty's texts, as Renaud Barbaras has catalogued: "clearly in the final analysis of the body in terms of sensing and sensed, touching and touched, subject of the world and part of the world. Such conceptual pairs are just so many displaced modalities of the duality of consciousness and object."[24]

The ontological situation is no less conflicted in Levinas. Why should we not consider Levinas's elemental philosophy in *Totality and Infinity* a monism? And the question of the transcendence of the human Other (*autrui*) as a reformulation of the problem of other minds? What makes these two thinkers post-dualist? What resources do they offer us for building theories of subjectivity and intersubjectivity that genuinely challenge the Cartesian and Kantian legacies? I contend that it is their phenomenological ontology of the body and its tendency to draw conclusions that *transgress* the bounds of phenomenological method that make the French phenomenologists allies of post-dualism. Additionally, at times we find Merleau-Ponty and Levinas reluctant to commit fully to the centrality of the body for fear that such a commitment would result in a fully immanent ontology inhospitable to the transcendence of the phenomenon, in Merleau-Ponty's case, and the Other, in Levinas's. Advances in contemporary philosophies of immanence give us more and more reason to see their fear as unfounded.

Using Kant as a contrastive perspective throughout, I will defend a corporeal ontology assembled from and against the phenomenological resources of Merleau-Ponty and Levinas. Corporeal ontology signifies a view of the subject as embedded in, immanent to, extended throughout, continuous with, and generated by its material environment and every one of the other bodies that populate it. This is not an endorsement of reductionism. On the contrary, it is partly a phenomenological thesis, and I will use phenomenological evidence to support it. I insist, however, that we need to move beyond the phenomenological perspective in order to account for the elements of embodied subjectivity that phenomenology's agent-centered methodology often disregards or puts out of play. This requires a careful articulation of the materiality of the body and its genesis, one which staves off reductionism and ventures certain speculative remarks about the life of the body. In short, the phenomenology of the body requires a non-phenomenological supplement in order to provide a comprehensive account of embodiment. I provide this supplement by attending to the sensitive/sensory[25] life of the body, by reworking the concept of sensation, and by enlisting a number of critics of phenomenology to build a theory of embodiment that remains forever nascent in Merleau-Ponty and Levinas.

In recent decades contemporary philosophy witnessed a turn to the body that threatened the dominance of dualist ontologies along with the dualist practical philosophies they generate. The literature of feminist, race, and queer theory attests to this. As does the literature of deconstruction.[26] The corporeal turn constitutes one of the most recent attempts to develop the post-dualist project and complicate our pictures of subjectivity, intersubjectivity, and community. This is because the body is now largely regarded as the locus of *all* aspects of subjectivity, not just the practical. The mind is no longer conceived as independent from, and thus invulnerable to, the operations of its material environment.[27] Indeed, it is dependent upon and, for some, identical to the environment. More on this later. When the subject is conceived *as* a body, as identical to its body, the problems as well as the solutions entailed in dualism begin to wither away; the problem of how the mind interacts with the body disappears. But the post-dualist framework also raises a number of new questions, particularly about the nature of the subject and the workings of its mind, its will, and its freedom to act. These are questions we will address along the way, and provide a closer look at in the concluding chapter. Moreover, we see the epistemological problem of other minds morph into the ontological problems of alterity and individuation. Intercorporeity, rather than intersubjectivity, more accurately describes the new problematic. Now, instead of asking how we *know* other beings, we are led to ask how it is possible for other beings *to be* other. What constitutes their difference and what makes possible our interaction with them? What is the nature of this interaction and is it possible to avoid violence as I engage the other? How, if individuals actually exist, does an individual become autonomous?

In the post-dualist framework the ontological and practical aspects of these questions cannot be separated. Because the subject is always already embedded in a practical environment and is in every way a historical product of that environment, what the subject *does* must be seen as identical to what the subject *is*. Ethics, politics, and ontology must be regarded as enmeshed at the most basic level. The remarks that follow attempt to stake out a position on this new terrain and to situate this position in both contemporary and historical contexts.

The Permanence of the Problem of Embodiment

Evidence that the embodied subject is currently enjoying great success, and will most likely continue to do so in the future, can be gleaned from the proliferation of works in feminist philosophy, critical race theory, and environmental philosophy, to name just a few of the places where the body is at the center of analysis. The continuing interest in the work of Merleau-Ponty and the emphatic return of Spinoza in disparate disciplines from political philosophy (Negri, Balibar) to neuroscience (Damasio), as well as recent attempts to retrieve the embodied dimension of Kant, Hegel, Husserl, and Heidegger lend further credence to the claim that the embodied subject is uprooting its Cartesian counterpart.[28] This suggests that the recurrent narrative which laments the forgetting or denigration of the body in the

Western philosophical tradition is losing its timeliness. This is a promising, if modest, victory over entrenched philosophical prejudices. Perhaps even more suggestive is the fact that the body has gained momentum in the philosophy of mind, particularly in studies of the embodied mind, a movement driven by thinkers like George Lakoff and Mark Johnson, Andy Clark, Alva Noë, Evan Thompson, Shaun Gallagher, Francisco Varela, Bernard Andrieu, Antonio Damasio, and others. This movement seeks to provide a non-dualist, post-Cartesian solution to the mind-body problem that not only takes seriously the progress of cognitive science, but also honors the first-person phenomenological perspective.

As Lakoff and Johnson acknowledge in their popular *Philosophy in the Flesh*, the embodied mind program owes a tremendous debt to the researches of pragmatism, especially the work of John Dewey, as well as the phenomenology of Merleau-Ponty. "We want to honor the two greatest philosophers of the embodied mind," write Lakoff and Johnson. They continue:

> John Dewey, no less than Merleau-Ponty, saw that our bodily experience is the primal basis for everything we can mean, think, know, and communicate. He understood the full richness, complexity, and philosophical importance of bodily experience.[29]

Although the challenge to Western dualism expounded in their text restricts its engagement with Dewey and Merleau-Ponty to introductory remarks, Johnson's more recent book, *The Meaning of the Body*, delves further into the philosophical debt incurred by embodiment theorists working alongside or as cognitive scientists.

The increased visibility of the body in the study of consciousness and subjectivity does not necessarily entail the reduction of the mind to the brain, or consciousness to synaptic/neural activity, although this is one possible outcome.[30] The interrogation of the body has produced a fertile variety of approaches, which have in turn yielded a range of unforeseeable problems and possibilities for rethinking the constitution of the body, its relations, and its place in the order of things, concepts, and meanings. Many of these approaches can be called materialist, but we must be careful not to assume that the embodied perspective always implies physicalism or positivism. As Johnson insists: "The brain is *not* the mind. The brain is one key part of the entire pattern of embodied organism-environment interaction that is the proper locus of mind and meaning."[31] This interaction is comprised of several irreducible dimensions: the biological, social, ecological, cultural, and phenomenological.[32] Indeed, Johnson offers a naturalistic thesis that is difficult to construe as reductive: "Meaning," he writes,

> is not just a matter of concepts and propositions, but also reaches down into the images, sensorimotor schemas, feelings, qualities, and emotions that constitute our meaningful encounter with our world. Any adequate account of meaning must be built around the aesthetic dimensions that give our experience its distinctive character and significance.[33]

It would seem that a balanced union of the material and meaningful remains a live option for both analytic and continental philosophers. As it should, if we desire a comprehensive account of experience. Like Johnson, I think this balance is best struck in the aesthetic dimension.

In my view one of the most important efforts made by the embodied mind folks is their attempt to undo the prejudice which says that our qualitative, imaginative, affective, and aesthetic experiences are *merely* subjective. This prejudice, as I have already indicated, only holds up in an ontology that sees subject and object, body and world, as inhabiting two distinct ontological realms, one internal and one external. What contemporary cognitive science is showing, however, is that the subjective (internal) and objective (external) worlds are actually continuous with each other.[34] The mind, in short, is extended throughout the environment and the environment permeates the mind just. Such evidence has consequences—which I will try to elucidate throughout—for how we conceive the structure of subjectivity as well as individuality and relationality. It suggests that "there is no Cartesian dualistic person" and that "there exists no Kantian radically autonomous person, with absolute freedom and a transcendent reason that correctly dictates what is and isn't moral."[35] Given that the post-dualist perspective undermines the basic distinction between internal psychic life and external corporeal life, theories of subjectivity are forced to acknowledge the essentially *liminal* nature of experience: all experience is a product of the body's transactions with environmental infrastructure and the other bodies that populate it. To quote Johnson again,

> meaningful form comes from the nature of our bodies and the patterns of interaction we have with our environment, and it is therefore shaped by our values, interests, and purposes as active agents. As Dewey insisted—and cognitive science confirms—thought is never wholly divorced from feeling, value, and the aesthetics of our embodied experience.[36]

Merleau-Ponty likewise advocates a transactional view of embodiment that we will explore in the following two chapters. For now it is enough to note that the classical dualist position not only proves itself prejudicial, since its terms have lost their reference it has become literally senseless. In order to foster the post-dualist perspective we have to unpack the carnal life of the body in its liminal aspects, at its points of intersection with other bodies, and once again see the aesthetics of embodiment as integral to subjectivity. Note that *aesthetics* here denotes the comprehensive sensory life of the body, from the perception of works of fine art to the dull sensations of everyday life. Throughout this book I am understanding aesthetics in an expanded sense that includes everything from the mundane to the fine, the participatory to the spectacular. Aesthetic events can be contemplative or deliberate, automatic or reactionary. Following Yuriko Saito, "the aesthetic" for me includes "any reactions we form toward the sensuous and/or design qualities of any object, phenomenon, or activity."[37] But it also includes active responses, as well as—and especially—those that we do not consciously form. Concomitantly, s*ensation* denotes the currency with which these body-world transactions take place.

At least since Heidegger phenomenology has defended a non-dualist thesis as it struggles against the prejudices of objectivism and dualism. There are, of course, countless non-phenomenological precursors to this general perspective: Parmenides and Anaximander; the atomists Democritus, Epicurus, Lucretius; Hobbes and Spinoza; Marx and Nietzsche; the American pragmatists. While the philosophers working on embodied mind acknowledge and cite from some of these historical resources, the fruits of their labors are often attributed to the latest research in cognitive science, cognitive linguistics, or emotion research. This not only obscures the history of the problem of embodiment, it also passes over a rich and conflicted body of literature which has much to contribute to the contemporary scientific debate. Such methodological decisions tend to reinforce the view that phenomenology is only valuable as a speculative, or merely theoretical, supplement to the sciences of the mind and that it lacks rigor or legitimacy when conducted on its own terms. Thus, Johnson admits that "phenomenology *leads* us to the primacy of movement, but it alone is not enough to prove the case. What is required additionally is empirical research from the cognitive sciences of the embodied mind."[38] While I do feel that phenomenology is best practiced synthetically, that is, in conjunction with the human and natural sciences, I think we need to be careful not to place it in the role of science's servant, or to underestimate/reduce its contribution to embodiment research.[39] Thus the necessity, assumed here, of excavating the history of French phenomenology to reveal the affinities and disparities between Levinas's and Merleau-Ponty's contributions to twentieth-century philosophy of the body, as well as their relevance to contemporary embodiment studies. When considered on their own terms I see the aesthetics of Levinas and Merleau-Ponty as indispensable for reconciling a pluralistic conception of embodiment, even if ultimately the two thinkers hold incompatible metaphysical positions.

A promising route opened up by the corporeal turn in philosophy offers the chance to rethink concepts that have been criticized right out of theoretical discourse. One of these concepts is sensation. Sensation is a concept with a confused history and a shifting, equivocal identity.[40] It is often conflated with or subsumed by perception, as exemplified in the term "sense-perception." It is often relegated to the realm of internal, mental states or reduced to physical stimulation. It is a concept that has been left behind because it belongs to a surpassed ontological and epistemological model, a simplistic causal theory of perception. The installation of the body at the center of the theory of subjectivity and the apparent collapse of the subject-object divide effected by Kant and post-Kantian idealism, however, has forced us to produce new ontologies and to attend to the new philosophical problems which result from this shift in perspective. Therefore, I would like to keep open the following question: *What happens when our bodies interact with their sensory (aesthetic) environment?* Entailed in this question is a series of ontological considerations that bear on the nature, power, and constitution of the body; the problem of corporeal individuation; the natural-artificial and human-nonhuman distinctions; the ethics of intercorporeal interaction; the reality of violence and death; as well as the problem of how to conceive sensation vis-à-vis perception and cognition. If sensation cannot be comprehended adequately by dualism, the possibilities for revitalizing sensation in the post-dualist landscape are multiple.

Situated at the intersection of the philosophy and science of the body, the fecundity of embodied mind theories would be enough to warrant a closer inspection of the history of the problem of the body. At the same time, given the promise of such research it is important to catalogue the nuances of the philosophical history of the body, and to raise and respond to the metaphysical questions it poses for contemporary studies. That is what this book does.

General Thesis

Phenomenology provides numerous resources for addressing the problem of sensation and for thinking through its place in corporeal ontology. Indeed, sensation constitutes the material basis of this ontology. The narrative I will weave about sensation tells how the return of the body has enabled the retrieval of sensation as a philosophically rich concept. Claiming Levinas and Merleau-Ponty as allies, I defend the thesis that sensation forms the basis of our intentional and intercorporeal experience. It immanently orients and integrates our bodies. It is pre-perceptual, pre-conceptual, and pre-personal, and its diachrony introduces a fundamental instability into the world of perception.

Phenomenology relies on a certain distance between perceiver and perceived, a distance which posits "phenomena" as the objects intended by subjects. Consciousness, for phenomenology, is always already polarized in this way; it is the point of departure for any phenomenological analysis. But if the body is constituted immanently, which is to say, generated by the material world, then the polarization of consciousness must itself be explained. When and how is the gap between subject and object introduced, ontologically speaking? Phenomenology does not ask this question. The primary relation between body and world maintained by phenomenology becomes methodologically problematic for phenomenology as such, to explain. Without the distance afforded by intentionality, which opens up and sutures the gap between perceiver and perceived, it is impossible for sensory phenomena to be apprehended as proper objects of intuition. Given the radical immanence of sensation, I contend that it never enters, as it were, the intentional gap, and therefore evades any possible phenomenological intuition.

Sensation lacks the transcendence necessary for the phenomenological observer to figure it against a background; it thus never rises, as such, to the level of explicit attention. As soon as it does it becomes perception, an afterimage of itself. Sensation's contours are never entirely defined or apparent; sensations transpire as non-phenomenal/non-intentional events. This notion contests Merleau-Ponty's crucial thesis that "a figure on a background is the simplest sense-given [*la donnée sensible*] available to us...."[41] Against his thesis I maintain that sensation makes sense (*sens*) and gives direction (*sens*) to our bodies at a *pre-intentional* level. To make good on this counter-claim and to unpack the dimensions of sensation, my view of embodiment synthesizes phenomenological and non-phenomenological perspectives that yield a metaphysical realism about sensation. This synthetic view impels us to build an ethics and politics that cultivate our aesthetic environment in enabling and affirmative ways.

Kant's Aesthetics and Critique of Sensibility

For historical context it is instructive to start with the Kantian legacy that remains so powerful in contemporary philosophy. Kant carries out an analysis of the aesthetic capacity of the subject in the early parts of the *Critique of Pure Reason*. His analysis marks a turning point in the history of the concept of sensation and exemplifies an attitude which still holds considerable influence today. To summarize Kant's impact it is fair to say that after him the legitimacy of sensation—as a unit of experience—becomes suspect; today it is permissible to lay claim to perceptions (composed, understood sensations), but sensations themselves are relegated to an amorphous, inaccessible, and ultimately unspeakable ontological plane that is never accessed by perception or cognition. Kant cannot afford to discard sensation completely, however, or else he would run the double risk of (1) succumbing to the absolute and subjective idealisms he argues against and (2) admitting that our representations correspond to nothing that actually presents itself to us.

The Transcendental Aesthetic of the *Critique of Pure Reason* lays out both the a priori and empirical components of sensibility. It radically claims that space and time, the so-called pure forms of intuition, are contributed to experience by the subject, they are not objective realities as in Newton's model. It also claims that the content of our intuitions, sensation, is provided by the objects we directly intuit in the world. In this respect Kant is an externalist about sensation. In his account of the subject-object relation, as well as his understanding of the subject as agent of thought and action, Kant is Cartesian in spirit; but he decisively advances beyond the Cartesian view by endowing the subject with the power to constitute the form of its world. Following Kant, Hegel deploys a brand of phenomenology that criticizes Kant's residual dualism, but Hegel also sacrifices the autonomy of objects along with the reality of sensations.

What is missing in all three of these views (Descartes, Kant, Hegel) is the practical or embodied dimension of sensation, or affirmation that it is sensation that delivers the materiality of the world to sensibility. Such affirmation can be found in the ancient atomists as well as Aristotle and later empiricists. It seems that Kant and Hegel, and to a lesser degree Descartes, are concerned only with the epistemological or logical value of sensation, a fact which leads them to minimize the ontological consequences of the sensory *encounter* that takes place between the world and the body of the observer.[42] Put otherwise, what they lack is a sense of the *volatility* attending sensibility and its function as immanent interface between sensing subject and aesthetic environment. A brief look at Kant's Transcendental Aesthetic in the first *Critique* reveals a failure to acknowledge the potential ontological disruption or diachrony harbored by sensibility. Davide Panagia aptly reminds us, however, that the immediacy of aesthetic experience (i.e., sensation) in Kant's third *Critique* "ungrounds our subjectivity." But Panagia explicitly means the subject as an agent of interestedness, judgment, and classification. Thus, what is ungrounded by sensation is the *control* the subject wields over the sensible, not the subject itself.[43] Entailed in Kant's oversight is the question of the legitimacy of his epistemological claim that sensory content is given unsynthesized by objects, that an object's qualitative unity is the product of subjective synthesis. Interrogating Kant on this point provides a bridge to the tacit idealism of Husserl's phenomenology, against which both Merleau-Ponty and Levinas launch their philosophical programs.

The Copernican revolution effected by Kant's *Critique of Pure Reason* ripples throughout contemporary philosophy. Its impact on modern and postmodern European philosophy, that is, the continental tradition, is nothing short of foundational. Indeed, it is not inaccurate to cite the Critical philosophy of Kant as the very origin of continental philosophy.[44] Given Kant's general importance in this history and his influence on the phenomenological movement in particular, it is necessary to delineate a few key points contained in his view. I will focus exclusively here on his view of sensation and his theory of sensibility since these are the theoretical objects under immediate consideration. This will enable us to draw a parallel between Kant and Husserl in order to connect the Kantian revolution, or what might be called the institution of constructivist epistemology,[45] to the institution of phenomenology.

Much contemporary philosophy regards Kant's suturing together of subject and object as nearly incontestable. Subject and object are codependent terms; their real distinction has collapsed. Against this claim I submit evidence that subjects and objects retain a kind of autonomy even if this autonomy is always caught up in relations. This is an idea that both Kant and I endorse, but there is evidence in Kant's own texts to suggest that his endorsement is not consistent with his constructivism, but akin to a metaphysical breach of his critical method. The burden falls on me to unpack this allegation.

The power and impact of Kant's irrevocable fusion of subject and object institutes our contemporary episteme, the era of what Quentin Meillassoux calls "correlationism." Correlationism is shorthand for the entrenched post-critical viewpoint which "consists in disqualifying the claim that it is possible to consider the realms of subjectivity and objectivity independently of one another." On this account, it may be legitimate to speculate about objects in themselves, but it is impossible to either think or know them. This view pervades so much philosophy after Kant that Meillassoux is compelled to conclude that "the central notion of modern philosophy since Kant seems to be that of *correlation*." Meillassoux continues:

> By "correlation" we mean the idea according to which we only ever have access to the correlation between thinking and being, and never to either term considered apart from the other. We will henceforth call *correlationism* any current of thought which maintains the unsurpassable character of the correlation so defined. Consequently, it becomes possible to say that every philosophy which disavows naïve realism has become a variant of correlationism.[46]

Phenomenology, as the philosophy/science which studies phenomena *as they appear to consciousness*, is by definition correlationism. One might even say that the subject-object correlation is the proper object of phenomenological analysis. This does not mean, however, that everything a phenomenologist writes reinforces or supports correlationism. I will try to make the correlationism of Merleau-Ponty and Levinas clear, as well as highlight the points at which their philosophies contest the primacy of the correlation. The remarkable tenacity of correlationism poses an obstacle to any metaphysical realism, including the one I espouse here. Constructivism is usually the default position of contemporary philosophy; its truth seems uncontestable.

Kant's revolutionary position holds that the objects of perception receive their form from, and so must conform to, our cognition of them. Cognition does not conform to objects. This view takes root, as noted, in the Transcendental Aesthetic of the first Critique.[47] Kant is concerned there not with a theory of the beautiful or a philosophy of art, but with the subject's capacity to receive sensory input from the external world. Sensibility is our capacity to be affected by objects; it is how objects are *given* to us.[48] He offers a theory of sensibility which is formulated in part as a response to classical empiricist accounts of sense experience, particularly those of the British empiricists, Hume and Hutcheson, for example. Kant agrees with the empiricists that cognition must begin with the experience of some object, but he contests the claim that all our knowledge is built up from what is given empirically, that is, from sensations. "There can be no doubt that all our cognition begins with experience," writes Kant. "But," he adds, "even though all our cognition starts with experience, that does not mean that all of it arises from experience."[49] He makes this distinction to set up a refutation of empiricism, but also because he understands "experience" as a composite phenomenon assembled from impressions received by the intellect. Once impressions are received the intellect applies concepts, either subsequently or simultaneously, to *produce* experience. Outside this production, which occurs within the subject-object correlation, there is nothing to experience. Ordinarily we believe the content of experience is given externally. But, says Kant, "long practice has made us attentive to [the cognitive element of all experience] and skilled in separating it from the basic material," provided by sense impressions.[50] Since experience is always more than the reception of sensory content, the given is never received in basic, raw form. That is, sensations are never received as sensations. How can Kant claim that they are given, then? Or rather, if sensations are always already worked up by the cognitive apparatus, what apart from linguistic necessity allows Kant to claim that anything like pure, unsynthesized sensory content exists at all? His schematic requires the concept of sensation, or the sensory manifold, to account for the content of experience, but beyond its basic architectonic value sensation seems to play no formative role in the constitution of experience. Nor does it have any influence on our capacity to constitute experience.

The empiricist position involves what Merleau-Ponty calls the "prejudice of the objective world." The *Phenomenology of Perception* thoroughly criticizes and opposes this prejudice with a non-Kantian alternative which maintains that knowledge of the world arises out of firsthand acquaintance with objects in themselves. Kant maintains that there is an objective (noumenal) world in itself beyond the (phenomenal) reach of perception, but that this noumenal world is unknowable. Merleau-Ponty eschews the notion of an objective realm that exists apart from the phenomenal, in favor of a theory which posits that the objects we perceive just are the objects of the noumenal world. These objects are constituted and individuated in perception, our only means of knowing them. He follows Kant to a degree, then, but transfers the constitutive power of Kant's transcendental subject to the body's capacity for "practical synthesis." Merleau-Ponty writes, "It is not through an intellectual synthesis which would freely posit the total object that I am led from what is given to what is not actually given; that I am given, together with the visible sides of the object, the invisible sides as well. It is, rather, a kind of practical synthesis."[51] The act of synthesis, or the individuation of objects, is said to occur through the body's commerce with things (Merleau-Ponty) rather than in the understanding or imagination (Kant).[52] For both thinkers, however, it is sense impressions that are purportedly synthesized. To see why this is true of Merleau-Ponty, who is often read as championing the priority of objects over sense impressions, we will eventually have to look closely at his concept of "sense experience" (*sentir*).

Kant's epistemological treatment of sensation has a clear ontological significance which contrasts with the view that sensations are purely internal events. Sensation denotes the material to be processed into experience by the understanding, and in this respect it is external or objective content. They are what *instigate* the production of experience. Kant writes: "The effect of an object on our capacity for [re]presentation, insofar as we are affected by the object, is *sensation*."[53] The material of sensation is provided to the subject from outside; it emanates from the objects which reside in the noumenal realm, the things in themselves. But Kant's epistemology, as is well known, has an uneasy time establishing the ontological divide between subjective and objective, phenomenon and noumenon, nor can he justify any causal interaction between these pairs.[54] His constructivism should prohibit any reference to things in themselves, as things are only knowable through phenomenal experience understood in a composite sense of the following sort:

Sensations + Concepts = Experience

This makes Kant's account of the *givenness* of sensation either speculative fantasy (something the Critical project aims to quell) or what Hegel calls a formal, "lifeless schema."[55] In either case, Kant undermines the volatility of sensation by situating it in a space inaccessible to the cognitive machinery of the transcendental subject—the noumenal. This is effectively what Samuel Todes argues in his somewhat neglected *Body and World* when he advances the thesis that Kant "imaginizes" perception and the ego and thereby underplays the materiality of subjectivity.[56] Todes's argument assembles roughly phenomenological evidence against Kant that is meant to show that the subject is not a disembodied, transcendental synthesizer of sensory content, but is itself a product of that content. Todes's thesis is worth revitalizing.

Todes argues for a pre-Kantian thesis, but from a post-Kantian/phenomenological perspective. Against the Copernican revolution he reasserts the idea that knowledge must conform to objects; more than that, he contends that the subject itself must also conform.[57] This is a consequence of the fact that perception is fundamentally practical, while only secondarily conceptual or imaginative. "On our view," writes Todes, "imagination presupposes practical perception because we must first *become somebody* by practical experience in the given world, before we can achieve self-expression and self-discovery by making a world of our own."[58] Our worldly productions, whether intellectual or material, are initiated in response to the world as it is found and as it demands to be handled. It is in the handling that we come know that this world is something other than what we make it.

Kant believes that he can ascertain from experience some a priori knowledge of the world, such as the pure forms of intuition: space and time. But a priori knowledge cannot guarantee that any content exists outside of experience and its transcendental conditions, only that when content is represented the form of its presentation is contributed by the subject. Consequently, it becomes difficult to explain how the subject could come into contact with, let alone find itself shaped by, truly autonomous objects or sensory content. For Todes, it is in the practical field of perception where objects await our interaction, yet even this lends no *certainty* about the reality of objects.[59] The phenomenal evidence of the perceptual field, writes Todes, determines the incorrigible existence of any given object "by way of some effective response to that object, and culminates by determining it as circumstantially outside us. This response, however, determines not merely the perceptual object upon which it is directed, but also the percipient from which it issues."[60] Only the dialogical interaction that occurs between the body and objects, so central to Merleau-Ponty's phenomenology of perception, can evince the material existence of these two terms. For Todes as much as Merleau-Ponty this dialogism gives the subject and object their particular form. It is not the spontaneous synthesis of the ego which performs this feat, it is the responsiveness of the active body with all its specific determinations: upright posture,[61] front-back asymmetry,[62] physical disability, gravitational attunement, institutional orientation, and so forth. This may not be enough to establish the autonomous reality of things, but it shifts attention away from the idea that space, time, and object-unity are products of the mind. The body is instead brought into focus, specifically as dependent upon what is outside it.

Todes raises a now common criticism of the Kantian subject when he claims that Kant "has no sense of how practice *makes the practitioner*."[63] For Kant, the world is but a reflection of our constitutive (imaginative, cognitive) capacities and we come to know ourselves only by first generating this world in experience. This puts him in the difficult position of accounting for how the material world is capable of shaping us at the most fundamental level. Against Kant, Todes aligns himself with many contemporary exponents of embodiment, both phenomenological and naturalist, who insist that subjects are produced as they explore and interact bodily with their environment, not before.[64]

It is possible to argue that Kant does not completely absent the body from his account of subjectivity. Angelica Nuzzo maintains that the body is far from missing in Kant's equation. If we look to the *Critique of Judgment*, for instance, we see the embodied dimension of sensibility highlighted by Kant. The experience of pleasure and displeasure in the face of aesthetic phenomena, notes Nuzzo, allow us to "*feel* ourselves a part of living (i.e., sensible) nature."[65] This pivotal feeling is basically corporeal. She concludes that "[Kant's] general aim is to attribute to human sensibility a new central place in philosophy, thereby steering the philosophical focus from the metaphysics of a 'disembodied soul' to the inquiry into an 'embodied mind'." In sum, Kant's modern view of sensibility is broad enough to encompass "the entire realm of the sensual: affections, intuition, sensation, feeling, and imagination."[66]

In her book *Ideal Embodiment* Nuzzo contends that Kant's theory of sensibility is actually a theory of *embodied* sensibility and that "transcendentally, the knowing subject of Kant's epistemology, the moral agent of his pure ethics, and the evaluating subject of his aesthetic theory of judgment is a rational embodied being."[67] Specifically, for Kant, the transcendental field is governed by a left/right asymmetry that corresponds to the asymmetry of our hands, and thus the a priori form of space (the formal aspect of sensible intuition) has the comportment of the body built right into it.[68] More than an empirical fact, this asymmetry is a transcendental condition of any possible experience.

Nuzzo gives plenty of evidence for the embodied dimension of Kant's transcendental sensibility in her analysis of his aesthetic theory.[69] She shows that Kant's innovative moment arrives when he makes the body a transcendental condition for aesthetics, a condition which is "formal" and "ideal," but at the same time corporeal.[70] We find Levinas eventually pursuing something analogous but less formal. For Kant, sensibility is the active reception of objects given and is "responsible for the fact that we are able to confront the reality of given objects."[71] But sensibility's activity extends further, since it also produces representations of objects and does so immediately, unlike thought, which is always mediated by sensibility. Sensibility guarantees that sensations received are never without form. Since Kant distinguishes between intuition and sensation he can designate intuitions as having objective content while assigning sensation a representational/subjective role as the formal *effect* of objects on our sensibility.

Nuzzo's attempt to display the embodied element of Kantian cognition is emblematic of the broader concern with embodiment in contemporary philosophy. One of a plethora of recent attempts to retrieve the body, it testifies to the inadequacy of the now-familiar narrative which laments the Western philosophical tradition's neglect of the body. I hesitate to contest Nuzzo's reading of Kant because she provides a compelling reading of Kant's aesthetics. Indeed, I do not think we are forced to either acknowledge the body in Kant or lament its absence. The question of Kantian embodiment is instead a matter of degree. Despite the embodied elements of Kantian cognition pinpointed by Nuzzo, the receptive function of sensibility must remain subservient to sensibility's formal aspect, as well as the activity of the understanding, in his philosophy. Consequently, Kant provides us with an account of sensing that *tames* sensation by reducing it to a logical placeholder in his diagram of aesthetic experience.[72] In other words, sensations are inferred from experience, not encountered in it. They can be conceived, but not perceived.

The question remains: How does the transcendental ego/body make contact with the material world? Looking at the first *Critique*, it would have to be through sensibility, since all rational judgment must pass through the senses. We have already seen, however, the problem with considering objects and sensations as given corporeally on the Kantian model. Kant distinguishes between intuition and sensation. Whereas sensation is simply empirical, or objectively given, intuition is simultaneously transcendental and empirical. Since we only ever intuit the appearance of objects, and therefore apprehend objects only through an a priori formality that provides them with the space and time in which they reside, we are prevented from claiming that sensation actually comes *from somewhere*, let alone that it is given materially. In other words, if sensations come from objects, but these objects cannot exist without the spatiotemporal conditions contributed by the subject, then objects cannot be an external source of sensations.

The tension I am trying to bring into relief is roughly this. Kant wants to give sensation a non-ideal source, namely, the objects of experience. This is to avoid the subjectivist view that when we sense, we only ever sense our own ideas or ideal content. But the spatiotemporal conditions of these objects are provided by the subject. So, if we subtract these conditions, what is left are pure sensory qualities without spatial or temporal coordinates, something difficult to imagine as anything other than a pure abstraction. If Kant's epistemology cannot actually establish that sensation has a material reality, this means that sensation, on his view, cannot be objectively given to sensibility, cannot instigate sensing, and cannot give form to the subject.

While the first *Critique* excludes sensation from the transcendental to affirm its non-ideal materiality, the third *Critique* opens up the embodied dimension of sensibility through an analysis of the feelings of pleasure and displeasure.[73] His analysis identifies the condition—affective (non-conceptual) intuition—that makes it possible for us to feel our participation in sensible nature. Despite Kant's discussion of affective intuition, I do not think he "[strengthens] the connection between sensation and feeling" at the ontological level, as Nuzzo suggests.[74] Read alongside the *Critique of Pure Reason* the recasting of sensibility in the *Critique of Judgment* does not quite resolve the problem of how to either establish or bridge the gap between the supposedly objective source of sensation and the subjective feeling of pleasure or displeasure. How can we be confident that our pleasurable aesthetic experience is a pleasure taken in something that is other than our own representation? Are we permitted on Kant's view to hold that aesthetic pleasure, which is an embodied response to aesthetic phenomena, is brought about by sensibility's reception of real sensations from real objects? If it is problematic to claim that sensibility actually receives material sensations from outside itself, it is problematic to claim that the corporeality of pleasure actually results from the corporeality of sensation. Without establishing the corporeality of sensation it is difficult to conceive aesthetic experience as an embodied, not just intellectual, response. What prevents Kant from achieving this, I suggest, is a wavering commitment to correlationism. In other words, his critical project is at once committed to the primacy of the subject-object correlation, but he nevertheless wants to claim that objects and subjects and objects do enjoy some kind of independence from each other. The independence claim finds little if any support in Kant's *Critique*, however.

Rather than reaching a decisive verdict I simply want to reiterate that Kant has effectively, and quite influentially, tamed the effects of sensation by insulating the transcendental subject from the material content of cognition. Accordingly, Kant's subject-object dualism, despite its tensions, prohibits sensation from actively constituting the subject. Now, I would not dispute that Kant has a transcendental view of embodiment, for Nuzzo gives a persuasive account. It fails to reunite the body of the subject to the material world, however, and this is because her argument explicitly resists such a reunion. As a result, the Kantian subject's identity remains beyond the reach of other bodies and material objects. Other bodies, moreover, must always be regarded as themselves constituted by the subject's sensibility and understanding. This has two ontological and practical implications that call for response. First, it is impossible for the subject's identity to be either formed or deformed by sensation. Second, the otherness of the material environment is reduced to the sameness of the subject's representational capacity.

Taming Sensation With Hegel and Husserl

Kant's pacification of sensation is ramified in Hegel's phenomenology. In the "Sense-Certainty" section of the *Phenomenology of Spirit*, Hegel addresses the problem of the given by rejecting the existence of a noumenal realm that provides the sensory input for cognition to process into workable knowledge. Hegel's refusal to infer the existence of pure sensory content eliminates the objectivity of sensation altogether, for it situates this content exclusively in subjective representations. This is because there is nowhere else to put it. In a sense, the symbiotic relation of subject and object disappears for Hegel because the object has become a concept—an ever-shifting and elusive concept, but a concept nonetheless. Since, for Hegel, the world is just the phenomenal appearance of human conceptuality, the sensory material of intuition *qua non-ideal material* becomes superfluous for thought. The subject-world correlation retains its primacy, with the result that the Hegelian object, more severely than the Kantian, is evacuated of its autonomy.

Hegel sees sensation as a prejudicial empiricist concept, one we use to explain the phenomena of experience without really comprehending the rationality of these phenomena. Sensation only makes sense as a concept in one of the infinite succession of appearances that make up the history of spirit. These appearances, whose shape derives from the conceptual framework used to make sense of phenomena are, as conceptual, presented to consciousness by consciousness.[75] Hegel's phenomenology tracks the transformation and interplay between these shapes. In the process, the sensible world becomes a fable for Hegel. The *Phenomenology* quickly sublates the empiricist prejudice of sense-certainty in its dialectic, replacing it with perception as a more advanced order of rationality. What the empiricist believes to be the direct *apprehension* of a singular sensory object reveals its truth as the *comprehension* of an object endowed with universal qualities: "So it is in fact the universal that is the true [content] of sense-certainty," Hegel says.[76] "I have this certainty *through* something else, viz. the thing; and it, similarly, is in sense-certainty *through* something else, viz. through the 'I'."[77] In Hegel the mediation of the world by the mind becomes a total mediation, further ensuring that the alterity and foreignness of the world can always be recuperated by the dialectic. Hegel foreshadows that,

"In pressing forward to its true existence, consciousness will arrive at a point at which it gets rid of its semblance of being burdened with something alien, with what is only for it, and some sort of 'other', at a point where appearance becomes identical with essence, so that its exposition will coincide at just this point with the authentic Science of Spirit."[78]

Hegel's discontent with the formalism of Kant's portrait of cognition induces him to "put flesh on Kant's architectonic."[79] Hegel's gripe is basically existentialist in character, in that he thinks that Kant is trying to understand experience before actually experiencing something.[80] This is why he begins the *Phenomenology* with sense experience, a move equivalent to jumping right into the stream of consciousness and letting oneself get tossed around in its waves, rather than trying to deduce the fluid dynamics of these waves from the shore. But it is also telling that he regards sense experience as something already shot through with universals, and so neither formless nor immediate at all. The stream of consciousness is, in effect, shown to be given through perception, not sensation. Such a tactic is standard not only for Hegel's phenomenology, but also for Husserl and his followers. Phenomenology of all stripes begins from the premise that we do not first experience sense impressions, formless qualities, but perceptual objects. The difference is that Hegel does not allow for the transcendence of the object; the object is a concept, not a substance existing in the material world. If anything, its transcendence is always a transcendence in immanence,[81] a notion endorsed by both Husserl and Merleau-Ponty.[82] Absolute transcendence of the object is prohibited by the methodological correlationism of all three thinkers. Just as in Kant, the form of the Hegelian object is the product of the conscious subject. But unlike Kant, this object has no other truth than the one bestowed upon it by the conceptual eye/I of the observer.[83]

Hegel's critique of Kant's ontological dualism targets sensation as a source of knowledge, specifically, as the origin of our representations. This is a reformulation of the Cartesian criticism of empiricism, demonstrated by the wax example in the *Meditations*, where Descartes shows that what we actually perceive in an object as it undergoes myriad qualitative changes is nothing sensible—which would only lead to skepticism—but an idea or representation. Hegel's critique of sensation goes further than

Cartesian skepticism, however. It leads to the abandonment of the concept of sensation as such. Although necessary to recount the odyssey of spirit, sensation is just a rudimentary form of experience that bears no certain knowledge and can easily be seen as simply prejudicial.

If we turn aside from Hegel's explicitly epistemological criticism, however, it becomes possible to see sensation as something other than a means to certainty. What we find in the empiricists, as well as Kant, is the idea that sensation is the instigator of experience. As such it possesses a certain kind of agency, one that eludes the subject's power of representation and which occasionally threatens its representational capacity. This sense of sensation vanishes in the Hegelian dialectic, but here we are precisely trying to recover it.

The material dimension of sensation drops out of Hegel's phenomenology, but not the post-Hegelian phenomenologies of the twentieth century, which uncover a different ontology of sensation. In his account of subjectivity, Levinas, for instance, revives the affective aspect of embodiment and champions sensation as a kind of element that nourishes the life of the body. Sensation also eludes and disrupts any attempt to fix it in a system of representation. There is nothing like this in Hegelian phenomenology. Merleau-Ponty, like Levinas, is not interested in working through the old epistemological debate. He instead constructs a new framework for thinking the correlation of body and world, but one which retains a vestige of the materiality of sensation. Neither Merleau-Ponty's nor Levinas's conception of sensation can be circumscribed by older models, but their novel character is, I think, most striking when refracted through those models.[84]

At stake when breaking with the idealist model that culminates in Hegel is not only an embodied conception of the subject, but also a rehabilitation of the concept of sensation and a practical philosophy that is founded in the aesthetic life of the body, not rooted at the intellectual level, like the Kantian imperative. An embodied imperative issues from the site where bodies interact with other bodies, where bodily transactions, yields, absorptions, resistances, and collisions occur. This is the place where sensations give and receive their form. Sensation is at the heart of all encounters, constituting and reconstituting the bodies involved. The concept of plasticity, developed as much by the American pragmatists as Catherine Malabou, will be the key to understanding this process.

Before turning to his French descendants, it is necessary to note the influence of the German idealists on Husserl's phenomenology. Merleau-Ponty and Levinas explicitly resist this aspect of Husserl's heritage. A common target is his sometimes implicit, sometimes explicit, idealism, which harbors important remnants of both Kant and Hegel. Those who would defend Husserl against this charge always seem to be fighting an uphill battle. This is because, as Tom Rockmore has shown, Husserl's "position is in constant dialogue with Kant's critical philosophy, to which he comes increasingly closer through the evolution of this position from descriptive phenomenology to transcendental idealism."[85] The call back to the things themselves has a Kantian ring to it, but for Husserl it is actually more like an Hegelian principle: to return not to mind-independent objects, but to the immediate phenomena of perceptual experience; proceed with reflection from there, without prejudging the matter at hand.[86] Despite his allegiance to the phenomena as such, however, Husserl retains a basic dualism that aligns him with Kant. Mark Rowlands frames the position, accurately I think, in these terms:

> Whereas for Kant, phenomena, experienceable things, are ultimately grounded in a noumenal reality, a reality of non-experienceable things, Husserl denies that phenomena require such grounding. There may or may not exist a transcendent, noumenal world, but if there is one we can neither know nor say anything at all about it. The physical world of which we can speak is not a transcendent world but one that must be understood in terms of actual and possible experiences. As such, it cannot exist independently of consciousness.[87]

The famous bracketing of the natural attitude which initiates the phenomenological method remains neutral about the things themselves and focuses the phenomenologist's attention solely on the given *as it is given*.[88] This means that Husserl—in a gesture of realist solidarity— does not discard the thing in itself, like Hegel, but, as a committed phenomenologist and with more restraint than Kant, refuses to speak about it. Only natural scientists and ordinary folks believe that when they talk about things they talk about the things themselves. But such talk is suspended by the phenomenological reduction, which drives a wedge between things in themselves and "what is really given in the phenomenological elements of representations."[89] Without fully rejecting their reality, Husserl leaves the things in themselves to the empirical investigators, and turns his attention to "intentional objects," the proper focus of phenomenological epistemology.

The given for Husserl, then, is not what comes from "outside" us. It is what is presented to intentional consciousness within the subject-object correlation. This includes the sensory material which, for Kant, remains a formal abstraction about the external world. So, on the one hand, Husserl tacitly retains the noumenon-phenomenon duality, but in a neutralized form, while at the same time situating the origin of the given *in* consciousness, and thereby forging another tacit alliance with objective idealism. This is the case in *Ideas* I and *Cartesian Meditations*, although the story is complicated by Husserl's turn to the body in *Ideas* II. As for objects and their sensible features, *Logical Investigations* complicates the matter further by offering a version of the sensible that is at odds with the idealism of *Ideas* I.

We saw that Kant's relegation of the material of sensation to the noumenal realm, oddly enough, disqualified him from claiming its objectivity. Consequently, his dualism has the effect of immunizing the subject from the instigation of sensation. Husserl's idealism, at least in *Ideas* I, has a similar effect: he once again domesticates sensation and mitigates its material dimension by subjectivizing it.[90] Like Kant and Hegel before him, he sees the subject as animating sensory content,[91] whereas I would argue, alongside Merleau-Ponty and Levinas, that *it is sensory content (sensations) that animates us.* We might pose this point of contrast in terms of what could be called the "principle of animation:" against the view which holds that the principle of animation is ideal or mental I offer the view that the principle of animation originates in the material environment, which means that subjects are constituted, practitioners are made, as corporeal events. Phenomenological idealism keeps the materiality of sensation at a distance, protects the subject from what would threaten its transcendental privileges. It conceives sensibility too intellectually and, consequently, the corporeal aspect of experience is drastically compromised.

It is not easy to figure out the sensory/material or so-called "hyletic" layer in Husserl's image of consciousness. As James Dodd has noted, "it is perhaps the most volatile concept in [Husserl's] corpus."[92] *Ideas* I explains that the notion of a hyletic layer is meant to replace what he called "primary contents" in *Logical Investigations*. Husserl describes primary contents as what "would be the contents of 'external' sensibility," although he is quick to point out that this does not refer to "some metaphysical distinction of outward and inward." At the level of phenomenological representation, then, these primary contents are the intuited ground upon which reflection is founded.[93] They include all the sensory content given in concrete experience, such as color and texture as well as the "sensile impressions of pleasure, pain, tickling, etc."[94] Primary contents no longer works as a concept in *Ideas* I so Husserl decides there to speak of "hyle" instead. In both cases Husserl is reconstituting what would otherwise be referred to as sensation: "sensation is hyle, that is, matter waiting to be charged with animating sense, awaiting an apprehension that will give it meaning."[95] The shift to the language of hyle allows him to emphasize the fact that the "sensuous stuff" of consciousness is immanent to, not independent of, consciousness.

Ideas I operates with a hylomorphism roughly Kantian in structure: what Husserl calls hyletic data are analogous to the first *Critique*'s sensory given.[96] Intentional acts give form to this data in the same way that the forms of intuition operate for Kant, even though Husserl refuses to proclaim that hyletic data are subject to an "animating synthesis" and even questions whether they play a constitutive role in intentionality.[97] The objectivity of the hyletic layer must be, as in Kant, *inferred* from perception: it is never experienced in its pure form or given to consciousness, since it is always filtered and formed by intentionality. Dodd even suggests that Husserl's idealism is stronger than Kant's: "Husserl's strategy is to claim that the sources of knowledge are not hidden, but 'are' only within an 'experience' that itself is a unity given in reflection—this is *against Kant*."[98] The inference to a mind-independent hyle is without phenomenological confirmation; it is without phenomenological evidence. Just as in Hegel and Merleau-Ponty, perception is the most basic mode of access to the given: "The *object-giving* (or *dator*) intuition of the first, 'natural' sphere of knowledge and of all its sciences is natural experience, and the *primordial* dator experience is *perception* in the ordinary sense of the term," writes Husserl.[99] Nevertheless, hyle serves as the ground of constitutive (noetic) acts of consciousness. Husserl locates hyle in something posited as non-subjective, the noematic nucleus (object essence), which provides the ideal limit of phenomenological intuition. The noematic nucleus is what persists throughout all of the adumbrations of any given intentional object.[100] It is, on Husserl's view, not the product of subjective constitution, but what is revealed through phenomenological intuition. Its role is merely formal, simply necessary to explain the intentional object's identity and the source of sensory intuition. The fact remains that for Husserl every object, even the "objective" noematic nucleus, is a correlate of consciousness.[101]

A tension similar to the one we noted in Kant is now apparent. If the hyletic layer is situated on the side of the subject, a layer of human consciousness, but is supposed to provide the non-subjective, non-ideal ground of noetic acts, what are we to make of the ontological status of the hyletic layer? Husserl is forced to postulate the reality of a non-intentional source of hyletic material in order to avoid idealism, but this can only occur through a betrayal of his allegiance to the evidence of the given ("the principle of principles"). A betrayal of this sort would carry him into the kind of realist metaphysics phenomenology wishes to suspend, but at the cost of his method's integrity.

Husserl distinguishes sensibility from the hyle which functions as the material basis of meaning-giving acts of consciousness.[102] He further distinguishes sensibility and hyle from the animating acts of consciousness, or noeses. He regards the hyletic layer, both formally and functionally, as "objective" while designating the phenomenal data of sensibility as the "subjective" manifestation of hyletic material. He writes:

> Both [hyle and sensibility] together compelled the old transfer of the originally narrower meaning of sensibility to the spheres of sentiment and will, to the intentional experiences, namely, in which sensory data of the spheres here indicated play their part as functioning "materials."[103]

He concludes that "we need a new term which shall express the whole group through its unity of function and its contrast with the formative characters...." This new term is "hyle," and it circumscribes both the affective and sensuous material that is formed by intentional acts and instilled with meaning by consciousness.[104] The formative acts of consciousness are designated as "psychical" in order to distinguish them from the corporeal and sensory,[105] but Husserl also emphasizes in response to Brentano's psychologism that both the noetic (Brentano's "psychical") and the material (Brentano's "physical") fall within "the stream of phenomenological being."[106] In short, both the matter and form of perception are located fully within consciousness. Sensation is stripped of its non-ideal, objective dimension.[107]

Because *Ideas* I is primarily concerned with the correlation of intentional acts and intentional objects, insofar as this correlation can be given a transcendental sense, the investigation of sensory material for its own sake remains subordinate to the project of transcendental phenomenology. In Husserl's words, an engagement with sensory material as such, or a "pure hyletics," "wins significance from the fact that it furnishes a woof that can enter into the intentional tissue, material that can enter into intentional formations."[108] *Ideas* I is then not the best place to find Husserl engaged with the corporeality of sensation, even if it is representative of his nascent philosophical perspective. It is better to look at *Ideas* II, where sensation (*Empfindung*) is dealt with explicitly with respect to the body and where the hylomorphic structure of consciousness—which regards sensation as amorphous and innocuous—is contested.[109]

Since Merleau-Ponty's notion of the lived body (*corps propre*) is an extension of Husserl's lived body (*Leib*) in *Ideas* II, it suffices to indicate here that Husserl's account of sensation in this text is quite different than the theory of hyle in *Ideas* I or primary contents in *Logical Investigations*. As Alia Al-Saji reads it, the second book of *Ideas* shows Husserl focusing "on the way the lived Body is constituted through the localization of ... sensings [*Empfindnisse*], i.e., the particular lived spatiality of the Body."[110] This is the prototypical concept of sensation I will try to elicit from the works of Merleau-Ponty and Levinas, as well as defend as the concept most faithful to the aesthetic life of our bodies. It is one which attends to the affective and kinaesthetic life of the body and, perhaps most importantly, reveals the materiality of sensation and the subject's reliance on this materiality.[111]

Sense Data and the Aesthetics of Embodiment

We have sketched some of the problematic aspects of the idealist and/or constructivist treatment of sensation, focusing specifically on where it locates sensation vis-à-vis the subject. In the case of Kant, sensation is found on the far side of cognition among the things in themselves. For the Husserl of *Ideas* I, sensation as hyle appears within consciousness, and merely functions as the "external" layer of intentional acts. In both cases, sensation is cut off from the body, allowed to neither enable nor threaten the constitution of the subject as such. By contrast, classical analytic philosophers sympathetic to empirical realism, Bertrand Russell and A.J. Ayer, for example, often speak of sensations (as opposed to sense data) as internal or subjective signs for something objectively given. Here is Russell: "Let us give the name 'sense-data' to the things that are immediately known in sensation," like color, texture, and so on. "We shall give the name 'sensation' to the experience of being immediately aware of these things."[112] With this distinction Russell draws the conclusion that we can infer the existence of objects which might cause our sensations, but these do not appear directly to the mind. Russell continues:

> Thus the various sensations due to various pressures or various parts of the body cannot be supposed to reveal *directly* any definite property of the table, but at most to be *signs* of some property which perhaps *causes* all the sensations, but is not actually apparent in any of them.[113]

This view of sensation is articulated within a realist ontology that posits discrete, fully formed objects existing outside the mind. Epistemologically speaking, these objects are made known to us through the sense data they transmit to consciousness. The process of perceiving and knowing thus begins in the object. Our minds subsequently reconstitute this data into the objects we perceive as outside us. When our reconstitutions correspond to the object in itself, we can claim knowledge of the object as it really is. Merleau-Ponty thoroughly criticizes this model under the name of the "constancy hypothesis" (PP 7-12/13-19) and in so doing steps through the door, opened by Husserl's *Ideas* II, to an embodied view of sensation.[114] The other trouble with Russell's view, and the empiricist view more generally, is well-documented by the idealist and constructivist response to empiricism.

My sympathy for the empiricist view is greater than Merleau-Ponty's. Despite its epistemological difficulties, the metaphysical realist in me likes that empiricism affirms the autonomous existence and qualitative unity of objects. Russell's sense data hypothesis, however, is problematic for at least a couple reasons. I think it is wrong to conceive sensation as internal, or as some kind of epiphenomenon of the mind. It is more than just a feeling or the subjective correlate of a physiological stimulus. Sensation provides a direct link to the world of objects, animals, people, and qualities. It is what presents objects, and that to which objects respond, whether practically, intellectually, or aesthetically. The transmission of sensation is, however, a bidirectional communication and exchange. On this construal sensations are regarded as external to the mind; however, this exteriority is not the whole story. If it were, then an unbridgeable ontological chasm would open between sensing subjects and the sensible world, replacing the equally objectionable subject-world correlation. There must be some bridge between external sensory content and sensibility. Sensation is that bridge.

Sensations travel. Every object possesses a unified sensory identity that can be apprehended or received by other objects. Its identity is transmittable, which is why it is possible to sense objects. Since sensing is not the literal consumption of an object, we might say that sensing is the reception, or taking in, of the object's sensory identity. There must be some way, then, that the object's qualities are detached and dispatched to our sensibility. There is, of course, a physical explanation for how this happens. Instead, what I am interested in exploring is the *metaphysical* aspect of sensation, for there are elements of sensation and sensing that are not accounted for by causal, mechanical, or even phenomenological models. Consequently, given the metaphysical nature of my project, I do not offer this text as a contribution to the embodied mind/embodied cognition literature, nor do I engage that literature at any great length. I do borrow from it at times. So, while it has much to say about the dynamics of sensation and perception, my account is philosophical and speculative. This is why a thorough discussion of the latest cognitive science and embodied mind research is absent from this book.

Some Theses On Sensation

The empirical realist has no problem positing objects as external to the mind. This is what realism does. Sensation is another story. In my view, sensations must be given some external status in order to preserve their objectivity and to explain their effectiveness on the body. Such objectivity is required to explain how bodies are *responsive* to sensations. So, two points that I take from realism: (1) objects and their qualitative unity exist independently of human subjects; (2) this objectivism leverages an externalist view of sensation.[115] The idealist critique of objectivism still holds: if it is the case that we never experience an object in itself, let alone raw sensory material; and that we can only ever know the world through the secondary qualities we perceive (à la Berkeley), then talk about mind-independent reality must be speculative. But it need not be *merely* speculative. Speculation becomes necessary to account for how our minds and bodies are affected by what is other—their dependence, vulnerability, activity, and destruction. One could object that this begs the question by assuming the existence of mind-independent bodies in order to argue for the reality of mind-independent bodies. On the contrary, if we do not posit the existence of autonomous bodies it becomes difficult to explain things like the constitution of the body, its responsive nature, as well as its eventual disintegration. We are forced to conclude, quite absurdly, that death is not a real event, but just an event *for us*.

The constitution of the world may be explicable by transcendental idealism, but it is difficult to see how such a view can explain the dissolution of the world. Kant gives us the conditions for the possibility of experience, but he never gives us *the conditions for the impossibility of experience*. In a word, if nothing other than the mind or consciousness or intentional objects exist, then what delivers violence and death to the subject? The materiality of the subject, that is, its corporeal engagement with a world of autonomous bodies, as well as its means of communication with this world, must be accounted for at both the physical and metaphysical levels. I think a revitalized realism about sensation, one which risks some speculative remarks, can do this. As speculative this realism must go beyond the correlationism of Kantian and post-Kantian critical philosophy as well as phenomenology.

We should avoid posing the question of sensation in terms of a false dichotomy: it is not the case that sensation is *either* a representational content, like Husserl's hyle, *or* an amorphous, discrete datum about which nothing meaningful can be said. Instead, sensation should be seen as a complex meaningful content composed of no less than six dimensions, enumerated here as theses to be elaborated throughout the remainder of this book and expanded in future work.

1. *Sensations are objective, real.* Sensations belong to independent bodies, animate as well inanimate,[116] and make up the singular qualitative constitution of these bodies. So, when Locke writes in his *Essay* that secondary qualities like color, sound, and taste are "nothing in the objects themselves, but powers to produce various sensations in us by their *primary qualities*,"[117] I would insist that this power really does reside in the objects themselves, specifically as their singular sensory composition and its attendant effects. This postulate takes root in empiricist anti-substance theories, including Hume's stageless theatre of personal identity and Berkeley's Lockean definition of the object as a collection of qualities.[118]

Sensations are *effective* insofar as they can bring about changes or engender responses in other bodies. For example, sandpaper *can* smooth wood because it *has* abrasion as a property. Or rather: its abrasive identity just is its capacity to affect wood abrasively. Similarly, we can enter an illuminated room because a light bulb or the sun is able to produce brightness, and a sound wave can shatter a glass because glass has fragility as a disposition and the sound wave has shattering power.[119] Sensations should not be restricted to their familiar role as qualitative or stimulating manifestations, for they are virtual *capacities* inhabiting objects and not mere potentialities;[120] or, if we insist on calling them properties, they must be conceived as transmittable rather than fixed to the substance in which they inhere.[121] It is not that the carpet *is* red, but that the carpet *can produce* red for color-sensitive bodies.

Throughout this book I will use the terms *capacity*, *disposition*, and *power* as synonyms that denote a formal structure (or property) of bodies. These terms denote real properties that entail determinate, although conditional, effects and/or affects. Dispositions are not merely possible or conditional, but *virtual*. They are real, but not actual, as Deleuze says. They exist in bodies, whether manifested or not. In Stephen Mumford's words, "To ascribe a disposition is to suggest possibilities of behaviour. It is to say that something could or would happen if the circumstances were right."[122] Later on I will explicate plasticity as the basic disposition intrinsic to bodies. Ontological dispositions will be shown to equal practical powers.

2. *Sensations are actualized relationally.* Relationality must be understood alongside, not in opposition to, objectivity. It is in their relations that objects exhibit their capacities, or deploy themselves. This does not mean that objects are reducible to their relations, however. Using the sandpaper example again, it can be said that sandpaper is abrasive only to surfaces that are receptive to abrasion. That is, only the right conditions can manifest its abrasiveness. A piece of wood will receive sandpaper sensations differently than a marble or glob of pudding. So, while sensations belong to objects as effective dispositions, they only *make sense* or *actualize* themselves when they enter relations with something that senses them. They never fully actualize themselves in any given relation, however. Something is always left in reserve. Other actualities remain dormant, as it were. Consider color, for example. As Alva Noë shows, color can be understood as the way a thing is disposed to change its appearance in color-critical conditions. To have a color, in other words, is to affect and be affected by the environment in specific ways that vary according to the specific dispositional capacity of a specifically colored object: "An object with a determinate color *acts on*, or *responds to*, its environment in a special way."[123] There is never a point at which this is not occurring. Relations are ubiquitous, but they do not exhaust the being of bodies.

Human perception is not a necessary condition for the manifestation of sensations. Abrasion makes sense to any surface that is susceptible to scratching. Sensations therefore display a *liminal* and *diacritical* aspect: they always express themselves in relations between objects (liminal) and are effective in different ways which are determined by the sensory capacity and susceptibility of the objects encountered (diacritical). The liminality of human sensibility is conditioned by the fact that the body is both part of and in some ways out of step with the world. It is immanent to, but also seems to transcend, the material world.[124] Diacriticality implies that sensations are always caught up in a differential sensory system, each system comprising a distinct, complex environment with countless folds and niches that afford singular encounters.[125]

It should be noted here that I insist on the relationality of sensation to acknowledge what Timothy Morton has called "the ecological thought," roughly the idea that every living and nonliving thing in the universe is interconnected, at all times. But interconnection does not necessarily eliminate alterity.[126] Sensory environments are always caught up in an ecology of sensations and qualitative forms, some of which are foreign, unknown, or unknowable. But as I have indicated, sensation is not purely relational, nor are bodies reducible to the sets of relations entangling them. Bodies, even when deployed in multiple relations, always hold something in reserve. Otherwise, how could they ever forge new relations? Sensation is best regarded as the *precondition* of relation; it is what enables bodies to enter into and exit alliances. It is the body's disposition/power which houses the architecture that allows it to shift allegiances.

3. *The practical value of sensation is ambivalent*. Sensations can enable and disable bodies, stimulate or violate them. Because sensations are ambivalent in this way, it is not possible to interpret them as merely subjective or internal. Some sensations result in the dissolution of the subject and their destructive capacity must be accounted for. Neither Merleau-Ponty nor Levinas adequately addresses this dimension of sensation. Sensory ambivalence provides the chance to build an ethics of embodiment which is based on our vulnerability to and nourishment by sensations.

4. *Sensations are a source of alimentation*. It has already been said that sensations must be in some sense objective if we are to explain their effectiveness, or what Aristotle refers to as sensation's dependence "on being moved and being affected."[127] This objectivity also accounts for sensation's capacity to nourish our senses and feed our bodies in the way that a melody, painting, or landscape has the power to transform or invigorate us, or how a contour of the ground orients our posture and gait. On this rendering, the Aristotelian distinction between the nutritive and sensitive faculties is collapsed. Sensation just is nutrition, alimentation. Without alimentation our bodies are left to languish in their habitual sensory circuits.[128] Alimentation and nourishment are two of the most significant elements I take from Levinas's corporeal ontology.

5. *Sensations are basically anonymous.* The anonymity of sensation is what prevents it from becoming an anthropocentric concept, one which would drive a wedge between the human and nonhuman worlds. Contra Aristotle, sensations do not rely on humans for their effectiveness; humans may feel the abrasiveness of sandpaper in ways that a piece of wood cannot, but this is only because humans (and some nonhumans) possess the power to translate sensations into affections or to process sensations into perceptions or cognitions or linguistic expressions, thus personalizing them. This is why I would say that perception is personal while sensation is not. The human ability to translate sensations into something personal speaks to the relationality of sensations, not to their objective constitution. It will be said that sensations are always attached to a particular object (Merleau-Ponty speaks not of red, but of the unique red of *this* carpet), but this by no means renders the quality qua quality proper to any particular object. They are, as it were, "transobjective." I will argue that our identity is constituted by the sensations we receive as well as the sensations we give off, but I will insist that these sensations do not belong to us, but rather we belong to them. Subjects, then, need sensations in a way that sensations do not need subjects.

6. *The time of sensation belongs to the past.* Sensations are almost universally regarded as phenomena of presence and equated with how they immediately manifest themselves to the senses. But the actualization of sensations requires a different temporal signature. Without the duration involved in the movement of my hand across a pane of glass, I cannot sense its smoothness. Over time sensations accumulate in the body (as habits, for instance) and leave a unique footprint on our body schema. This sedimentation may lead to a desensitization or inattention to familiar sensations, a condition involving practical consequences, like a diminishment of adaptability. Insofar as sensations are virtually real, their existence prior to actualization belongs to the past, to what Merleau-Ponty calls "a past which has never been present." In a sense, then, the reality of sensation remains forever past, shattered as it is when it manifests its efficacy at the level of present attention, perception, or reflection. It therefore challenges the priority given by Heidegger and others to future-oriented human projects. Again, sensation is the precondition of these projects.

These six theses arise out of a rereading of the corporeal ontologies of Merleau-Ponty and Levinas. But neither Merleau-Ponty nor Levinas subscribes to all six of sensation's dimensions. Complete adherence to these theses requires that we formulate an independent position which is in some respects at odds with the French phenomenologists. This position emerges in this book and has its most elaborate expression in the last two chapters, wherein I attempt to develop an original view of the embodied subject's reliance on sensation.

Three Body Types

The modern view which sees sensation as merely subjective or dependent on objective, "primary qualities," does not adequately address the reality of sensation. Some contemporary philosophers have tried to respond to this inadequacy, and it is their attempts to do so that orient the analyses of the following text. Additionally, I suggest that the inadequacy in question arises because sensation is always kept at a safe remove from the subject and that this gesture is informed by a dualist ontology that conceives the body as separate from the perceptual and intellectual operations of the subject. Such a view obscures the subject-object relation as well as the nature of the intercorporeal community. My cursory history of the fate of sensation in the post-Kantian milieu serves not as an indictment of modern idealism *tout court*, but rather as an heuristic with which to understand the corporeal phenomenologist's desire to inject sensation with new life. The problem now is to give an account that adheres to the volatility of sensation and captures the aspects of experience left out of the Kantian/Husserlian model. The resolution of this problem reveals not only a more complex picture of sensation itself, but also demonstrates the central function of sensation in the processes of corporeal individuation, the constitution of bodily identity, and intercorporeal commerce. Such an understanding motivates my critique (understood in the Kantian sense) of the phenomenology of the body and the development of a practical theory of corporeal power.

My own view of the body as plastic emerges through an exploration of the phenomenologies of Merleau-Ponty (Chapters 2-3) and Levinas (Chapter 4), with whom I travel up to the point at which they no longer pursue the questions that I would like answered by a theory of embodiment.

Admittedly, these questions are my own concern and are motivated by a materialist impulse that neither phenomenologist attempts to satisfy. Merleau-Ponty's *reversible body*, which is developed in response to the modern theory of sensation and really begins to take form in the chapter on "Sense Experience" (*le sentir*) in *Phenomenology of Perception*, is treated first. There are traces of the reversible body at play in *The Structure of Behavior* and this model is modified in texts like "Eye and Mind," "Cézanne's Doubt," "The Child's Relations with Others," and *The Visible and the Invisible*, but the most substantial articulations appear in the *Phenomenology*, which nowadays is often overshadowed by the ontological promise of *The Visible and the Invisible*. My view is that the earlier text is by no means superseded.

Partly in response to an apparent ethical defect in Merleau-Ponty's own philosophy, Levinas deploys what I call the *susceptible body*. If Merleau-Ponty's body downplays its passivity in favor of its competence or grasp (*prise*) of things, consequently misrepresenting the volatility of sensitive life and posing an obstacle to the solicitations of other bodies, then Levinas provides an account of the body which overstates the vulnerability of the body and obscures the enabling effects of sensation. Notably, however, he does provide unique resources for thinking sensation in its transcendental and alimentary functions, as well as its affective and material dimensions.

The *plastic body* I eventually endorse against the phenomenologists (Chapter 5) is a reconstruction built from components found in both Merleau-Ponty's and Levinas's texts, most important of which is the carnal sensibility they offer as a replacement for the Kantian model. Following James, Dewey, and Malabou, among others, the plastic body balances what I see as two extreme yet opposing descriptions of the body-world relation. Once this balance is struck we then have an account of embodiment that provides an alternative to the correlationist view of sensation and subjectivity, narrows the gap between phenomenology and non-phenomenology, and provides the basis for a practical philosophy grounded in the aesthetic life of the body (Conclusion).

Chapter 2

Synchronic Bodies and Environmental Orientation

> Let us return to sensation and scrutinize it closely enough to learn from it the living relation of the perceiver to his body and to his world.
>
> Merleau-Ponty, *Phenomenology of Perception*

At this point we have a historical framework in place to situate the reformulation of sensation in Merleau-Ponty and Levinas. This chapter and the next focus on what Merleau-Ponty has to say about the body's constitution, the aesthetics of embodiment, and the nature of sensation. They adduce the divergence between sensation and perception as Merleau-Ponty understands it, principally in the Sense Experience (*Le Sentir*) chapter of *Phenomenology of Perception*. My purpose is to exhibit Merleau-Ponty's ontology of the body, paying specific attention to the practical function of sensibility, and ultimately to challenge his thesis that the intercorporeal relation is fundamentally synchronic and reversible. My critique results in the claim that if we maintain Merleau-Ponty's thesis that the perceptual life of the body is the bedrock of experience, then it becomes difficult to explain the asymmetry of violence and the reality of hostility, as well as the death of the body and *a fortiori* the disintegration of perception entailed in death.

The Centrality of the Body

It is undeniable that Merleau-Ponty makes the body central to his philosophy of the subject and that the ideality of the real—defended by countless thinkers before and after him, including his Gestalt allies—is contested by his theory of embodiment and his primacy of perception thesis. By putting the body at the base of his analyses, indeed at the birth of the world, he puts the body immediately in touch with the objects of *human* perception and argues for the codependent, dialogical constitution of subject and object.[129] By making perception primary, he shows how things and persons, minds and ideas—in short, determinate entities as such—arise out of the indeterminacy, or nascent figuration, of the perceived world. Sometimes he equates body and perception; other times he casts the body as an instrument or vehicle of perception. Most commentaries resolve this inconsistency by showing that Merleau-Ponty means to overcome mind-body dualism by relocating consciousness from the mind to the lived body, or they excuse him for carelessly invoking the dualism he clearly rejects. There is no conscious mind "within" the body: it is just *the body itself* which is conscious. This is his explicit view.

It is not always noted, however, that the body is only important for Merleau-Ponty because it is essential to any account of the nature of perception. His introduction of the body into the discourse of perception is meant to challenge classical philosophers of mind (Descartes, Hume, and Kant, for instance) as well as the dominant psychological theories of his day, particularly behaviorism. The body imbues the primacy of perception thesis with a practical perspective that redefines the objective world as a series of adumbrations and meaningful forms determined by the corporeal constitution of the subject. It is precisely the embodied dimension of perception that is missed by the classical philosophers on Merleau-Ponty's view. As for his opponents in psychology, they fail to acknowledge that a mechanistic view of behavior overlooks the vital role that meaning plays in human consciousness. Behaviorism remains beholden to the actuality of stimuli, even when it does talk about anticipation. Anticipation, as the behaviorist views it, is always a mechanical reaction to stimulation, not a creative or interpretive encounter with meaningfulness. Human consciousness, in Merleau-Ponty's estimation, "has the ability to orient itself by the *possible*, the *virtual*" and these capacities are to be located in the structure of perception.¹³⁰

Despite his corporeal orientation, it could be said that Merleau-Ponty is not really interested in the body as a *material* entity. He is only concerned with how the body's situatedness shapes perceptual experience and the sense of the world. He is not immediately interested in addressing the metaphysical questions which surround the body or incarnation, nor is he bothered about reconciling the phenomenology of embodiment with the research of the physical sciences, as the current efforts of neurophenomenology and embodied cognition are attempting. Or rather, he would prefer to explain empirical research on the basis of phenomenology, not the other way around, as is the trend today. The body as perceived and lived, as given phenomenally to the consciousness inhabiting it, is his primary object of description. Most of what he says about the lived body is evidently given to perception; it is neither speculative nor deductive. He thus adopts Husserl's distinction between *Leib* and *Körper* in order to set the latter aside and focus exclusively on the former. His analyses are undeniably founded upon this distinction.

Körper is the determinate, objective body of science. It is known from the third-person standpoint. It is the physiological body that functions in many ways below the level of consciousness and that is constantly degenerating and regenerating with the passage of time. *Leib* is the conscious body, the body that experiences the world as a network of meaning instead of as a field of causal interactions. When the lived body (*Leib*) is in pain it confronts that pain with horror or with patience. By contrast, pain for the objective body (*Körper*) is little more than a physiological change of state and is legible not by the body itself but only by an external observer trained to read its biological or neurochemical data.¹³¹ Whenever Merleau-Ponty is explicating the life of the body it is the lived body he intends to describe. His object of study is, to be sure, circumscribed by a methodological decision: his adoption of phenomenology and its strict adherence to what appears (as given) to consciousness.

The problem of the body is not simply, for Merleau-Ponty, a matter of simple description or a vindication of first-person experience. It represents the problem of how "there is *for us* an *in-itself*" (PP 71/86), or how it is possible for perception to immanently order the perceptual field while at the same time revealing the world as a transcendent phenomenon. To reconcile this apparent paradox Merleau-Ponty interrogates the fact that perception is never divorced from a body's perspective on things. In order to disclose the significance of perspective, he is forced to come to terms with the ontological meaning of the body. Therefore, instead of considering the body as an "obstacle" to be overcome, or as a material thing, Merleau-Ponty conducts a critique of the body as the very condition of possibility for disclosing the world (PP 68/82). He posits that "The object-horizon structure, or the perspective, is no obstacle to me when I want to see the object; for just as it is the means whereby objects are distinguished from each other, it is also the means whereby they are disclosed" (PP 68/82). This means that our corporeity not only circumscribes our finitude, our determination as creatures locked within a given spatial and temporal horizon, but that horizonality, or the figure-ground structure, is basic to perception, knowledge, and the individuation of bodies. It is a transcendental condition of experience.

It must be kept in mind that inserted in the middle of the figure-ground structure is a "third term." This is the body (PP 101/117).[132] Since the body plays such a pivotal role in the structuring of perception, and therefore the world, it is necessary to outline the ontology of the body to reveal Merleau-Ponty's general theory of perception and, consequently, being. After all, he does say that the perceiving subject *is* the perceived world (PP 72/86). To understand Merleau-Ponty's theory of the subject and how it interacts with the world, we must first know what makes up the lived body.

Perception and the Lived Body

It would seem that by beginning with perception Merleau-Ponty is mainly concerned with epistemological questions, or at least with the question of how we access and apprehend things. This is implied when he says in "The Primacy of Perception" that his project is "not a question of reducing human knowledge to sensation [*sentir*], but of assisting at the birth of this knowledge, to make it as sensible as the sensible, to recover the consciousness of rationality" (PrP 25/67). As well, M.C. Dillon's classic *Merleau-Ponty's Ontology* is curiously oriented by a classical epistemological problem: Meno's paradox.[133] This right away suggests that Merleau-Ponty is occupied with unraveling our *knowledge* of the things themselves rather than the things *themselves*. Moreover, by closely following Husserl, it would seem that Merleau-Ponty is endorsing some form of idealism, even if not the strong transcendental type.[134] But Merleau-Ponty actively criticizes idealist presumptions by repeatedly pointing to the incongruity between perception and things perceived. Thus, while his primacy of perception thesis works as a response to a host of epistemological viewpoints,[135] it also advances an ontological position which speaks to the constitution of both subjects and objects, and finds these entities manifesting an autonomous life of their own that actively resists cognitive synthesis or total comprehension.[136]

The double epistemological/ontological concern marks a tension within Merleau-Ponty's methodological starting point: immanent perceptual phenomena. How can specifically human perception reveal to us what ultimately exists in itself? That is the paradoxical question Merleau-Ponty's phenomenological ontology seeks to answer. The paradox is ostensibly resolved when Merleau-Ponty recognizes that the duality of subject and object, in-itself and for-itself, is *founded* by perception, rather than presupposed by it.

> The first philosophical act would appear to be to return to the world of actual experience which is prior to the objective world, since it is in it that we shall be able to grasp the theoretical basis no less than the limits of that objective world, restore to things their concrete physiognomy, to organisms their individual ways of dealing with the world, and to subjectivity its inherence in history. Our task will be, moreover, to rediscover phenomena, the layer of living experience through which other people and things are first given to us, the system 'Self-others-things' as it comes into being; to reawaken perception and to foil its trick of allowing us to forget it as a fact and as perception in the interest of the object which it presents to us and of the rational tradition to which it gives rise. (PP 57/69)

The apparent immediacy of perception, which "is no longer the impression, the object which is one with the subject, but the meaning, the structure, the spontaneous arrangement of parts" (PP 58/70), is defined in non-objective terms and cannot be dissociated from the network of concrete meanings that are exchanged at the intercorporeal level. Perception is not first a matter of intuitive apprehension or judgment, it is a dialogue of physiognomies— corporeal arrangements whose sense is deciphered and rendered determinate by the body's practical know-how.

John Sallis identifies three important characteristics of perception. These encapsulate the ontological consequences of Merleau-Ponty's primacy of perception thesis. By designating perceptual experience as primary, Merleau-Ponty shows that perception is original, autonomous, and foundational.[137] All our reflections, and thus everything we know, have their origin in perception. The fund of perceptual experience is already there before our senses, full of animation, form, and meaning. Perception is not produced by the subject: the subject always finds itself inhabiting, from a singular perspective, a phenomenal field whose horizon is forever receding and whose figures are always shifting their look. For phenomenology, the resistance this field offers to our gaze reveals it to be beyond our comprehension and in some sense prior to us. The phenomenal field, in short, is not a human fabrication. It conditions human fabrication. The open, ever growing perceptual field that Husserl calls the *Lebenswelt* comprises phenomenology's version of the transcendental (PP 61/74; VI 185-186/239).

Whereas for Kant the transcendental ego is what unifies and stabilizes the sensible realm, for Merleau-Ponty only a subject situated within an environment is able to negotiate the coordinates that characterize experience and furnish itself with the material that founds understanding, judgment, reflection, and action. "A subject so aloof from the world as to be able to constitute space as pure form would be no more capable of distinguishing 'up' from 'down' than would a subject so subordinated to the world as to be merely receptive of non-oriented sense-content," says Sallis.[138] Perception and constitution are what takes place *between* subjects and objects. It belongs neither to the subjective nor the objective side of things, but rather *involve* (folds, envelops) the subject and the object at once. The fundamental opacity or ambiguity of this involutionary movement resists objective circumscription and prevents the evidence of perception from being "absorbed into the circuit of reflective thought."[139] The object given in perception is never given completely, yet we nevertheless observe and interact with it as a unified thing (PrP 15/47).

By designating perception as the birthplace of the world, while at the same time imbuing this place with an irreducible ambiguity, Merleau-Ponty poses a considerable challenge for anyone asking, "What exists?" Is it a disfigured world eventually figured by perception, or is there some figuration prior to perception? Is matter nothing without perceptual form, or is matter always already formed? For phenomenology, it seems necessary to always reformulate this question as: "What meaning can I discover, given my finite, corporeal constitution?" Of course, this echoes the Kantian critical question, "What can I know?" But Merleau-Ponty modifies the Kantian problem, which attempts to draw the limits of rational knowledge, by turning the synthetic act of cognition into a problem of synthesis whose solution is the lived body. As Sallis puts it, "The body, to which is linked the whole series of reductions that indicate the need for synthesis, is, in a sense, the agent of the synthesis that is needed."[140] This does not mean that Merleau-Ponty simply replaces Kant's transcendental ego with a lived body that remains free of the effects of history. The body is always already "saturated with its object" (PP 215/249) and a history, and thus not the proper origin of the world. The body that performs the synthesis of perceptual experience is never completely "aloof" from the world because there is always something impersonal and improper about the body (PP 215/249)—a foreignness inhabiting it—unlike its self-identical doppelganger, the transcendental ego. Moreover, despite its capacity to "withdraw" from the world in reflection, the lived body always remains tied to its world by an intentional thread (PP 72/86).[141] The subject-object correlate is irreducible; it colors everything that can be said about the reality of things and the life of the subject.

The need for a transcendental faculty of synthesis becomes superfluous if the body already accomplishes the coordination of experience. Now, Merleau-Ponty does not say that matter is formed prior to perception, but he also does not say that it is not formed. He says that the genesis of form is traceable by examining perception, which, again, does not tell us something explicit about things but rather about how we know them. "In positive terms, Merleau-Ponty's task is to retrace, beginning at the level of profiles, the constitution of the object, in such a way as to show how at each level there is already a synthesis initiated within the matter itself without there being any need for an extrinsic act of synthesis."[142] The body is able to accomplish this retracing because it is inserted directly into the perceptual horizon and serves as the anchor "in a total system of possible profiles in their correlation with certain motor possibilities."[143] The body is always converging in practice upon an optimum perspective, or an increasingly coherent system of appearances, but never absolute knowledge of the object itself (PP 301-303/347-350). The object always evades the reach of perception despite perception's increasing ability to make sense of or manipulate it. Although perception is foundational, it discloses objects as independently constituted, and never reaches complete convergence with the object.

In a frequently cited working note to *The Visible and the Invisible* Merleau-Ponty acknowledges that by beginning with perception in *Phenomenology of Perception* he prevented himself from articulating the kind of non-dualist ontology that he was working out in his later texts. When he admits that "The problems posed in *Ph.P.* are insoluble because I start there from the 'consciousness'-'object' distinction" (VI 200/253), he realizes that it is impossible to bridge the gap between subject and object, as well as lived body and objective body, if these binaries remain cast as ontologically distinct. He thought that, by beginning with perception, subject and object could be shown to achieve their (abstract) distinction from out of the more primary unity of perception, considered as a dynamic intentional nexus. Ultimately, the argument runs, it is the body's practical competence that carves out the contours of reality: "My body is the fabric into which all objects are woven, and it is, at least in relation to the perceived world, the general instrument of my 'comprehension'" (PP 235/272). It is clear that it is only through the body—here portrayed as a kind of prosthetic of the understanding—that the world is organized into semi-discrete and discrete objects of perception. But is this an ontology of what exists or an ontology of embodied perception?

The lived body problematically possesses a kind of double life. On the one hand, Merleau-Ponty wants the body and its practical aims to provide the transcendental background against which perception is generated (consider his privileging of "spatiality of situation" over intelligible Newtonian space in PP 100/116). On the other hand, Merleau-Ponty insists that the body always finds itself caught up in a world populated with objects, people, meanings, and ideas. He maintains the first position in order to escape a naturalistic or positivistic conception of subjectivity. He maintains the second position in order to avoid charges of idealism or immaterialism. These evasions force him to maintain a view of the embodied subject as both generative of, and generated by, its perceptual world, a view which has become more common than it was in the 1940s. The generated world is identical to (or at least correlated with) the perceived subject insofar as the subject is what gives form to the world, by orienting its spatiality, for example (see PP, chapter 3). The objective world that generates the body is what harbors the perspectival and practical environment we always find ourselves within, and which resists us when we try to encompass it in theory or practice. The objective environment would be the world in which things store their unseen profiles, the forgotten world of anonymous, non-intentional sensory existence which lines the visible world (PP 215-216/250-251). As objective, or "invisible," it can only be inferred from the evidence of the visible.

By bracketing the objective world as well as the body taken as physical object, and beginning with the world *as perceived*, Merleau-Ponty gives himself over to a sustained phenomenological interrogation of the aporetic, somewhat Schellingian, query, "How can my body serve as both the origin of the world and its product?" His book-length reply details the ways in which the body primarily interacts with its world at the phenomenal level, that is, at the level of perception. This interaction is several times characterized as a dialogue of reciprocal determination. Subject and object codetermine each other, exchange forms, and trade meanings (PP 127, 129, 132/148, 150, 154). Neither subject nor object enjoys privilege of determination.

This maneuver, that is, beginning an ontological investigation with perception, raises questions about the pre-perceptual genesis of the body, particularly at the material level. Some of these questions are addressed by Merleau-Ponty, but we must ask whether his account of the pre-perceptual genesis of the body falls within the scope of phenomenology or whether it must have recourse to a supplementary speculative metaphysics, a question of absolute origins. I will argue that Merleau-Ponty's phenomenology does draw upon a metaphysics of the body, but that this metaphysics derives from and transgresses his phenomenological investigations.

Merleau-Ponty acknowledges that the primacy of perception thesis is reminiscent of an idealist epistemology that assumes the constitutive power of consciousness. But if the body is what makes perception part of the objective world while at the same time serving as the condition of that world's appearance, then a kind of distance must be introduced between the material world in which the body is an object of science and the lived world in which the body engages a meaningful existence. Otherwise, how can he explain the body's frankly *transcendent* constitutive power? As Merleau-Ponty remarks, "If my consciousness were at present constituting the world which it perceives, no distance would separate them and there would be no possible discrepancy between them" (PP 238/275). Whence the discrepancy? Whence the escape from immanence?

Merleau-Ponty answers that what makes the body more than a physical object is the distance opened within consciousness by the polarization of subject and object effected by *intentionality*. Intentionality is both what animates the body as a subject, but also what keeps it necessarily correlated with the world. It enables transcendence, but only ever a transcendence within immanence. Like the figure-ground structure, intentionality is an ontological fact of existence (PP xvii/xii). In principle, it holds that conscious life and knowledge are inextricably bound up with the historical horizon in which we act, interpret, and exist. At the corporeal level intentionality structurally links my lived body, my objective body, the body of the other, and the objects of the world. Each comprises a quasi-independent node of the perceptual web, but each node is nevertheless always correlated with the others.

The Materiality of the Body

Merleau-Ponty's lived body must be decidedly "closer" to the material world for his phenomenology to challenge the idealist phenomenology of Husserl. That is, the lived body must really possess a kind of materiality that is unappreciated by Husserl. To achieve this materialization, Merleau-Ponty must posit a pre-perceptual life of the body, a life lived before constitution. Otherwise, the body is reducible to its perceptual activity: *esse est percipi*. Merleau-Ponty must allow that the body's capacity for perception is not merely the result of its own ideal activation, and that its constitution is not comprised only of "existentials" that "operate in perceptions" but remain unperceived themselves (VI 178, 180, 189/232, 233-234, 243; see PP 238/275).[144] Upon reflection the phenomenal field must show itself to have already been a field full of extant bodies. Without a site of genuine intercorporeity Merleau-Ponty would have to resort to a quasi-theological account of the incarnation of consciousness in the body, or leave the birth of consciousness, along with the gap between self and other, shrouded in mystery.

Faced with the threat of immaterialism and despite the constraints placed on his discourse by the phenomenological perspective, he does not pass over in silence the pre-phenomenal constitution of the body. He delimits its materiality from an ontological, rather than physiological or biological, perspective. This requires some speculative deviation from his commitment to phenomenological method.

When I say that Merleau-Ponty "speculates" about the constitution of the body, I mean that he admits elements into his account of subjectivity that are not disclosed phenomenologically. Methodologically, his phenomenology displays a hybrid form, foregoing as he does the quest for scientific purity exhibited in so many of Husserl's texts. It is a mixture of phenomenological description, empirical research, and metaphysical speculation. Disentangling these threads is not always easy. Merleau-Ponty's ambiguous deployment of method is partly what enables him to escape the fate of subjective idealism; it is what Lakoff and Johnson admire when they call Merleau-Ponty an "empirically responsible" phenomenologist.[145] For instance, in order to explain the rigidity of psychological prejudices like racism and their influence on the structuring of perception, Merleau-Ponty appeals to the genetic, historical, and physiological dimension. He does this not to show that perception is always forced to conform to a reified biological or social structure (Child 107/15), but to argue that heredity and social conditioning are co-constitutive of the individual and his or her attitude toward others. He writes that it is not the case that "the way in which the child structures his social environment is unrelated to the hereditary or constitutional dispositions of his nervous system" (Child 108/16). The individual is never simply determined by his or her environment. The individual operates between the biological and the social, "*takes a position* in the face of [these] external conditions" (Child 108/17, my emphasis). Here we see the phenomenological supplement to the biological. The child's perceptual prejudices are the result of a "single global phenomenon" that emerges from certain natural determinations and social conditioning, but against which the child is able to make his or her own meaning (Child 108/17). To comprehend the genesis and alteration of this meaning it is necessary to see how perception is both something given (as social prejudice and physiology) and enacted (in the body's meaningful responses to its perceived environment).

Unfolding the constitution of the body means giving an account of the genesis of its many dimensions with a view to exposing how these dimensions make up the "new definition of the *a priori*" discussed at several points in the *Phenomenology of Perception* (for example, PP 220-222/255-257). The corporeal a priori is addressed from at least three aspects which do not always display a coherent relationship: (1) the primacy of perception thesis, (2) the body as the hinge of perception,[146] and (3) sensation as the body's original communion with the world. The primacy of perception thesis says that the things we encounter are conditioned by, which is to say, oriented according to, our field of perception. This field is coordinated by the (partially anonymous) constitution of our bodies and their (often impersonal)[147] capacity to practically synthesize the world (PrP 14/45-46). Of particular importance for this synthesis is the *schéma corporel*, or body schema,[148] along with a number of other components which function transcendentally in Merleau-Ponty's view of the body as reversible. These will be examined momentarily.

Although it operates as a transcendental, the lived body is never fully detached from external bodies, objects, and other persons.[149] The material world and the body *as subject* are co-transcendentals or codependent, we might say. This is Merleau-Ponty's original philosophical innovation.[150] The body for him is not "an agency underlying the organization of experience" or "the foundation of transcendental constitution."[151] He does argue, however, that the body organizes the space it inhabits into functional and practicable places, although he does not mean to say that places are generated spontaneously by individual bodies. Instead, the body's organizational capacity "is a response to the questions the world raises," which means that its transcendental function "is inconceivable apart from its receptive, responsive, centripetal role before the givenness of the world, its existence as flesh amidst the flesh of the world."[152] When we speak of Merleau-Ponty's transcendental perspective, we must always keep in mind that his is an impure transcendental, a set of conditions that are themselves conditioned by the body's mutable history. This "historical *a priori* is constant only for a given phase and provided that the balance of *forces* allows the same *forms* to remain" (PP 88/104). Merleau-Ponty's discussion of habit provides the concrete key to the historical a priori, a powerful notion that underlies much of the discussion of corporeal genesis below.

Dillon's defense of Merleau-Ponty's non-Kantian transcendental philosophy does not fully appreciate the difficulty of escaping Kantianism/correlationism, especially for the phenomenologist. On the one hand, the primacy of perception thesis opposes the Kantian model by claiming that the phenomena of perception are *prior to* the divorce of subject and object, subject and object being abstractions conditioned by the primordial layer of perceptual experience. The transcendental is generated not by a pure lived body, but by the lived body's phenomenal, intercorporeal encounters in the "system 'self-others-world'" (PP 60/73). In Dillon's words, "The lived body is not a transcendental subject; it is a phenomenon situated among other phenomena within the world horizon."[153] Merleau-Ponty further displaces the constitutive role of the subject by speaking sometimes of the thing as the source of the body-subject's unity (PP 322/372). But how can the thing provide the lived body's unity if the thing's unity is merely an abstraction from perception, which is itself conditioned by the lived body, which is merely a phenomenon? Merleau-Ponty maintains that neither body nor object possesses priority; it is their dialogue, communion, or intertwining which is primary. But if he wants to displace the constitutive role of the subject, then he must posit the externality of other bodies a priori. This, however, is disallowed by the primacy of perception thesis as well as the general phenomenological perspective Merleau-Ponty adopts from Husserl.

To sidestep idealism and ground embodied perception in intercorporeity, Merleau-Ponty needs the lived body to be the product of intercorporeal encounters rather than their condition of possibility. This requires him to commit to both an ontological realism about other bodies and a correlative dualism that enables his subject-object dialogue to be truly dialogical. His realism is most evident in his treatment of sense experience, where he looks beyond what is given phenomenally to perception in order to speak about what lies below the level of intentionality; his tacit commitment to dualism in the *Phenomenology* gets recast in terms of reversibility in *The Visible and the Invisible*, arguably to the detriment of alterity.

Sometimes he speaks to the contrary, but there is neither a pure a priori nor a pure a posteriori in Merleau-Ponty.[154] For instance, he says that the habituated body schema "remains forever anterior to perception [*qui reste toujours en deçà de notre perception*]" (PP 238/275), which would seem to indicate that the body schema is always prior to the existence of the world, and is therefore an ahistorical a priori. The body and perception would be non-identical in such a case, the former always already constituted prior to the appearance of the space-time of perceptual events. But since temporality is always indexed to embodiment for Merleau-Ponty, there would appear to be no body before time or time before the body. "We must understand time as the subject and the subject as time," he says (PP 422/483).[155]

If the body and perception are identical—that is, if there is no body before perception and no perception before body—it is necessary to make sense of the latency of the lived body, the body lived unconsciously, prior to reflection and in the background of explicit perception.[156] As Merleau-Ponty writes in "Eye and Mind:" "There is that which reaches the eye directly, the frontal properties of the visible; but there is also that which reaches from below—the profound postural latency [*latence posturale*] where the body raises itself to see…" (EM 187/85-86). This is the body in the grip of the corporeal world, constrained by the exigencies of its embodied experience, and always locked in a circuit of habits and default practices.

When posited from the phenomenological point of view the primacy of perception thesis has the disadvantage of not really explaining how it is possible for the body—its habits, body and postural schemata, behavioral circuits, style, or physiognomy—to be constituted prior to its own perception. And yet, these things must already be in place for perception to function. Indeed, phenomenology does not allow us to speak of an "anonymous" or "impersonal" body that underlies conscious perception and precedes the differentiation of my body from the body of the other (PP 240/277; Child 119/33). Such a dimension must be admitted, however, unless we are willing to concede that the body perceives every event or alteration that affects it, even the imperceptible. This would be stretching the meaning of perception too far, I think. Like Merleau-Ponty (VI 200/253), I see the troublesome status of the impersonal/imperceptible as a methodological problem that limits his early work but which can be overcome by adopting an ontological perspective, as he does most explicitly in *The Visible and the Invisible* when he shifts from the language of consciousness and object (dualism), to the language of the flesh of the sensible (monism).[157] It remains to be seen whether he abandons the subject-object correlation as a presupposition of his thinking of being, or if his later work retains the basic correlationism of the earlier.

Is Perception Really Primary?

Despite his focus on first-person human perception, Merleau-Ponty's earlier texts have plenty to say about the pre-perceptual and anonymous elements of the body. While an adequate metaphysics of corporeal individuation may be lacking in the *Phenomenology of Perception*, there is a healthy ambiguity that attends the transcendental status he assigns to the body. For instance, a structure like the body schema might be designated as a pure a priori if it can be shown to possess an immutable, or ahistorical, element (PP 142/166; SB 189/204). Are their immutable structures at work in the *Phenomenology*? I believe there are.

What I suggest in this discussion of the primacy of perception thesis is that, if perception is in a strong sense essential to the configuration of being, it is not clear how we are to conceive the materiality of the body *prior to* perception. And yet, if it is the body that perceives (PP 238/275), and this body is the product of "a past which has never been present" (PP 242/280), then we are obliged to speculate about the metaphysical genesis of this body. On Merleau-Ponty's view we are forced into the position of thinking the body as the condition of possibility of experience while simultaneously upholding the view that both body and world are the products of perception. To make salient this issue it seems necessary to distinguish the body, as what *gives rise to perception*, from perception *as an embodied activity*. This distinction would lend primacy to the body as corporeal and render perception a secondary activity of the body. In other words, corporeality and perception would not be equiprimordial. It will be objected that this distinction is precisely what is contested by all of Merleau-Ponty's work on perception. In response, I would maintain that if we push the primacy of perception thesis to its limit, what we end up with is the limit of human knowledge, or the finitude of thinking about the origin of perception. The objective body may only be knowable through perception, and in a sense borne of operative intentionality, but this does not explain how consciousness itself gets off the ground. If, by Merleau-Ponty's logic, the existence of consciousness depends on the body (or, in Spinoza's language, the mind is the idea of the body), should we also say that the body exists because of consciousness? Or because of perception? That does not seem quite right. And Merleau-Ponty agrees.

The distinction I propose between the perceiving body and the preperceptual body is spurred by an asymmetry in Merleau-Ponty's text between the body and perception, two terms that are supposed to be synonymous and therefore symmetrical. There are moments, however, where perception is distinguished from and subordinated to the body, although the converse does not occur. This subordination, when it occurs, challenges the primacy of perception thesis by shifting the transcendental character of perception to the level of corporeal sensibility. That is, sensation becomes the transcendental condition of perception. Support for this interpretation is found in the "Sense Experience" chapter of the *Phenomenology*, where the privilege of perception is called into question while Merleau-Ponty attempts a delimitation of the difference between sensation and perception. It is here that we see the most radical elements of Merleau-Ponty's transcendental philosophy, as well as his most fecund flirtations with the concept of sensation.

To substantiate these points I will defend the deliberately provocative thesis that Merleau-Ponty, while attempting to account for the body's relation to the world, gives priority—perhaps unwittingly—to sensing, not perceiving. The priority is granted from an ontological/metaphysical perspective, decidedly not from a phenomenological one. Let me be clear: I am orienting my investigation at a level not explicitly engaged by Merleau-Ponty, so I am not criticizing him for failing to discern what I am concerned with here, namely, the ontology of sensation. With this caveat, we will now pursue the following basic questions: (1) *What constitutes this body that orients our perceptual field?* Merleau-Ponty has plenty to say about this. (2) *Where does this body come from, and how is it individuated from the ambiguous field of the sensible?* First we will unpack some of the primary elements of the body and show that Merleau-Ponty consistently conceives the body as reversible, that is, synchronized with its environment. A close look at his analysis of sensibility reveals the mechanics of reversibility.

Synchronization and Habit

We have seen how the problem of the body is a problem of perception. We must now uncover what this lived body *is* that coordinates and conditions the subject's capacity for perception. Indeed, this capacity is what gives meaning to the world as perceived. Where does it come from and of what is it made? The lived body is not explicitly thematized in our everyday operations, although we are always in some sense aware of it. Many of its components exist in the background as we carry out our mundane activities, and we rely on its stability and health as we go about our business. Most of its physiological activity proceeds without our attention. When the body becomes ill or is disturbed in some other way, it announces itself like Heidegger's broken hammer and becomes an object requiring examination.[158] In these cases it presents itself as an obstacle to be overcome rather than a vehicle or tool that allows us to navigate our environment with facility. Under normal circumstances our bodies are attuned to their material situation and function together as an uninterrupted unity. As Shaun Gallagher puts it,

> When the lived body is "in tune" with the environment, when events are ordered smoothly, when the body is engaged in a task that holds the attention of consciousness, then the body remains in a mute and shadowy existence and is lived through

>   in a non-conscious experience. But when the lived body loses its equilibrium with the environment, it suddenly appears at center stage, announcing itself as painful, fatigued, distorted, clumsy, embarrassed, etc.[159]

This does not mean that we inhabit two ontologically distinct bodies or that the body can be divided into multiple ontological levels.[160] It means that the lived body is most of the time absent or withdrawn from perceptual experience while at the same time conditioning that experience.[161] It can assume various degrees of conspicuousness, but for the most part it is inconspicuous.

Equipped with this image of the normal mode of embodiment, I want to argue that the texts prior to *The Visible and the Invisible* catalogue a series of correlations between body and world that prefigure the concept of flesh, a concept which provides a promising and problematic depiction of the body-world relation. These correlations can be found, among other places, in Merleau-Ponty's discussions of habit, style, physiognomy, and body schema. Admittedly, the language of "correlation" prejudges the matter at hand by smuggling in dualist/objectivist terms when these terms are precisely what Merleau-Ponty's phenomenology aims to dispel. However, given that perception always "takes advantage of work already done" (PP 238/275), there seems to be at least a minimal, or qualified, ontological objectivism at play in Merleau-Ponty's phenomenology. He believes in a world that precedes and will outlast human perception. Moreover, Merleau-Ponty's use of terms like "communion," "dialogue," and "synchronization" suggests that perception in the *Phenomenology* can be thought within a dualist framework, even if this framework is only to be understood as the result of a more originary unity of subject and object. In short, the correlationist prejudice is operative in the language employed in Merleau-Ponty's exposition of perception.

The emphasis on synchronization expresses Merleau-Ponty's desire to take the middle road between rationalism and empiricism, and to strike a balance between active and passive conceptions of embodiment and perceptual synthesis. The body is not fully responsible for creating the world in which it exists, he contends, but neither is it completely vulnerable to all of the impressions inflicted upon it by material events. It is an entity whose actions are partly enacted according to its desires and partly dictated by the impersonal contours of its physical locale. As Madison puts it, "The subject of perception is not the free subject, the master of itself which realizes itself to be a unique individual."[162] Because the body is bound up with the world and given a form or "logic"[163] that it does not give itself, its capacity for action, its existence as an "I can" rather than an "I think," is determined by the "unreasonable promiscuity"[164] it carries on with its environment when it is not reflecting on itself. The pre-personal unity of the body conditions perception and everything perceptual experience entails. As Morris shows, "the body only perceives through its anticipatory motor explorations" which are informed by motor and body schemes that "allow the body to bring the past into the present, and thus articulate the present in a way that would otherwise be impossible."[165] Let us look at the elements of this past.

Perhaps the central correlation of body and world is *habit*. Merleau-Ponty's account of the habituated body is closely tied to discussions of the body/postural schema, physiognomic perception, and behavioral circuits, each of which is supported by what he calls an "intentional arc." The intentional arc names the set of skills or (non-representational) disposition that predisposes an agent to perceive and act in the world with optimum facility. It subtends consciousness and draws together the various threads of the practicable environment into a meaningful horizon of possibilities. It does this by first unifying the senses into a synchronized system that lends sensory coherence to perception. This is what Merleau-Ponty means by "synaesthetic perception" (PP 229/265). The body is not just a reflex mechanism, it is a physical entity capable of interpreting, making sense of, and adapting to the disparity of stimulation it constantly receives. The "personal core" (PP 134/156) of the body "brings about the unity of the senses, of intelligence, of sensibility and motility" and "goes limp" in illness, as the famous Schneider case reveals (PP 136/158-159). Habits are crucial because they provide the body with its historically informed behavioral identity, in the form of latent or sedimentary sets of actions that make its surroundings familiar and workable, allowing it to sense and perceive without always having explicitly to appeal to the personal core of consciousness. Habit gives the intentional arc a certain regularity.

Habits provide the body with a stable practical form. This means that, for the body that possesses a stable identity, they are not merely supplemental or ancillary modifications of a blank corporeity. Or rather, insofar as we acquire them from our cultural and social environments they are a kind of original prosthetic, not unlike language (Child 99/4-5). They comprise a substantial part of who we are, how we experience, and what we can do. Habits allow us to sink our attention in the present without having to attend at each moment to what the body is presently doing or going to do. Taken as a unified system the body is, Merleau-Ponty says, "my basic habit" [*l'habitude primordiale*] (PP 91/107). In order to free itself from the environment the body adopts "pre-established circuits" that give it the space to pursue its intellectual projects. As he says, "it is an inner necessity for the most integrated existence to provide itself with an habitual body" (PP 87/103).[166] This is a view shared with William James, who maintains that habit condenses and simplifies the movements required to complete a particular task, thus habit "diminishes fatigue" by freeing up attention.[167]

Habit, for James, is a material phenomenon that is registered both on and in our bodies. He holds that our repertoire of habits "depend[s] on sensations not attended to," which means that our "body's attitude" or proprioception subtends the series of movements which make up a given habitual action, like buttoning a shirt or brushing one's teeth.[168] The body's attitude is written in the body and, like Merleau-Ponty's intentional arc, what enables the body automatically to make sense of a particular series of sensations and unify them into a coherent habitual action. As he explains in *The Principles of Psychology*, "the phenomena of habit in living beings are due to the plasticity of the organic materials of which their bodies are composed."[169]

Merleau-Ponty does not share James's naturalistic/neuroscientific interpretation of habit. For Merleau-Ponty habits are not stored in the physiology of the body as muscle memories or neurological patterns. Habits are an acquired power built upon the body's unified capacity to grasp an environmental directive and imbue that directive with a meaningful "motor significance" of its own (PP 143/167). The sedimentation of a habit in the body is always permeated, as Edward Casey notes, by the "intentional threads that go back and forth between the body and its ever-changing phases, which are continually reanimated by current experience."[170] In short, habits are anchored in the intentional arc.

The acquisition of a habit involves the "rearrangement and renewal of the body schema," which underlies the habituation process as an "immediately given invariant" (PP 141, 142/165, 166; translation modified). The body schema is an invariable corporeal structure, an open system of motor potentiality that is receptive to the cultivation of habit but not itself capable of being dissociated from the lived body. It remains open because it is arranged according to the shifting practical objectives of the subject, which are not determined in a vacuum but arise in a historical horizon and are always motivating new projects. The subject sets his or her tasks according to the layout of his or her situation and the practical possibilities it presents, while habits reorient the body schema according to the singular way these possibilities are inhabited. Correlatively, the body schema is structured as a response to concrete conditions; it is a dynamic form that is at once shaped by material forces and regulated by the intentional arc and existential milieu of the embodied agent. Casey writes, "the habituation which such inhabitation accomplishes involves a delicate dialectic between the implied passivity of enclosure ... and the activity of getting to know our way around in a given circumstance."[171] There is never a point at which this dialectic is not underway, which is why Merleau-Ponty says that space "is already built into my bodily structure, and is its inseparable correlate" (PP 142/166).

The sedimentation of habits in the lived body releases the subject from the immediacy of the present and enables the "movement of transcendence" that characterizes Merleau-Ponty's conception of volition. The movement of transcendence—which is, paradoxically, enabled by a habitual will—is never a movement toward absolute transcendence. It is always a relative transcendence, more like a reconfiguration of the immanence of being in the world. In his discussion of being in the world we find a decisive statement of Merleau-Ponty's embodied, correlationist view of transcendence:

> The world is inseparable from the subject, but from a subject which is nothing but a project of the world, and the subject is inseparable from the world, but from a world which the subject itself projects. The subject is a being-in-the-world and

> the world remains "subjective" since its *texture and articulations* are traced out by the subject's movement of transcendence. (PP 430/491-492, my italics)[172]

As we know, this is not an endorsement of idealism. It does, however, indicate that Merleau-Ponty sees our capacity to transcend any present situation as predicated upon the immanent organization of that situation by the body's perceptual activity. Conversely, this activity must be seen as a mode of the fundamental passivity of the body. The world, too, turns the subject into a project. There is a certain plasticity underlying this dialectical relation. Despite the apparent symmetry, however, there is a sense in which the plastic correlation of body and world—that is, the immanence of embodiment—is dominated by the projects/projections of the subject. This is because the "texture" of the world is an "articulation" of the subject's practical freedom, which means that the constraints imposed on the subject by the world are, in a sense, self-imposed. Moreover, Merleau-Ponty seems to suggest that the world would be a desolate wasteland without the texture afforded it by subjectivity. It is not so much that the subject possesses a mysterious power to escape immanence, but that Merleau-Ponty's immanence is never pure. It is always already crisscrossed with avenues of transcendence traced out by the subject. Perception guarantees the *complicity*, which is not to say identity, of subject and world because it has intentionality at its center. Intentionality, as we know, binds subject and object while it simultaneously polarizes them. Its difference is subtended by a fundamental sameness. The complicity of intentionality remains asymmetrical, however, for it is the subject that introduces perception into the world and initiates the movement of transcendence. The asymmetrical relation accounts for the ability of the subject to cultivate *its own* habits.[173] Without the movement of transcendence habits could only be imposed on the body from outside. The body possesses a basic creativity that allows it to habituate itself from within.

Just as tissue, neurons, blood, bone, and all the rest work together to form our physiological system, the habits we adopt, cultivate, and inherit make up the lived body's non-biological armature. Without the economizing effect of habit our bodies are destined to expend their energy on simple reflexive behavior or waste it relearning how to perform operations performed many times before. Our bodies are normally not restricted to these modes of existence. Much of our lives are routinized and we perform many tasks as if we were automata. But our automation is only apparent. Habitual activities actually enable us to expand our range of spontaneous actions, which is what Merleau-Ponty means when he says that "habit expresses our power of dilating our being in the world, or changing our existence by appropriating fresh instruments" (PP 143/168). Although automatic, they amplify the range of our freedom.

The armature of habit is no less fundamental than the biological constitution of the body. It is true that Merleau-Ponty says that habit is "merely a mode" of the body's fundamental capacity to transform a spontaneous action into a personal gesture (PP 146/171, translation modified), that habit particularizes the body through repetitious and regular acts. In contrast to the substantial, teleological self of Aristotle or Aquinas or Kant, self-identity for Merleau-Ponty "is maintained through time not by virtue of an unchanging underlying entity, but through repeated action."[174] Habit, then, is ontologically basic to embodiment. More strongly, the body subject *is* a habit. As Casey shows, the primacy of habit is twofold. First, habit is the corporeal manifestation of a past that lives on in my body as its unreflective history. "In this way habit takes the lead over the very body it requires for its own realization." Second, habit forms the basis upon which corporeal style and personal expressivity rest. It mediates between the general, anonymous body and the sculpted body built up by our culture and conduct.[175] In Merleau-Ponty's words:

> Although our body does not impose definite instincts upon us from birth, as it does upon animals, it does at least give to our life the form of generality, and develops our personal acts into stable dispositional tendencies. In this sense our nature is not long-established custom, since custom presupposes the form of passivity derived from nature. The body is our general medium for having a world. (PP 146/171)

Habits are what enable the body to comprehend its environment, to achieve a "harmony between what we aim at and what is given, between the intention and the performance" (PP 144/169). This understanding is of course not intellectual, but inscribed in the body as the physiognomy and corporeal *sens* (meaning, direction) that at once opens and limits our field of perception (PP 152/178).

Before we achieve the freedom to cultivate our own habits we must have reached a workable state of corporeal equilibrium. The forces and impulses we are born with must be tamed in order to make life manageable. Only then are we free to take up the world as a field of equipment. In a sense this is already done for us as we enter into the circuits of behavior maintained by our culture. As Alphonso Lingis puts it, "One is born with forces that one did not contrive. One lives by giving form to these forces. The forms one gets from the others."[176] As human beings we are delivered directly into a world whose form has been shaped by human artifice and techniques of civilization. These forms are technologically produced and conducive to the kind of beings we are. Cultural artifacts are ideally made to enable the postures that we normally adopt as we take our position in the environment. The built places that receive us as newborn infants already have us in mind, or they at least anticipate that our bodies will resemble those which came before. When they do not we rebuild them or adapt our postures accordingly, or the body endures the labor of forced adaptation and potential debilitation. The network or circuit of places made to accommodate our corporeal physiognomies constitutes the meaning of our built environment, the infrastructure of our culture.

The development of the lived body that Merleau-Ponty describes is supported not just by the foresight of architects, but also by natural/cultural atavisms that live on in our human bodies. Following André Leroi-Gourhan, Lingis explains,

> Unlike other mammals, which make their way head first, the nose is no longer in contact with the environment; the eyes have become the directing organ. The upright posture disengaged the hands from the terrain; they now become coordinated with the eyes. As humans begin to alter and reconstruct the environment about them, new functions are taken on by different body parts and organs.[177]

So, it is not just that our bodies are born into habitable spaces that will enable the acquisition of habits. The ways in which we as humans have come to inhabit our environment are ingrained in the physiology of our species, and therefore operate to construct the postures we assume. This point echoes, from an evolutionary perspective, Merleau-Ponty's remarks about the symbiotic relation between the child and its world. Here he is showing a degree of sympathy with James's more naturalistic perspective:

> In fact, from the time of his birth the child who will have prejudices has been molded by his environment, and in that respect has undergone a certain exercise of parental authority. Consequently, there is no moment at which you could grasp, in a pure state, his way of perceiving, completely apart from the social conditioning that influences him. Inversely, you can never say that the way in which the child structures his social environment is unrelated to the hereditary or constitutional dispositions of his nervous system. ... And so the internal characteristics of the subject always intervene in his way of establishing his relations with what is outside him. It is never simply the outside which molds him; it is he himself who takes a position in the face of the external conditions.
> (Child 108/16)

Ultimately, the individual is neither social nor natural at its start. He or she is both at once. The space between these two organizational forces—nature and culture—possesses an "elasticity" [*élasticité*], says Merleau-Ponty, because it can manifest both reactive and active responses within the child (Child 108/16).

Synchronization and Affective Circuits

The body is similarly caught up in circuits that are basically affective. Affective circuits lend our bodies an emotional identity by economizing the things we feel.[178] Since the body is never without its passions, never without a certain emotional disposition or mood, its affectivity must be regarded as constitutive of embodiment.[179] It can be argued, as Lawrence Hass does, that it is affectivity that separates us from the world of inanimate things.[180] Our affects imbue our intercorporeal encounters with a resonance that can energize us (joy) or enervate us (sadness). But it is not just personal encounters that are laced with affectivity—it is the entirety of aesthetic experience. This insight is behind the almost essentialist discussion of color in the *Phenomenology of Perception*, where colors are said to have a "felt effect" and a "motor significance" that explains why, for instance, "red signifies effort or violence, green restfulness and peace" (PP 209-211/242-244).[181] This is not to say that our bodies are hopelessly at the mercy of sensory stimulation. As Merleau-Ponty argues, "The subject of sensation is neither a thinker who takes note of a quality, nor an inert setting which is affected or changed by it, it is a power which is born into, and simultaneously with, a certain existential environment, or is synchronized with it" (PP 211/245). Sensory and affective circuits carry our bodies along, pushing and pulling them, because our bodies are *of* the sensible realm and informed by its sensory contours. Yet we retain the ability to seize upon and transform their meaning, and thus transcend ourselves through aesthetic/affective creation. "I cannot be caught in immanence," says Paul Klee.[182]

Gail Weiss explains how the intentional arc enables a series of disparate affects to be drawn together into a personal circuit of emotion. The intentional arc acts as the internal circuitry of the lived body in the sense that it is always running in the background as the (normal) subject sets out to enter into new and habitual series of tasks. Unlike the habitual circuits that we find in James, where the body runs according to an established set of neural pathways that correspond to its observable behavior, for Merleau-Ponty it is the body's intentional arc that allows it to engage in habituated activities unthinkingly. "This intentional arc," writes Weiss, "provides human beings with an affective sensibility that enables the integration of quite dissimilar experiences into a synthetic whole."[183] For Merleau-Ponty it is the intentional arc (which is reducible neither to the physical nor the representational) that underpins the body's competence, its coherent and almost effortless way of moving, acting, gesturing, and expressing itself corporeally. Or more specifically, it is the habituation of the body's intentionality through practical interaction with the environment that establishes the intentional arc as the grid upon which the world is always diagrammed.[184]

There is evidence to suggest that the emotional life of the brain is at least as fundamental to the lived body's normal functioning as the meaningful dialogue it carries out at the perceptual level. The point here is not merely that the lived body cannot perform without having an emotion and that this emotion is localized in the brain. It is the more salient point that the meaning culled from the world by the lived body is always in part produced by the affective valence of our situations. A situation, as Johnson understands it, is a complex event which occurs *between* an organism and its environment. It is analogous to what Merleau-Ponty means by our existential situation, or being in the world. Drawing from the philosophy of Dewey as well as the neuroscience of Antonio Damasio, Johnson argues that,

> Emotions are key components of complex processes of assessment, evaluation, and transformation. As such, they are integral to our ability to grasp the meaning of a situation and to act appropriately in response to it. Most of this ongoing processing and action is never consciously entertained, but it is nonetheless *meaningful* to us, insofar as it constitutes an important part of our maintaining a workable relation to our surroundings.[185]

Without emotion it is difficult (or impossible) for our bodies to determine whether or not their present environment is safe to inhabit. Without emotional assessment the body cannot rationally act or free itself from the defensive posture in which it remains vigilant against imminent threats. By the same token, the body cannot read hostility or security into the land without having fashioned an intentional arc that enables it to judge another body as congruent or incongruent with itself. Affectivity and intentionality are woven together, infused in the body's sensibility.

Anticipating a bit, I would say that Merleau-Ponty too often focuses on the intentional life of the body while neglecting its affective and material life. In this he remains very much a proponent of the subject as calculative agent, as actor. It is not that he fails to see that these two dimensions of embodiment—activity and affectivity—are intertwined and equiprimordial, but that he tends to *pathologize* those moments when the body loses its competent hold on the world or when its intentional arc loses its coherence.[186] This results in an inadequate view of how the body acquires its identity and maintains its integrity vis-à-vis the environment. In the same way, he tends to overlook the physical or material aspects of how objects and emotions orient the body's activity.[187] The dialogue of subject and object—which forms the kernel of Merleau-Ponty's narrative regarding the primacy of perception—is driven by the exchange of meanings *intended* by the conscious body, not by unregistered (autonomic) signals received from the environment or mundane sensations that fail to solicit attention. It is, for the most part, only figures or forms which stand out against a horizon that attract Merleau-Ponty. He has considerably less to say about insignificant and "neutral" situations, as well as situations where the body is so overwhelmed that its intentional threads are severed and the figure-ground structure is torn asunder.[188] I am thinking here of what Foucault refers to as "limit-experiences." It is the *immediacy*, it seems to me, that is significant about these situations (often painful) that Foucault describes as pushing our bodies to the edge of their power threshold, and thus enhancing their capacity for pleasure. It is true that our bodies recover from/adapt to the extreme situations that test their limits—that these situations solicit our bodies in a particular way that often allows them to incorporate the lesson of the situation—but the situation as disruptive event, not just its stable outcome, must also be considered integral to the body's historical identity.[189]

(Dis)Orientations

Objects, for Merleau-Ponty, have a hand in regulating the intentionality and material form of the body. "The keyboard," explains Shannon Sullivan, "has a particular shape and manner of operating that call for a specific bodily comportment in order to use it."[190] There is a plurality of significance transmitted to the body by the keyboard that can be accommodated in a variety of ways; the body must adapt itself to these meanings if it wants to dialogue with, rather than dominate, the object. Entailed in this is the idea that my body does not perceive the material world without that world confronting it with a meaning that I have already projected onto it. Sullivan writes: "The keyboard has a meaningful place within my world because, through my body's familiarity with the keyboard gained through the repeated use of it, a piece of plastic and metal has become an extension of my intentionality." She continues: "My intentionality turns a heavy object into a paperweight; it is because of my need to hold papers down that a random stone nearby becomes a cultural object."[191] These descriptions imply that ultimately the lived body, not its object, controls the order of perceptual significance, the circuits of meaningful behavior, and to some extent the very form of the objects it confronts.

There are instances, however, when the materiality of the world seizes upon our bodies and perception is unhinged. And these are not pathological moments, but constitutive of normal lived experience. Lingis describes the orgasmic body as one whose seizure is not merely a failure of the intentional arc, but the result of a decomposition of the body's postural schema itself. "Does not the orgasmic body figure as a body decomposed, dismembered, dissolute, where postures and dynamic axes form and deform in the limp indecisiveness of the erotic trouble? Is it not a breaking down into a mass of exposed organs, secretions, striated muscles, systems turning into pulp and susceptibility?"[192] In a different context George Yancy describes a scene wherein the body of a white woman is given over to involuntary gestures that cannot be explained with a Pavlovian reflex theory or a theory of dialogical perception. Something else is required to account for the "ambush" of the black body—the visceral response solicited in a white woman when the body of a black man enters her elevator. She may tell herself that she knows this body; that she has a handle on what a black body is and what it wants to do; that she has no reason to clutch her purse closely. Yancy writes how "she may come to judge her perception of the Black body as epistemologically false, but her racism may still have a hold on her lived body."[193] Despite herself, she tenses up, her body recoils. She does not search the man's body to bring its true sense into relief; nor does she objectify him. She has no need to: his darkness symbolizes a threat that her sensibility registers with lightning quickness. *She* becomes self-aware, nearly to the point of paralysis. She averts her eyes and fixes them straight ahead, trying to overcome her body's racism.[194] But it is not that the black body's gaze has turned her into an object, as Sartre would say. It is the very darkness of the man's body, his sensory and symbolic constitution, that arrests the white woman's movement. He remains an ambiguous presence, his darkness gripping her in such a way that her intellect and volition become helpless.

Yancy's work draws insight from Merleau-Ponty, but even more from Fanon's *Black Skin, White Masks*, a book wherein Fanon explicitly takes up the concept of the body schema to interrogate its function in intercorporeal relations. Ordinarily, the body schema is described as the "implicit knowledge" possessed by the body that enables it effortlessly to reach for the cigarettes at the corner of the desk, or lean backward to retrieve the matches buried in the desk's drawer.[195] Such postural facility is experienced by the white body whether it is in its office or out in public. The black body, by contrast, is not afforded this facility when the gaze of a white body descends upon it. Recalling such an encounter, Fanon describes himself as once upon a time "completely dislocated" by the white gaze, which apprehended and returned his body to him "sprawled out, distorted, recolored, clad in mourning...."[196] "What else could it be for me but an amputation, an excision, a hemorrhage that spattered my whole body with black blood?"[197] In this scene of confiscation what gets excised from Fanon's subjectivity is precisely his body schema, or at least its enabling function. It is replaced by a "racial epidermal schema" that, if anything, disables his body by entering it into an economy operating according to hues and tints, shades of light and dark.[198]

As objectified, the black body becomes laced with legends, symbols, myths, and fantasies—all of which are woven into it by the look of the white person and supported by what Fanon calls a "historico-racial schema."[199] This schema, which is situated anonymously *below* the body schema, hijacks the black body, summoning it to be more than a practical, competent corporeality—what Merleau-Ponty calls an "I can." Merleau-Ponty plainly says that it is our competent embodied perception that weaves the fabric of the real (PP x/iv-v). Fanon reminds us that it is the perception of the white body that traces the contours of the world and forces the non-white body to respond accordingly. "I wanted to come lithe and young into a world that was ours," laments Fanon, "and to help build it together."[200] Alas, this world came readymade for him. To summarize this contrast, we might say that whereas the white body is *solicited* by the world to actively complete it, the black body is made to *perform* in a world that has always already been completed for it. It is in this economy of colored skin that the dialogical theory of perception exposes one of its limitations.

Perceptual experience, vision in particular, can never be divorced from the historical and cultural milieu that orients the body's postural schema.[201] Corporeal orientation is what enables a simple look to confiscate the other's body and elicit from it involuntary movements and emotions like shame or fear. This orientation is invariably underwritten by race, among other social factors. As Sara Ahmed describes it, corporeal orientation is the point at which a body's world unfolds. This world, we learn from Merleau-Ponty, expands outward from its center by the appropriation of language, tools, and other technologies. And just as our instruments become invisible once we have adapted ourselves to them—once they become *zuhanden*, as Heidegger says—whiteness disappears as a category that normatively structures the historical a priori of experience, not only for white bodies but for non-white bodies as well. At any given moment this disappearance is already accomplished. The norm is set in place. Consequently, a racialized world oriented by whiteness dilates the white world while simultaneously contracting the non-white world.[202]

All bodies depend upon the familiarity of this white world for their work. Getting things done or "doing things," writes Ahmed, "depends not so much on intrinsic capacity, or even upon dispositions or habits, but on the ways in which the world is available as a space for action, a space where things 'have a certain place' or are 'in place'." If the body is always already racialized and oriented by whiteness, then the body schema is fundamentally structured by the world of whiteness and compelled to "inhabit whiteness" in order to navigate the world with facility, as if it were at home in whiteness, even when that body is black or brown.[203] This, of course, entails that the non-white body is never at home unless its home is the world of whiteness. The orientation of whiteness is precisely what puts "physical objects ... styles, capacities, aspirations, techniques, habits" within our grasp.[204] Conversely, failing to inhabit whiteness puts many things out of reach.

Reading Merleau-Ponty's *Phenomenology*, it often seems that the world he has in mind is for the most part a world filled with things to be handled or manipulated, a world within reach of anybody or any body whatsoever. Merleau-Ponty's world is one of practical abilities. This world downplays how in the process of getting things done the functional use of everyday objects neglects their sensuous aspects, which require a more attentive, impractical, or contemplative approach in order to access, accommodate, and adapt to them.[205] To be sure, the manipulation of things leads to better understanding; this is where knowledge and know-how come from. But we can manipulate things because we are things ourselves, sensitive things. Sensing enables us to orient ourselves toward goals and order our surroundings into a meaningful habitat. For some of us this habitat is more accommodating than it is for others.

The problem of other bodies, different bodies, is certainly considered in the *Phenomenology*. So is sensing. Sense experience is considered at length. But the exemplary scenes in Merleau-Ponty's text involve a human being confronting some inanimate object. This encounter anchors the norms of perception. When the human is incapable of maximizing its grip on the object, that is, when the human is unable to adjust its body to the physiognomy of another body, Merleau-Ponty signals a pathology (PP 136/158). Yancy's description of the "elevator effect," Fanon's theory of the racial epidermal schema, and Ahmed's assessment of racialized corporeal orientation, however, reveal corporeal incompetence and dissymmetry as marginalized but no less prevalent norms of embodiment. We too are manipulated by objects, symbols, and orientations—and not just in ways that enable our bodies or expand our perceptual grasp.

Identity: Physiognomy and Style

Merleau-Ponty's account of color perception in the *Phenomenology* underscores his more general point that the body's communication with its environment happens primarily at the level of perceptual meaning, or what he often calls "physiognomy" or "motor physiognomy" (PP 209/243). The subject is not a pilot navigating the body from within or merely an organic mechanism. The subject is able to negotiate its surroundings because its corporeal composition is legible by other bodies, and other bodies are legible for it. Bodies possess the power to read and respond directly to both formal and qualitative features. Merleau-Ponty insists that perception is always laced with sense, and it is this sense that enables the body to respond to "sensations."[206] To say that colors induce the body to move in specific ways because they display a certain physiognomy is to say that sensory experience is always figured, that even colors are never experienced as detached from a significant horizon.[207] The body can negotiate this horizon because it possesses its own physiognomy, one which is arranged by the physiognomy of the world and displayed in the arsenal of gestures it typically deploys (PP 143/168).

Merleau-Ponty deploys many concepts to characterize the original unity of body and world. In the *Phenomenology* it is perception, physiognomy, and style; in the course on nature, it is natural environment and the Earth;[208] in *The Visible and the Invisible*, it is the flesh of the sensible, "this generality of the Sensible in itself, this anonymity innate to Myself," as Merleau-Ponty puts it (VI 139/183). Individual bodies for him are always cut from the same impersonal cloth—personal individuation is something achieved, not given. The meaning of the personal, however, can only be understood against the backdrop of a pre-personal milieu, whether this is nature, the sensible realm as such, or the world as the sum total of profiles or an eminently expressive style:

> The natural world is the horizon of all horizons, the style of all possible styles, which guarantees for my experiences a given, not a willed, unity underlying all the disruptions of my personal and historical life. Its counterpart within me is the given, general and pre-personal existence of my sensory functions in which we have discovered the definition of the body. (PP 330/381)

The concept of style gives us a clue to Merleau-Ponty's understanding of corporeal identity, which is something dynamically constituted by environmental conditions and repetitive encounters. It must be maintained; it is not given. Our bodies are products of the sedimented meaning that constitutes our cultural milieu and the physical makeup of habitable space. These conditions comprise the always tenuous historical a priori which provides the mutable, phenomenal ground upon which the world is synthesized, understood, and modified by the body-subject.[209] Born into a stylized environment which calls upon it to adopt a compatible bodily comportment, the body is not *inscribed* with a style as much as it coherently expresses a historical embeddedness, a set of social and physical limitations, constraints, and possibilities. The body is "a certain style informing my manual gestures and implying in turn a certain style of finger movements, and contributing, in the last resort, to a certain bodily bearing." Its identity is, in a word, "a work of art" (PP 150/176).

Style is not fixed in the visible form of the body, nor is it an abstraction from the many postures a given body exhibits. A style is nothing other than the specific animation of a body, the invisible force that renders it recognizable in its singularity (PP 327/378).[210] As Graham Harman writes, "style is a real force that animates the qualities [of a body]."[211] Style is not spontaneous expression, however, and in the last analysis the general style of the natural and social worlds serves as the condition of possibility for the emergence of individual style, which is to an extent determined by its historical and natural milieu.[212] "Expression," therefore, "has the form not only of a creative, but also of a *responsive expression*."[213] Style is an eminently consistent kind of response to how things are.

By defining it as style, Merleau-Ponty lends a determinate fluidity to corporeal identity. "A style," he writes, "is a certain manner of dealing with situations, which I identify or understand in an individual or in a writer, by taking over that manner myself in a sort of imitative way, even though I may be quite unable to define it" (PP 327/378). Style is not only recognizable, it is transferable as well as somewhat vague and elusive. It is precise, but difficult to trace. Husserl might call it "anexact." Style, of course, is recognizable across an array of individual examples and generalized from those many examples. "One can hear a newly discovered Charlie Parker recording and," notes Harman, "immediately recognize the style; one can and will say that 'that solo is really classic Bird', even though up till now it was not part of the known Parker oeuvre."[214] Beyond a certain threshold of differentiation, however, a specific style begins to break up and lose coherence, perhaps morphing into another style. We can imagine a masterful jazz musician like Parker deviating so far from his usual delivery so as to approximate John Coltrane. Like plagiarism, this can happen intentionally or by accident, unbeknownst to the plagiarist. In such an instance, what would be left of Parker? Has he not in a sense become Coltrane, insofar as Coltrane's musical style is the extent of his (audible) identity? In a strong sense Parker and Coltrane just are the sounds they produce, especially for the millions who do not know them personally. Merleau-Ponty gives a visual example in *The Visible and the Invisible*, explaining that a pebble or a shell exhibits an identity that persists throughout "their variations" but "within certain limits." On this principle of identity bodies maintain their identity so long as their sensible modifications do not disintegrate the style that animates them, whether this style is self-generated, borrowed, or remixed from already available styles. Identity is lost when a body moves "beyond a certain range of their changes" (VI 161/213), or crosses a stylistic threshold.[215] Merleau-Ponty does not fully explore the causes of these deviations in identity, but he gives one of the best accounts of what style means for identity.

For Descartes, by contrast, it is the mind that judges an object's identity as continuous throughout its modifications, or that determines a cloaked figure perceived from some distance to be a person rather than an automaton.[216] It is this same mind which, removed from the mutable world of extended substance, retains its identity and subsists through every modification of the body. For Merleau-Ponty it is the body that recognizes another human being beneath the cloak. And it is the cloaked figure's style of moving that gives it away. "It is through my body that I understand other people, just as it is through my body that I perceive 'things'" (PP 186/216). The dialectic of recognition becomes a dialogue of styles that unfolds without the mediating judgment of the mind. "The concept of style," writes Linda Singer, "secures the Other's direct accessibility as a distinctive way of inhabiting the world. ... His integrity is not that of a conceptual consistency, but of an existential project which is directly present, even if I cannot reconstruct its inner workings."[217] In Merleau-Ponty's words, the other is for me "an unchallengeable style" that relays its identity to my own body's identity and makes the other "in principle accessible to me as I am to myself" (PP 364/418; SB 222/238).

Style is one of the most supple phenomena adduced by Merleau-Ponty. It "ensures my existence of a stability, while allowing for the possibility of growth and change."[218] James, as we will see, refers to this stable instability as *plasticity*. Merleau-Ponty, for his part, directs us to the fluid constitution of bodily integrity. He defines the intercorporeal realm as a sphere of immanence where bodies communicate, influence, and reinforce each other. This communication is at once personal and anonymous, inherited and created.[219] But corporeal style remains always dependent upon the body schema, which offers a constant stability amid the flux of intercorporeal dialogue. Gallagher points out that the body schema should not be regarded as something standing between subject and object as mediator or "screen" (SB 219/236), but rather, "insofar as it is dynamic in taking up certain postures and thus situating the body in respect to the environment, it remains experientially invisible—absently available."[220] It is there and not there, operating in the "active role of organizer" of sensations as something that "reflects and determines the posture that is taken up by the lived body in its everyday situations."[221] This seems to suggest that the activity of the body schema plays a more fundamental role in the organization of perception than any other component, including style, habit, or sensibility.

Identity: Body Schema

Faithful to phenomenological doctrine, Merleau-Ponty contends that a figure against a background is the simplest form of experience. Experience tells us this. But his point is not merely empirical. Lest we interpret his observation as a simple empirical truth, he notes that "this is not a contingent characteristic of factual perception" (PP 4/10). It is an ontological truth, a truth about how the world is structured transcendentally. And like all transcendentals in Merleau-Ponty, it is historically conditioned by perception. As Elizabeth Grosz points out, the body schema (she says "body image") is at work in the structuring of this a priori. She writes,

> The body image is necessary for the distinction between figure and ground, or between central and peripheral actions. Relative to its environment, the body image separates the subject's body from a background of forces; but also within the body, the body image establishes the distinctions—between movements of limbs, say, and the rest of the body—which provide it with its corporeal context. A single movement reorients the whole of the body, creating what might be called a gait or posture, an individual and cultural bodily style.[222]

Sullivan refers to this orienting of the environment/other as "projective intentionality" and, like Grosz, sees such a view as troubling from a feminist ethical perspective: Instead of being an account of the dynamic, co-constitutive relationship between self and other, the model of intersubjectivity offered by Merleau-Ponty tends toward that of a subject's monologue with itself that includes a domineering erasure of others in its projective 'communication' with them.[223]

Although invaluable for understanding the corporeal structure of lived experience, Merleau-Ponty's account of the body schema is often blind to raced, gendered, and other forms of embodiment.[224] I would add that he equally neglects unfigured experience, or the experience of sensing what is ungraspable—for example, wind, cold, sunlight; the elemental or atmospheric in general—that does not stand out in relief against a backdrop. This blind spot in Merleau-Ponty's ontology, which ties the structure of the world to the constitution of the body schema, informs his view that body and environment, subject and object, are synchronized or reversible, and that our primary mode of engagement with the world is our familiar manipulation of things as well as their innocuous solicitation of us.

We have already seen that habits are specific rearrangements of the general body schema, which serves as the variable invariant, as it were, against which the modifications of the body are registered. We have seen, moreover, how Fanon, Yancy, and Ahmed call into question the normative historicity of the body schema, and how Grosz and Sullivan raise problems about its constitutive activity. It then becomes possible to say that the body schema's dynamic relation with its environment is constitutive of its individuation and that its apparent invariance (PP 141/165) applies only to its *function* as active regulator of movement, but does not apply to any determinate regulations themselves. These regulations are normative, determined culturally, historically, intercorporeally; they configure and are configured by the world we perceive. Despite its historical variance the body schema nevertheless operates for Merleau-Ponty as the dominant organizing principle of perception. From the perspective of lived experience, then, the world must appear as complicit or synchronized with the body-subject's practical agenda, even if this agenda is laced with anonymous, impersonal, and unconscious prejudices—with alterity.

On the one hand, it is possible to characterize Merleau-Ponty's conception of the body schema and habit as plastic, as does Weiss.[225] This does not mean that the lived body's structure begins as a blank, undifferentiated slate and only subsequently becomes schematized and habituated. The lived body requires habits and body schemata in order to perceive, and without them "perception is impossible," says Merleau-Ponty (Child 122/37). They are a basic condition of perception, not just an outcome of it. These basic structures maintain their stability while remaining open to modifications that would restructure them. The modifications could be perceptual or physiological. Since perception is internally linked to the body's constitution (in as much as the body is part of the world of perception), any restructuring entails a new style of movement, and thus a new perceptual experience. As Merleau-Ponty writes, "This link between motility and perception shows at what point it is true to say that the two functions are only two aspects of a single totality and that the perception of one's entry into the world and of one's own body form a system" (Child 122/38).

On the other hand, Merleau-Ponty seems resistant to the idea that the lived body is fully plastic, completely open to external modification or destruction. There appears to be something indestructible about the lived body. Insofar as it is a living (human) body, and not a body reduced to its objective relations in the world—a merely material body—it maintains a set of transcendental invariants that do not succumb to the effects of material transformation or physical breakdown. Or, put differently, it is not clear on Merleau-Ponty's analysis how these invariants could ever be directly affected by material forces; they themselves are not material and they have no material basis. They are, as it were, incorporeal corporealities. Included among these, the body schema, consciousness, and intentionality serve as the limit conditions of the embodied subject, that is to say, the conditions that compose the agent to whom the world appears and from whom the world receives its meaning, but who also remains out of step with the world's physicality. The difference of the lived body is precisely its non-physical constitution.

Also among these invariants is the figure-ground structure of perception, something only possessed by beings with bodies like ours. The figure-ground structure is grounded in the body schema, which suggests that the body schema must be always present in some form for the body to perceive. If this is true, then perception must submit its primacy to the body's postural latency, which is internally related to perception but also determined by the body's physical, physiological, and generally material dynamics, some of which are not perceptual and can be metaphysically separated from the perceptual system. Put otherwise, the lived body is dual in nature: it is both physical and non-physical, material and transcendental. These aspects are internally related and inseparable, but it is clear that Merleau-Ponty favors the lived body as in some sense constitutive of objectivity, including the objectivity of the physical body. But could the lived body exist without the physical, objective body? Is the lived body transcendental in the strong sense, the condition of possibility of the objective body? It seems that it would have to be if it is the case that perception is the condition of possibility of the world. This would also mean that the lived body cannot be fully destroyed by the physical world, that something of it transcends the body's materiality. Merleau-Ponty's language of flesh and incarnation suggests a "spiritual" dimension to the lived body, although he is careful to avoid that term.

The lived body is essentially the perceiving body. Perception is what gives the body its life. But perception depends upon the body schema, which is vulnerable to imperceptible forces. While the dialectic of perception may work to reconfigure and reorient the body schema, material forces threaten to destabilize/deschematize it, along with the figure-ground structure of intentionality and even perception itself. An unschematized body is longer capable of distinguishing figures or grounds and is not, therefore, able to enter into dialogue with its environment. Such a body would not be "lived," in Merleau-Ponty's terms; it would be reduced to an object. But the lived body *is an object*; its objectivity is the site of its living. Without it there is no place for perception or consciousness to occur, no place from which the body schema or figure-ground horizon can organize the world of perception. The latter are not the pure conditions of possibility for the world to appear, for they themselves cannot appear without the objective body that functions as their material locus.

All of this is to say that the lived body is discontinuous with the material world in which it is embedded. There is a diachrony that marks the interface of body and world. And yet, in Merleau-Ponty's view, body and world are synchronous with each other. They are ontologically parallel and internally related, co-constitutive. What I am suggesting is that this is true only at the level of perception, but not at the deepest level of their relation—sensibility.

Since, on Merleau-Ponty's view, perception presupposes a functioning body schema, and the body schema is acquired dialogically, body and world must be synchronized for perception to occur. Otherwise, the body schema could not develop and the dialogue could not occur. I think this synchronization is required for Merleau-Ponty's conception of reversibility, which is implicit in the *Phenomenology* and explicitly emphasized in *The Visible and the Invisible*. It is responsible for his view that subjects and objects are basically articulations of a single sensible element called the flesh, where "seer and visible reciprocate one another and we no longer know which sees and which is seen" (VI 139/183). If the subject-object relation is fundamentally diachronic, however, then it is not properly reversible. It is asymmetrical. And it is sensibility, I will argue, alongside Levinas, that introduces asymmetry into the subject-object relation.

A Synchronous Sensibility

The language of synchrony is employed by Merleau-Ponty on many occasions to describe the body-world relation. It is a recurrent trope in his texts. He speaks, for instance, of impersonal biological life and personal life as for the most part operating in concert, the former being "practically taken for granted" as something "I rely on to keep me alive." As he frames it, we exist "without being able either to reduce the organism to its existential self, or itself to the organism" (PP 84/99). Citing the biography of Saint-Exupéry, Merleau-Ponty notes that on rare occasions our organic life can be almost completely suppressed by our personal life: "It may even happen when I am in danger that my human situation abolishes my biological one, that my body lends itself without reserve to action" (PP 84/99). Later in the *Phenomenology* he explicitly notes the synchronization of the biological and the human, yet lends a certain primacy to the biological:

> as we have indicated above, biological existence is synchronized [*embrayée*] with human existence and is never indifferent to its distinctive rhythm. Nevertheless, we shall now add, "living" (*leben*) is a primary process from which, as a starting point, it becomes possible to "live" (*erleben*) this or that world, and we must eat and breathe before perceiving

and awakening to relational living, belonging to colours and lights through sight, to sound through hearing, to the body of another through sexuality, before arriving at the life of human relations. (PP 159-160/186)

Instead of taking this as a glimpse into Merleau-Ponty's tacit naturalism, we should see it as an example of his "empirically responsible" phenomenology, but an example that seems to oppose his primacy of perception argument. From an existential point of view the biological does not come first; the human is not built upon the organic body. The lived body expresses, reciprocally, the physiological and psychic because it always already finds itself absorbed in a meaningful circuit of behavior. Its biology must be understood and expressed within its lifeworld.

This is one of the reasons why Merleau-Ponty speaks on the one hand of an original syncretism of body and world, but then quickly dispels the notion that sensing (*sentir*) is ever without a human sense (PP 211/245). And yet, he speaks of sensibility as belonging to an anonymous life of the senses that thrives "on the fringe of my own personal life and acts." He writes, "Each time I experience a sensation, I feel that it concerns not my own being ... but another self which has already sided with the world, which is already open to certain of its aspects and synchronized [*synchronisé*] with them" (PP 216/250). Now, this is a form of synchrony that the lived body is not in control of, for it is established imperceptibly and concerns the body as something that senses before it perceives, that lives materially before it grasps meaningfully. It hints at an aesthetic dimension operating below the radar of perception.

It is here that we see Merleau-Ponty catching sight of the immanent relation between sensing and sensed that characterizes his notion of flesh. More important for us, however, we are shown the diachronic point at which the body-world relation becomes a volatile one. It is at the level of sensing that the body is at its most vulnerable, where its hold on the world and its capacity to dialogue with other bodies is not yet accomplished, and is even susceptible to experiences that could dismantle its integrity. It is here that body and world become unhinged.

Sensing relies on a synchronization or synthesis of the senses (with each other and with their proper objects) whereby each organ's unique means of exploring is brought together in the intersensory realm of perception. Perception is made possible by the "domain of sense itself, the community of significance between [the visual and tactile] being inadequate to ensure their union in one single experience" (PP 225/260). This union, as we have seen, is effected by the body and the intentional arc that allows it to actualize the "motor potentiality" of an object and thereby effectively grasp its meaning. Merleau-Ponty writes:

> I am able to touch effectively only if the phenomenon finds an echo within me, if it accords with a certain nature of my consciousness, and if the organ which goes out to meet it is synchronized with it. The unity and identity of the tactile phenomenon do not come about through any synthesis of recognition in the concept, they are founded upon the unity and identity of the body as a synergic totality. (PP 316-317/366)

Thus, the dialogue of subject and object, of styles and physiognomies, only occurs when the lived body is capable of conforming itself to the "logic of the world," that is, when it is capable of synchronizing with it (PP 326/377).

In his treatment of sensibility/sense experience Merleau-Ponty seems to acknowledge the diachrony of sensation and its capacity to disrupt body-world synchrony. But, as we will see, he is reluctant to assign explicit primacy to sensing over perceiving. Indeed, these distinct modes of experience—the former unwieldy, the latter organized—are either conflated or collapsed in most of Merleau-Ponty's descriptions. Understood as a preperceptual and anonymous mode of embodiment, the volatility of sensing poses a threat to the synchronization of body and world. It opens the body to forces foreign to perception.

The concept of flesh developed in *The Visible and the Invisible* follows up the idea of synchronization with the insight that seer and seen, touching and touched, are reversible or chiasmic phenomena. The subject-object dialogue, which retains the dualist form, is transformed into an immanent ontology that regards subjects and objects as individual expressions of the sensible in general. I would not want to go so far as to say that such a move "reduces the other to the same" or eliminates alterity from intercorporeal relations. However, I do agree with Levinas when he says that "[there is a] priority of the flesh ... to the detriment of another ambiguity or ambivalence, that of the enigma of sensation-sentiment, which is played out in the passivity of the *senses affected* [*sens affectés*] by the sensorial, between the pure undergoing or suffering and eventual pain, and the *known* [*su*] of knowledge that remains behind as its residue or trace."[226] Later I will return to this insight.

Not unlike the idealists, Merleau-Ponty tames the volatility of sensation in two ways: first, by defining it in terms of synchrony and treating it as something that for the most part enables our perceptual competence; and, more radically, by invoking a "fundamental narcissism of all vision," which is supposed to describe the mode of being of the flesh. The general reversibility signaled by this portrayal of the sensible may indeed pertain to peaceful and mundane experiences of otherness, but it neglects the many ways that sensation can disable us, as well as the uncertainty, if not danger, involved as our bodies move from one sensory environment to another. It does not do justice to novel or extreme sensations, and it downplays the reality of hostile or deadly environments. In a word, it mitigates the vulnerability of our bodies.

As noted, Merleau-Ponty does recognize a layer of sensation that operates "below" perception. As pre-perceptual it does not solicit dialogue with the lived body. Instead, it remains out of sync with lived experience and descends upon the body with a volatile proposition.[227] Merleau-Ponty's emphasis on body-world synchronization obscures the asymmetry of intercorporeity at the level of sensation. This results from his desire to assimilate sensing (*le sentir*) to the model of perception as "communion," which tends to regard otherness as generally hospitable. The thesis of reversibility can only be advanced by ignoring the resistant alterity of the material world, that is, at the peril of sensation's volatility. This is why neither the phenomenology of perception nor the ontology of the flesh can adequately address the problems of embodiment and why the metaphysics of bodies we find in Spinoza or Nietzsche,[228] for instance, must also be consulted in order to decipher the meaning of the body.

In giving an account of subjectivity and the immanence of the body-world relation Merleau-Ponty makes significant advances past Kant and Husserl by developing concepts such as style, physiognomy, and habit. These concepts allow him to speak coherently about perception and intersubjectivity as corporeal interactions that do not require the mediation of an immaterial transcendental subject or disembodied mind. For this reason, Merleau-Ponty can be regarded as a kind of materialist.[229] This ambition becomes even more apparent when he is writing about sensing, or when he speaks of the "carnality" of the flesh in *The Visible and the Invisible*. There his theory of embodied perception shifts its focus from the form of perception to the material of perception—that is, sensation, or the sensible as such. It is in his analysis of sensing that we can best see Merleau-Ponty trying to secure the immanence of body and environment. His commitment to immanence, however, is limited by his commitment to the primacy of perception thesis and his methodological commitment to the principle of intentionality. Both of these reintroduce a measure of distance, or transcendence, into immanence. The limit of his materialism appears when his theory of habit is contrasted with a neurophysiological account like that given by James.

At this point and beyond I remain agnostic on the question of whether or not Merleau-Ponty succeeds at establishing the materiality of the world and making concrete the phenomenological subject. That is, it is not clear to me that he has the resources to argue for the material reality of the body or its world. What is clear is that in his attempt to do justice to the subjective and objective sides of experience he tends to provide more substantial arguments for the constructivist view of the subject. This is no reason to abandon his path in favor of another, but it does call into question the degree to which his corporeal descriptions distance him from the idealism of Husserlian phenomenology.[230]

Chapter 3

Perception, Sensation, and the Problem of Violence

> The body is a strange thing, and when it is caught up
> in an accident involving non-human forces, there is no
> predicting the result.
>
> Aira, An Episode in the Life of a Landscape Painter

Merleau-Ponty begins his rehabilitation of sensation as early as *Phenomenology of Perception*. After rejecting the modern view of sensation as a discrete unit of content that must be assembled by the mind with other units in order to build the objects of perception, he endorses a view of sensation as *sensing* (a more appropriate translation of *le sentir*, sense experience)[231] which is adapted primarily from Erwin Straus's *The Primary World of Senses*, on the one hand, and Husserl's *Ideas* II, on the other. His idea of sensing regards it as "that vital communication with the world which makes it present as a familiar setting of our life" (PP 52-53/64-65). He thus makes sensation central to his post-dualist perspective and incorporates it into the primacy of perception thesis he champions. The trouble is that he uses the concept in several, not always compatible, ways. Its reference shifts throughout his texts. Although I will not catalogue every nuance of *le sentir* or *la sensation*, I will adduce some of the divergent uses of "sensing" in Merleau-Ponty's texts. At the same time I will argue that one particular usage best captures the significance of sensing, namely, that sensing is the body's primary mode of engagement with otherness; that it operates below the level of intentionality (and therefore perception); and that it is even more basic than operative intentionality, which Merleau-Ponty identifies as the "natural and antepredicative" form of perception. The operative form of intentionality negotiates the body's first contact with the phenomenal field, "furnishing the text which our knowledge tries to translate [via explicit judgments] into precise language" (PP xviii/xiii). It is tacit, "unconscious." Like operative intentionality, sensing denotes a certain imperceptible continuity between body and world, and it is fundamental to Merleau-Ponty's corporeal philosophy. While his privileging of perception often elevates the perceiving subject above the perceived object, there is a pervasive sense in which the dialectical relation between subject and object is primary for him. He does not fully appreciate, however, the subject's passivity in this dialectic.

A Healthy Ambiguity

It is notable that Merleau-Ponty recognizes a distinction between sensation and perception. Indeed, it is this distinction that motivates the present analysis of his work. Whereas perception is constantly striving to pull objects out of their ambiguous presence and into workable relief from their background, it is sensation that occasionally threatens to break up the synchrony enjoyed by perceptual experience. To claim that such interruptions are merely invitations to explore the undiscovered meanings contained in the perceptual horizon, as Merleau-Ponty and his commentators often do, is to miss the qualitative difference between an experience that beckons our attention (perception) and one that directly engages—sometimes forcibly—our bodies (sensation). This is not to say that sensation marks the suffering of the body, but it is sometimes that. He writes: "With the problem of sense experience, we rediscover that of association and passivity" (PP 53/65). Perception, by contrast, is never merely passive; nothing just "happens" to the lived body. That is, there are no non-subjective perceptual events (PP 411/470). There are, however, "vital event[s]" that occur unconsciously (Nature 174). Are these events sensed, perceived, or both? Neither? It is not clear how they are phenomenologically disclosed.

Sensation is often assimilated to perception in Merleau-Ponty's texts. When this happens there is a problematic reduction of the alterity of sensation, as well as a glossing of the problem of passivity posed by sense experience. Once again, a healthy ambiguity inhabits the border between sensing and perceiving and Merleau-Ponty knows this, even exploits it. The ambiguity makes it difficult to know whether he intended to differentiate rigorously two ontologically distinct layers of experience, or if he desired simply to demarcate two aspects of perception: the affective/passive and the intellectual/active. My view is that he explicitly regards sensing as a mode of perception, but in his explication of *le sentir* he also uncovers a lost dimension of embodiment that cannot be readily recuperated by his model of perception. The question now becomes, does Merleau-Ponty attempt to incorporate the "problem of sense experience" into the problem of perception? Or is there something about sense experience that proves intractable for the phenomenology of perception? At the end of the day, the ambiguity that motivates these questions proves irresolvable and yet, precisely for this reason, worthy of interrogation.

Perhaps anticipating that a simple privileging of embodiment is not sufficient to liberate phenomenology from transcendental idealism, Merleau-Ponty suggests that it is the "primary layer [*couche originaire*] of sense experience [*sentir*]" that allows perception to "break with the critical attitude" (PP 238, 239/276). It is here that Merleau-Ponty most deliberately departs from his idealist precursors in order to chart the existence of an experience not prey to any kind of subjective synthesis. By beginning with what is phenomenally sensible, he begins with an always already synthesized form/content instead of positing a discrete form and content that are only brought together by a unifying faculty.

> I start from unified experience and from there acquire, in a secondary way, consciousness of a unifying activity when, taking up an analytical attitude, I break perception into qualities and sensation, and when, in order to recapture on the basis of these the object into which I was in the first place blindly thrown, I am obliged to suppose an act of synthesis

which is merely the counterpart of my analysis. (PP 276-277/275; cf. PrP 25/69)

The classical approach to experience begins with abstractions, not with what is given, and is responsible for the mistaken view that the subject's role in experience is to provide the chaotic world of sensation with formal order. Merleau-Ponty's concern is to keep the subject always in touch with the objective world and to demonstrate that this immanent relation is the source of the content of perception and, by consequence, the form of the world. This results in the view that the world does not achieve any *explicit* form unless it is in dialogue with a human agent, which sounds like idealism. "The thing is inseparable from a person perceiving it, and can never be actually *in itself* because its articulations are those of our very existence..." (PP 320/370). Oftentimes the subject of perception is described by Merleau-Ponty as immediately in touch with a semi-determinate, but never amorphous, world of things always on its way to becoming more precisely formed and therefore more hospitable to the body's motor capacity. This ambiguous and anonymous "lifeworld" provides the transcendental conditions of perception (PP 365/418-419).[232] More fundamental than the lifeworld, I would suggest, is the realm of the sensible.

Anonymity

Both sensation and perception are occasionally designated as anonymous, as when Merleau-Ponty writes that "Sensation [*sensation*] can be anonymous only because it is incomplete." Or: "Perception is always in the mode of the impersonal 'One'" (PP 216, 240/250, 277). These remarks have generated consistent criticism from feminist philosophers who charge that by affirming the reality of an anonymous body, Merleau-Ponty overlooks the role that gender plays in the construction of experience. This criticism is justifiable, but it does not apply to all of the senses of "anonymous" employed by Merleau-Ponty. That is, it does not apply to the anonymity of sensation insofar as sensation is something undergone by the body unconsciously or pre-personally. Before explicating this level of sensation we need to see what else is anonymous for Merleau-Ponty.

There are at least four sites of anonymity noted by Merleau-Ponty. First, there is the pre-communicative stage in the psychogenesis of the child, where his or her body is not yet distinguishable from the body of another. Here "there is not one individual over against another but rather an anonymous collectivity, an undifferentiated group life" (Child 119/33). Second, there is the anonymity of habitual actions. It is true that a person's habits inform their style, and thus their personal identity. But to the extent that habits can be triggered unthinkingly or operate automatically, they possess a certain anonymity. Third, Merleau-Ponty sometimes speaks of the body in general, by which he means the organic body that lives "as a prepersonal cleaving to the general form of the world, as an anonymous and general existence" (PP 84/99). The idea of a general—that is, gender-free, race-free, ability-free—body "beneath" the personal is problematic because, as Sullivan argues, it suggests a neutral ground upon which our bodies communicate with other bodies. But, the objection runs, no such ground exists, as our bodies are always individuated by habits and other historically particular bodily behaviors. When I assume that the gestures of the other are understandable because we share a common body, then I run the risk of deciphering the other in terms of my corporeity (or the myth of a universal body), rather than trying to *achieve* a site of communication that preserves the other's particularities.[233]

Johanna Oksala rejects the view that an anonymous body subtends the intersubjective relation and that intersubjectivity is something that needs to be achieved. She argues that the body-subject is historically generated all the way down by "language, tradition, and community."[234] Even the anonymous body is structured by environmental and social conditions. We have already seen that Merleau-Ponty does not quite offer a fully historicized lived body, that there are certain structural invariants that assume different modes but are ontologically immutable. Or, as Butler argues with reference to his treatment of sexuality, Merleau-Ponty's appeal to "the universal structures of bodily existence" "prefigures the analysis of lived experience, investing the body with an ahistorical structure which is in actuality profoundly historical in origin."[235] Whether or not he subscribes to an invariant general body, it seems that Merleau-Ponty recognizes at least one anonymity that is radically ahistorical: the anonymity of sensation, "which remains forever anterior to our perception." This is the fourth site of anonymity, the transcendental mode of sensation.

Modes of Sensation

There are two forms of sensation at play in Merleau-Ponty's philosophy, one that he criticizes (call it "substantive" sensation) and one that he endorses (call it "transitive" sensation). The transitive form is conceived under two registers: the phenomenological and the transcendental. It is implied in his term "sensing" (*sentir*).[236] Despite what has been said about the impurity of Merleau-Ponty's transcendental philosophy he does provide a concept of sensation that is close to a pure a priori. Sensation, on this reading, serves as a necessary, unconditioned condition of perceptual experience. But to argue for the *primacy of sensation* in Merleau-Ponty, as I am here, it is necessary to contrast the notion of sensing developed in the "Sense Experience" chapter of *Phenomenology of Perception* with the classical conception of sensation (*la sensation*) found in modern philosophy, which Merleau-Ponty critiques in the opening chapter of his text.

The classical notion of sensation views sensations as data, as discrete bits of material received from the external world and processed by the mind into representations of that world. Merleau-Ponty rejects this view as a fiction that betrays the evidence of experience, but he does not provide a full-fledged alternative to the modern view. Likely fearing that he would merely be replacing one abstraction for another, he elects instead to turn to the evidence of lived experience, that is, the world of perception. His positive thinking about sensation, then, is overshadowed by his critique of sensation as a "unit of experience." This is unfortunate because his own view of sensing forms the basis of his theory of painting in essays like "Cézanne's Doubt" and "Eye and Mind," and it is crucial to understanding that theory. Since he proclaims that "any theory of painting is a metaphysics" (EM 171/42), an understanding of his conception of sensing can reveal important features of his metaphysics.

The classical view of sensation which Merleau-Ponty rejects gets reinforced in everyday language when we speak of sensations as discrete properties that cause us to see a book as red or to feel it as smooth, for example. Red and smooth, we say, belong to the cover of this book and it is these properties that affect, separately, our visual and tactile senses. Color is received by the eyes; texture is apprehended by the fingertips. It is *the* book that is red and smooth, and it is the task of the mind to reassemble these stimuli into representations that correspond to the objects that produce them. The problem with this view is that it places metaphysical prejudices ahead of experience (PP 5/11) and results in a backward view of the nature of things and how we know them, according to the phenomenologist. As Taylor Carman puts it,

> Nowhere in our perceptual awareness do we come across discrete qualitative bits of experience fully abstracted from the external, perceptually coherent environment. ... This is in part just to say that perceptual experience is *intentional*, that it is of something, whereas impressions, sensations, and sense data are supposed to be the nonintentional stuff from which the mind somehow extracts or constructs an experience of something.[237]

We perceive *things*, not sensory units. Sensation, phenomenology teaches us, is inferred from perception when we reflect on how it is that an object, which is "not completely our work," can transmit its qualities to us (PP 37/46). This classical (and quotidian) line of thinking assumes that objects exist apart from us, fully formed with sharp boundaries and fixed properties. It puts an objectivist metaphysics and naïve realism ahead of the ambiguous content of perception, which for Merleau-Ponty is the first and final arbiter of what exists. "Experience," writes Carman, "rarely exhibits such sharply defined features ... and no analysis of perception into discrete attitudes with crisply defined contents intending isolated qualities can capture the peculiar 'perceptual milieu', always at once a 'behavioral milieu', in which things show up for us under meaningful aspects."[238] When we attend to what we are actually given, we never discover sensations. Instead, we find figures against backgrounds and semi-determinate bodies which become more determinate as perception catalogues their adumbrations. We find qualities that entice and repel us, a sensible realm that perception "infuses" [*imprègne*] with significance and style (PP 34/43).

What is required is a concept of sensation that does not reduce the style of the sensible to the intentional life of the perceiving subject and does not completely subject the materiality of sensation, its affective and imperceptible directive force, to the formality of the understanding or practical orientation of the body. Shying away from the language of sensation, Merleau-Ponty speaks of sensing as "an experience in which we are given not 'dead' qualities, but active ones" (PP 52/64). This is what I am calling the shift from a substantive notion of sensation ("dead qualities") to a transitive one ("active qualities"). In Merleau-Ponty's terms, sensing is that "vital communication with the world" which makes it feel like home, familiar and manageable. Sensing "invests the quality with vital value, grasping it first in its meaning for us, for that heavy mass which is our body, whence it comes about that it always involves a reference to the body" (PP 52-53/64-65). By interpreting it as communal Merleau-Ponty indicates that sensing has active and passive dimensions. Sensing receives the world and seizes it. By making sensing a corporeal event he puts the subject immediately in touch with the object itself. But, of course, this is an impure immediacy, mediated by the invariant structures that keep the body out of step with the physical world.

The insistence that sensing is a bodily event at once active and passive is taken over from Husserl and Erwin Straus, both of whom contest the Aristotelian idea that sensing is analogous to a piece of wax receiving the imprint of a seal. In addition to the sensations that fill our representations, Husserl's *Ideas* II describes the role that kinaesthetic sensations (*kinaestheses*) play in the constitution of perception. Kinaestheses are the non-representational sensations that guide motility. They denote "one's inner sense of the movements, tensions and possibilities of one's own Body," as Alia Al-Saji puts it. As the body moves about its environment, negotiating its contours and encountering other bodies, it responds almost automatically to the directives and solicitations communicated to it. This practical know-how, or *competence*, requires no mediating idea or judgment in order to be executed, although it typically draws on established habits. As Al-Saji says, "there is no question of mimesis between kinaestheses and the qualities of the perceived thing. It is rather by moving around things and tracing their contours that kinaestheses make perception, as a concrete dynamic process, possible."[239] She concludes: "Kinaesthetic sensations are hence a function of my Body's orientation in the world; they are my way of feeling the active engagement of my Body with an outside."[240]

A similar view of the function of sensation—as non-representational, directive—is found in the work of Straus, a figure to whom Merleau-Ponty's *Phenomenology* appeals and whose analysis of sensing clearly influenced the latter's own position. In *The Primary World of Senses* Straus argues that Descartes is responsible for the pervasive view that sensations are ideas, merely mental events. "As mere ideas of color, light, and the like, sensations to Descartes lack any intrinsic contact with physical things. This relationship is only inferred...."[241] On this view, the subject has sensations but does not properly receive, let alone suffer, them. This is because the subject who senses, for Descartes, is "removed from time and becoming" and "receives indifferently and unmoved."[242] For Straus, this entails the elimination of the "life" of sensing, by which he means its dialogical or communal character as well as it affective force. He writes:

> All sensory impressions are answers to questions; they are not simply there in the way in which the physiological processes underlying them are. We receive sensory impressions insofar as we orient ourselves within our primary relationship with the world by questing, seeking, expecting.[243]

Sensing and knowing are sharply distinguished in Straus's view. When we know something, we grasp its meaning by suspending our vital commerce and rendering an explicit judgment about the thing in question. This image of cognition is analogous to what Merleau-Ponty calls intentionality of act. "Sensing," which is closer to Merleau-Ponty's operative intentionality, is "a sympathetic experiencing. It is directed to the physiognomic characteristics of the alluring and the frightening," says Straus. He continues, in language echoed in *Phenomenology of Perception*,

> When we grasp an expression, a communion is established which seizes and changes *us*, which holds and confines us; while in knowing, it is we who seize the world, who appropriate it and detach ourselves from the particular, attaining the full scope of an horizon which, ultimately, we transcend.[244]

We see Straus here appreciating the ambivalence of sensation, its ability to provide us with appearances as well as their capacity to direct and transform our corporeal identities. Moreover, we see him anticipating Todes's insistence that practice *makes* the practitioner. He even acknowledges the disabling potential of sensation: "it is just in sensations of pain that we feel the world attacking and invading us."[245] It is this last point that gets covered over when the perceptual field is regarded primarily as a totality of tools or equipment to be handled, or when the synchrony of body and world is stressed too emphatically.

Straus's theory of sensing is useful here because it brings out the material, vital dimension of sensing that is endorsed by Merleau-Ponty but sometimes overshadowed by his commitment to describing perception in instrumental terms. Straus demonstrates that the body's sensibility is neither limited to the passive reception of stimuli, nor is it the Kantian faculty that projects a spatiotemporal grid into the sensible field. As Barbaras says of Straus,

> sensibility must be apprehended in the form of sensing, understood as a specific mode of relation, as the communication of the living being with a world. Sensing is the mode according to which the living being *as such* is linked with the world (and this is why it defines a common ground between human and animal), it designates the living being's originary mode of existence.[246]

Straus's view of the lived body is more naturalistic than what we usually find in Merleau-Ponty. In his course notes on nature from the Collège de France Merleau-Ponty does, however, adopt Straus's philosophical biology of sensory communion.[247] But it is not so much a biological conception of human embodiment that Straus is interested in articulating. He is much more concerned to draw a phenomenological distinction between the affective and cognitive modes of existence, or what he calls the "pathic" and "gnostic" modes. These modes correspond for Straus to sensing and perceiving, respectively, and significantly *are discontinuous with one another*.[248] Needless to say, Straus spends most of his energy unpacking the mode of sensing, which Barbaras says "corresponds, in fact, to a mode of immediate communication, to a sympathy with the world that does not entail any thematic dimension."[249]

Although he does not explicitly draw such a definitive distinction between sensing and perceiving, Merleau-Ponty displays a marked interest in the immediate, affective dimension of body-world contact. When describing the transitive form of sensation, or sensation as communion, he refers to it, as already noted, as the "primary layer" of perception. It would be difficult for him to acknowledge that this layer is made up of "non-intentional stuff," for this would contradict the doctrine that experience is always of full-fledged things and, moreover, it would require him to give an account of how perception, which is thoroughly intentional, can commune with the non-intentional. Phenomenology could not provide such an account. This may be why Merleau-Ponty holds back from drawing a sharp distinction between sensing and perceiving. It is not always clear precisely what their relation is for him. Is one is ontologically primary or are they ontologically equiprimordial. One thing is clear, however: sensation is not seen as just the inferred material of perception or the passive reception of stimuli. It is a corporeal event undergone by the subject and constitutive of the subject's integrity.

A purely physiological perspective cannot capture the phenomenon of sensation because it is blind to the intentional dimension of sensing, as the *Phenomenology* argues:

> Sensation is intentional because I find that in the sensible a certain rhythm of existence is put forward—abduction or adduction—and that, following up this hint, and stealing into the form of existence which is thus suggested to me, I am brought into relation with an external being, whether it be in order to open myself to it or to shut myself off from it. (PP 212-213/247)

We glean from this passage that "intentionality" does not just denote the fact that all sensory experience is directed toward an object. It suggests that sensation involves electing to be taken into or removed from a situation. Furthermore, there is here an overlapping of intentionality and affectivity. To sense is to be directed by an external object, to be carried or assailed by its rhythm. This is what it means for sensation to have a "motor physiognomy" or "living significance" (PP 209/242-243). If it is the case that "the world ceaselessly assails and beleaguers subjectivity as waves wash round a wreck on the shore" (PP 207/240), then we must regard the directives of sensation as fundamental to the constitution and power (*puissance*) of subjectivity (PP 210, 211/244, 245). We will see this theme recur in some of Levinas's writing on sensation and aesthetics.

Sensation is able to play a part in the arrangement of our subjectivity because sensibility is internally related to our postural schema and the practical objectives it means to accomplish. Lingis writes that "the postural schema is not simply a diagram of the way all the parts are equilibrated: the body does not tend to a state of rest, but tends to maintain a state of tension centered in a particular direction." This centering is directed by the body's posture, "that is, the motile way the body centers and converges all its receptor surfaces upon an objective."[250] But we also cannot forget that the body "is itself a sensible being that continually schematizes itself, makes a gait of its movement, a gesture of its displacement, makes of each of its here-now particular configurations or positions into a posture or attitude maintaining itself or varying itself continuously."[251] This means that the body's rhythm remains always susceptible to the sympathetic and antipathetic physiognomies of its environment. The way in which environmental determinations constitute the body's power (or freedom) is addressed in my conclusion.

For the most part Merleau-Ponty regards sensing as an amicable affair, the mutual completion of subject and object. He speaks of it, after Straus, as a "sympathetic relation" with objects. "Apart from the probing of my eye or my hand, and before my body synchronizes with it, the sensible is nothing but a vague beckoning [*une sollicitation vague*]" (PP 214/248). Despite the fact that consciousness is "saturated" with the sensible, Merleau-Ponty insists that "the sentient and the sensible do not stand in relation to each other as two mutually external terms, and sensation is not an invasion of the sentient by the sensible" (PP 214, 215/247-248).[252] The tireless influx of sensory stimuli is no affront to the subject's sensibility, but rather an invitation to mutual animation. Sensation under this rehabilitated model is the primary mode of contact with being, neither completely active nor passive, and the means by which bodies originally and ordinarily respond to one another. Since sensation, for Merleau-Ponty, is not temporally prior to perception, we might be better off calling it the *edge* of perception.

Painting the Body

Exactly what Merleau-Ponty means by sensing is perhaps best illustrated when he is writing about painting. The painter, unlike the scientist, is someone who defers his or her manipulation of objects and in this deference "returns to the soil of the sensible" (EM 159, 160/9, 12). Bypassing the practical aspect of things the painter tries to capture the birth of the thing by depicting the self-organization of its qualities and its "internal animation" (EM 182/71). This is possible, says Merleau-Ponty, because the painter's body is "immersed in the visible" and can be used by the visible to give artistic expression to its many senses (EM 162/17-18). The painter swims in a sensory ocean that directs his or her body's affective and motor capacities into aesthetic expression, but only if the painter is willing to *lend* his or her body to the visible. The task of the painter's body is to express the nascent meaning of the visible. And this is precisely what painting is: it is the "transubstantiation" (EM 162/16) of the sensible from the sensory field to the canvas, a process which is made possible by the complicity of sensitive subjects and sensible objects.

By situating the painter and painted on the same plane—the visible—Merleau-Ponty is able to collapse the distinction between art and nature, on the one hand, and the distinction between reality and representation, on the other. These distinctions are replaced by a general economy of sensation and expression, which is to say that the aesthetic dimension becomes for Merleau-Ponty the means by which the material and imaginary realms enter into communion. He cites Cézanne in "Cézanne's Doubt:" "Art is a personal apperception, which I embody in sensations and which I ask the understanding to organize into a painting" (CD 13/22). To do this, the painter must become an articulation of the sensible, the mechanics of which are key to grasping Merleau-Ponty's non-dualist, non-representational theory of painting.

At the heart of his theory is the idea that the painter and the painted, the seer and the seen are made of the same flesh. In "Cézanne's Doubt" there is a flesh of nature, whereas in "Eye and Mind" (which is contemporaneous with *The Visible and the Invisible*) it is the visible/sensible that defines the flesh. In both instances Merleau-Ponty wishes to demonstrate how subject and object participate in a "locus of reversibility"[253] which permits them to work together in expressing the aesthetic dimension of being. In the role of painter the subject catches onto the rhythm of the visible and allows it to commandeer his or her body's intentions and gestures. In this way "the visible world and the world of my motor projects are each total parts of the same Being" (EM 162/17). It is this overlapping of seer and seen, this chiasm of visibility, that prohibits us from positing a distinction between the interiority of the subject and the exteriority of the world. It is what makes painting, at least in the case of Cézanne, a non-representational act.

To understand the act of transubstantiation carried out by the painter, the image to be rendered and the gestures required to render it must be understood as continuous with each other. There cannot be an absolute difference between the sensible and its artistic expression, for this would violate Merleau-Ponty's doctrine of the flesh, which maintains that seer and seen are but two sides of a single visibility, indeed visibility as such (EM 163/19-20). As Michael B. Smith writes, "Merleau-Ponty's aesthetics of painting is grounded in a metaphysics of vision, and vision, in turn, in an ontological description of the body subject as a seeing seenness."[254] Visual representation is not carried out by the viewer; it is "'incited' [*excitée*] to think by the body" (EM 175/51). For the painter this thinking is embodied in the painterly gesture itself. The unique contours of the visible spectacle seize upon the painter's body and, catching the painter in a circuit of immanence, induces the body to adopt a physiognomy that expresses the "carnal formula" of the sensations to be painted. This entire process is made possible by the reversibility of visibility or, more generally, the "duplicity of sensing" which is the animating principle of both body and world (EM 164/23, translation modified). We may wonder whether this duplicity is not mediated, on the painter's side, by reflection. But let us set this question aside for now.

As Merleau-Ponty's aesthetics makes clear, sensing occurs neither inside nor outside the subject. It is a liminal event, originally responsible for the style assumed by the painter's body and, consequently, her artistic style. "Style is what orients and shapes in view of a revelation," says de Waehlens.²⁵⁵ Before it becomes a defining trait of an artist, or an object of reflection for the artist, it "germinates at the surface of the artist's experience" (ILVS 53/66).²⁵⁶ The "exigency" of style is therefore compromised by over-intellectualized or mannered treatments of the sensible. Intellectualism in philosophy and objectivism/realism in art both eliminate the contingency of experience and thereby undercut its ambiguity with abstractions (PP 38-39/48-49).

An individual's style is a singular manner of accessing the real or negotiating its rhythms. These rhythms are first received, as directives of *sens*, by sensibility. Secondarily they become habits, gestures, signature techniques, or clichéd expressions. The problem, for someone concerned with portraying their immediacy, like Cézanne, is to portray these directives as they are delivered to sensibility "to make *visible* how the world *touches* us" (CD 19/33)—without imposing a form that is not given by the sensible itself. The style of the painting should reflect the immanent negotiation of subject and object that takes place at the level of "viscous, equivocal" appearance, rather than at the level of pragmatic manipulation or cool reflection (CD 17/30). "The painting," writes de Waehlens, "gives visible presentation to what is not visible for the pragmatic eye, and is normally 'possessed' by the sense of contact: movement, volume, lightness, or mass, as they obviously are presented in the work of Degas, for example."²⁵⁷

It is Cézanne's painting, argues Merleau-Ponty, which is exemplary in its attempt to render for perception the "chaos of sensations" (CD 13/22). This gives us more reason to think that Merleau-Ponty understands sensation as something other than perception, since chaos is certainly not of a piece with perceptual life. Cézanne's work is populated by figures which seem to be on the verge of breaking down or losing their form; or, on their way to metamorphosing into altogether different figures. Chaos lurks within them. They attempt to bring to appearance what Merleau-Ponty refers to as the "unstable, and alien" element of "natural perception" (PP 225/260). Cézanne, he writes, "wanted to depict matter as it takes on form, the birth of order through spontaneous organization" (CD 13/23). If this organization is to be truly spontaneous, not mediated by the artifices of technique or idealization, then Cézanne would have to develop a style that matches the immediacy of his theme: the emergent sensory order, or the world as it acquires its aesthetic contours. In short, he would need to compose the chaos of sensation. Merleau-Ponty writes:

> The outline should therefore be a result of the colors if the world is to be given its true density. For the world is a mass without gaps, a system of colors across which the receding perspective, the outlines, angles, and curves are inscribed like lines of force; the spatial structure vibrates as it is formed. (CD 15/25-26)

This conception of spatiality is antithetical to Kant's in that it makes spatial organization a product of the sensory manifold, thereby locating the principle of animation in the matter, rather than the form, of perception.[258]

What allows the painter to be animated by the sensible? Like his or her chosen subject, the painter possesses a physiognomy that can adapt to the physiognomy or "motif" of still-life objects, landscapes, the faces of portraiture (CD 17/29). The motif, which is "no more than a combination of colors," provides the body of the artist with directives that initiate the creative event, "an event which grips [the] body, and this grip circumscribes the area of significance [*sens*] to which it has reference" (CD 16/27; PP 235/272). Art is not first and foremost an act of symbolism. It is an affective reconfiguration engendered by the body's sensibility. The artist's body "is an object which is *sensitive to* all the rest, which reverberates to all sounds, vibrates to all colors, and provides words [or lines, colors] with their primordial significance through the way in which it receives them" (PP 236/273).

Merleau-Ponty's discussion of Cézanne suggests a conceptual, but perhaps not real, distinction between sensation and perception. This is discernible in his remark that Cézanne breaks with the Impressionists by rejecting the latter's attempts to "capture, in the painting, the very way in which objects strike our eyes and attack our senses." This attack, he says vaguely, occurs at the level of "instantaneous perception" and appears as the chaos of sensations invoked above (CD 11/19). The *Phenomenology of Perception* likewise implies that sensation is part of perception, and yet distinguishable from what is ordinarily perceived—whole, medium-sized graspable objects projected against a background. Most tellingly, he writes: "What is called sensation is only the most rudimentary of perceptions, and, as a modality of existence, it is no more separable than any other perception from a background which is in fact the world" (PP 241/279). In a manner different from Straus, Merleau-Ponty finds continuity between sensation and perception because he wants to avoid making the latter the "form" and the former the "matter" of experience. Because no phenomenological distinction exists for him, no real distinction exists.

The Diachrony of Sensation

Despite his allegiance to the thesis that all consciousness is both directed toward some object and always projected against a horizon of meaning, Merleau-Ponty does suggest that a non-intentional form of sensing exists. This he describes as "forever anterior to perception," a provocative formulation that opens a distinction between sensing and perception, and points to an originary, pre-phenomenological encounter with the sensible, one that belongs to the prehistory of perception. When Merleau-Ponty speaks of the anonymity of the body, it seems to me that it is this encounter he intends to highlight, and not the general or neuter form of the body. Moreover, his view of sensibility situates sensing on a transcendental level, or in "a kind of original past, a past which has never been present" (PP 242/280). It is into this original past that perception must reach in order to apprehend what *there is* to perceive. Or rather, perception must nourish itself on the sensations that make up its irretrievable past. Without sensation, consciousness cannot survive. This is because, as Al-Saji argues, "perception lags behind sensibility—so that consciousness and being do not coincide, despite Merleau-Ponty's claim in the 'Temporality' chapter [of *Phenomenology of Perception*]."[259]

There is, then, *more* than a conceptual distinction to be drawn between perception and sensation. The case can be made that the pre-personality of sensation should take ontological precedence over the personality of perception in Merleau-Ponty's philosophy, although, as we have seen, he usually folds these disparate experiences into the image of perception as communion, as *sentir*. There is a fundamental diachrony, or non-coincidence, at the heart of perception that breaks up its synchronization with the world. This diachrony is introduced by sensation. Levinas takes up this point and uses it, like Deleuze, against Merleau-Ponty. Diachrony is the work of sensation, the "primary layer" of sense experience "which at once grounds perception and assures its opacity and non-coincidence," in Al-Saji's terms.[260] Upon this shifting ground lie at least three other layers which constitute the perceptual experience. Merleau-Ponty outlines these in a discussion of hearing.

The different layers of sound are only identifiable once the unified experience of listening, say, to a piece of music is analyzed by reflection. After making this phenomenological point Merleau-Ponty ventures to speculate about the multidimensional sensation of sound itself: "there is an objective sound which reverberates outside me in the instrument, an atmospheric sound which is *between* the object and my body, a sound which vibrates in me 'as if I had become the flute or the clock'; and, finally, a last stage in which the acoustic element disappears and becomes the highly precise experience of a change permeating my whole body" (PP 227/263). Merleau-Ponty here describes the liminal nature of sensation—it "is *between* the object and my body"—as well as its capacity to directly reconfigure the body. This reconfiguration might manifest itself in dance, which is arguably the most obvious example of "a change permeating my whole body" or the body communing with its auditory environment. Given Merleau-Ponty's description, however, we should hesitate to posit dance as a primary or "instantaneous" reconfiguration. What comes first is the "objective sound which reverberates outside me in the instrument." Physically, a sound wave. This reverberation reaches us in a highly complex situation, against a background of noise and silence, and in principle could drown out this background by reaching an oppressively loud volume. That is, the sound is potentially hostile to the body and the body's potential communion with the aural environment. This potential resides in the fact that sensation's liminality places it at the threshold of the world *as perceived*. Sensation reverberates whether anyone is there to perceive it or not; it is not beholden to the mechanics of perception.

On average we do not experience the pure reverberation of an instrument outside of an aural context, and yet Merleau-Ponty says that this objective sound occurs in the instrument rather than in our ears. This compels us to think of our perception of sound as delayed. Our ears arrive late to the event of sound. This is because we must "*learn* to perceive according to Merleau-Ponty," says Al-Saji.[261] The world possesses rhythms that solicit synchronization from our bodies; it challenges us with dissonant rhythms; it meets our bodies' groping with inconvenient designs and incapacitating sounds. Some of these we can catch onto, others not. Our sensory environment is not always ergonomically advantageous: it contains sensations that are alien and unstable, but whose meaning nevertheless saturates us (PP 214, 215/248, 249). Perception "converts the elements of the sensory encounter into recognizable and representable identities" and effects a "transformation of the inherent ambiguity and intertwining of the sensory—a transformation that the sensory suggests but as a result of which it comes to be overlaid and forgotten qua sensory life."[262] On this reading, sensory life becomes the virtual dimension of perceptual life.

Always beyond the reach of perception, but nevertheless serving as the "unreflective fund" that provides it with phenomenal content, the sensory life of the body reveals itself as the anonymous, objective ground of any actual perception (PP 242/280). In Al-Saji's words,

> Perception may be a prospective actualization, but it is experienced as the discovery of what was always already there. It is this anteriority that makes objects appear real to us—our experience of their presence being given through their inexhaustibility and alterity. This inexhaustibility is due to the coexistence and non-coincidence of rhythms in sensory life, a life which at once constitutes the ground of perceptual experience while being irreducible to perceptual form. What allows the experience of anteriority to be more than an illusion for Merleau-Ponty is that it relies on, and holds the trace of, a more original delay—that of sensory life as forever past with respect to perception.[263]

It is not so much that Merleau-Ponty subscribes to the view that there is an anonymous body subtending the historically and culturally inscribed body, but that he affirms a carnal sensibility whose resources cannot be exhausted by an individual's consciousness or singular perceptual experience. Sensibility is basic to the pre-personal identity of the body and constitutive of an "unconscious" dimension of subjectivity. Put otherwise, only a portion of what the lived body senses makes its way into perception, and even less becomes the object of reflection. When Merleau-Ponty writes that "Perception is always in the mode of the impersonal 'One'," we must take this to mean that perception is at every moment the renewal of the synthetic act which reaches into the past while projecting into the future in its attempt to fix the object of perception before us.[264] This entails that perception is an "ever-recurrent failure" [*échec perpétuel*] to hold onto what is given in sensation (PP 240/277).

Perception apprehends a phenomenal field which is "never presented in any other way than integrated into a configuration and already 'patterned' ['*mise en forme*']" (PP 159/186). Following Gestalt principles Merleau-Ponty holds that no sense experience happens outside of the horizon subtended by my personal intentional arc and the historical/cultural horizon in which I am always situated. This phenomenal field, however, cannot be identical to the field engaged immediately by the senses, for the latter is marked by a singularity which resists entry into the intentional horizon. Sensibility, then, remains bound to a pre-personal field wherein "each sensation, being strictly speaking, the first, last and only one of its kind, is a birth and a death" of the body that receives it. Moreover,

> the subject who experiences it begins and ends with it, and as he can neither precede nor survive himself, sensation necessarily appears to itself in a setting of generality, its origin anterior to myself, it arises from *sensibility* which has preceded it and which will outlive it, just as my birth and death belong to a natality and a mortality which are anonymous. (PP 216/250)

The carnality of the subject inhabits two distinct spheres, the practical-personal, on the one hand, and the sensible-impersonal, on the other. They never operate in isolation from each other, and this fact calls into question the primacy of perception and the primacy of body-world synchrony.

The tension between the personal and impersonal body is palpable in Merleau-Ponty's reluctance to disengage sensation from perception and allow the former to devolve into the formless data of the empiricists or the pure sensory manifold of Kant. This is why sensation appears sometimes as a rudimentary form of perception (thus guaranteeing perception's inherent form) and at other times as the transcendental condition of perception (which ensures Merleau-Ponty's anti-idealist credentials). In the last analysis Merleau-Ponty wants to maintain the primacy of perception while at the same time championing the immediacy of sensing which is clearly endorsed in his analysis of Cézanne's painting and its ability to express the dialogue of physiognomies that is the body-world relation. If there is a truly anonymous and pre-perceptual form of sensing acknowledged in the *Phenomenology*, then there is reason to suggest that the sensations undergone by the body's organs point to a transcendental field that is better depicted by the Impressionists, however speculative or non-phenomenological their aesthetic might be.

Merleau-Ponty tells us that Cézanne breaks with the Impressionists over their impossible desire to portray how objects strike our senses (CD 11-14/19-23). The Impressionists are wont to paint what would be the pure a priori of perception, that is, sensation, whereas Cézanne's painting exhibits sensible nature as it emerges into an organized form. On this reading, the Impressionists would be the painters of a "non-thetic, pre-objective, and pre-conscious experience" that depicts "sensation as a private phenomenon" (PP 242/279). It is this private sphere that is most problematic from the perspective of a perception which is, according to "The Primacy of Perception," fundamentally intersubjective (PrP 17-18, 26-27/52, 70-71). As Merleau-Ponty writes in "The Philosopher and His Shadow:"

> The fact is that sensible being, which is announced to me in my most strictly private life, summons up within that life all other corporeality. It is the being which reaches me in my most secret parts, but which I also reach in its brute or untamed state, in an absolute of presence which holds the secret of the world, others, and what is true. (Shadow 171/215)

Sensation, then, becomes problematic because it harbors a form of solipsism, a view which Merleau-Ponty ardently resists. The touch of sensation opens the body to the world of objects, others, and communication. But in itself it cannot be accessed, represented, or articulated. The problem of solipsism raised by the "aesthesiological" is resolvable only when it is assimilated to perception, for perception, writes Merleau-Ponty, "is never a matter of anything but co-perception. I see that this man over there sees, as I touch my left hand while it is touching my right" (Shadow 170/215). As he says elsewhere, perception is always already reversible. If there is solipsism, then it must be wrested from the intersubjective sphere and therefore no solipsism at all.

Merleau-Ponty's entire critique of sensation derives from his observation that we do not really encounter much of what the classical empiricists and rationalists say we do. For the most part he is right: we do not perceive sense impressions or sense data. We perceive things. Against classical theory he maintains that we only arrive at the imperceptible through analysis, which must necessarily begin with the perceptible. This may be true phenomenologically, but it does not foreclose the possibility that, ontologically speaking, perception is a derivative experience, subtended by a more rudimentary experience of embodiment. Merleau-Ponty acknowledges the existence of imperceptible encounters with things, which is why I think the realist strand of his analysis of sensing supports the thesis—even if he does not advance it himself—that perception derives from the transitive form of sensation. When he speaks of the sound reverberating in the instrument before it reaches the ears of the listener, he acknowledges the primacy of an aesthetic atmosphere that is anterior to perception. Here resides the anonymous sensory experience that saturates our bodies and cannot be recuperated by the subject-object dialogue. *The Visible and the Invisible*'s concept of flesh develops this anonymous sensibility into a general theory of being.

Reversible Bodies

The flesh (*la chair*) radicalizes insights from the *Phenomenology* by replacing the latter's residual subject-object dualism with a monistic account of the sensible. In the early text our bodies and the bodies of others (human and nonhuman) are said only to achieve full expression through the co-constitutive dialogue of perception. This dialogue is made possible, explains *The Visible and the Invisible*, because both subject and object belong to a common "element," the sensible as such, or the flesh. It is this element that brings together while at the same time separating the poles of perception: "the thickness of flesh between seer and the thing is constitutive for the thing of its visibility as for the seer of his corporeity" (VI 135/178). The separation of bodies, then, is derivative of the fundamental "narcissism" at the heart of the sensible. In *The Visible and the Invisible* it is no longer perception that gives birth to discrete objects, but the so-called dehiscence (*écart*) of the flesh. Dehiscence is the name Merleau-Ponty uses to describe the fission of the sensible into sentient body and sensible world; it denotes the coiling back or enfolding of being performed in sensing:

> [The flesh] is the coiling over of the visible upon the seeing body, of the tangible upon the touching body, which is attested in particular when the body sees itself, touches itself seeing and touching the things, such that, simultaneously, *as* tangible it descends among them, *as* touching it dominates them all and draws this relationship and even this double relationship from itself, by dehiscence or fission of its own mass. (VI 146/191-192)

At bottom it is the dehiscence of flesh that constitutes my body as an individual that senses and gains it the necessary distance from what is perceived (VI 140/185). Since individuation results from the separation (*écart*) of the flesh, understood as a single element, it entails a kind of reversibility between bodies. At the crossing where reversibility occurs, "perception is born" (VI 154/202).

By "reversible" Merleau-Ponty means that at any moment the one who sees can become the one seen, or the one who touches can become the touched. The possibility of a passive body becoming active or an active body becoming passive is immanent to embodiment as such. He holds that the reversibility of the sensible is analogous to what happens when I touch my left hand with my right. This is the narcissistic element of the flesh: "the seer and the visible reciprocate one another and we no longer know which sees and which is seen" (VI 139/183). Sensing is here attributed not to individual subjects who exist apart from their worlds, but to the flesh as a substance that divides itself into sensible and sentient beings. This is the primary dualism of *The Visible and the Invisible*, it seems to me. The *Phenomenology*'s anthropocentric dualism has been mitigated here, but at the same time a new dualism, embedded in the rhetoric of "chiasmus," arises. While intended as a figure that could overcome the *Phenomenology*'s undesirable dualism (as identified by its author), the chiasmus injects a new duality into the heart of Merleau-Ponty's monism of the flesh. Consequently, the figure of the chiasmus "does not solve anything, because in order to work, both terms [subject and object, seer and seen] must be preserved even as they are cancelled at another level."[265] The sensible-sentient chiasmus is what signals the dualism troubling—or short-circuiting, however you want to see it—the monistic ontology of *The Visible and the Invisible*.

What remains unclear is how the flesh becomes sentient in the first place, why some beings achieve sentience while others remain merely sensible. "For if the body is a thing among things, it is so in a stronger and deeper sense than they," Merleau-Ponty asserts (VI 137/181). One way to overcome the sensing-sensed dualism is by broadening the scope of sentience to include any entity that can receive sensory stimulation. If stimulation is regarded as an objective event, and is not confined to the interior life of humans or other living animals, then we can begin to speak of the sensations experienced by inanimate objects. This is one way to abolish *The Visible and the Invisible*'s dualistic conception of the sensible, but one which also commits us to a new, perhaps Whiteheadian, metaphysics of sensation.

Merleau-Ponty explicitly points out that the presumed reversibility of sensible and sentient is always imminent, but never accomplished (VI 147/194). In other words, my left and right hands cannot both be touching each other at the same time; one of the pair must play the role of passive object while the other actively senses it. More generally, sentient/subjective and sensible/objective never fully synchronize because reversibility has an asynchronous core. It must be stressed that the impossible coincidence at the center of reversibility is, in part, a product of the analogy of self-touching chosen by Merleau-Ponty. The asynchrony of reversibility is therefore a consequence of his analogy to self-reflexive behavior and does not seem to apply to what we typically consider an intercorporeal relation. Nor does it apply universally to sensing or tactility.[266]

What if the always deferred synchrony of reversibility is not like attempting to catch sight of one's own shadow by quickly turning around? Consider how smelling, tasting, and hearing do not bear the kind of symmetry necessary for reversibility. Sure, I can be smeller or smelled, but the scent that invades my nose is in no position to take in my scent. The same could be said of a taste or sound. These sensations are more invasive than the tactile and give us a good idea of the basically irreversible or dissymmetrical nature of sensing. Something like a handshake, by contrast, appears to offer a better analogy for reversibility.[267] But even the handshake proves irreversible—perhaps it is exemplarily irreversible—since the strength and delicacy of the persons shaking will most likely be disproportionate, a matter of unequal force. This is why Beata Stawarska argues, rightly I think, that the concept of flesh performs a "massive reduction of the specifically *intersubjective* experience of the body manifest in an encounter with another embodied person to the corporeal dynamic operative within the body proper."[268] Self-touching offers us a helpful image of reflection, but not entirely an accurate account of the intercorporeal encounter.

In her work on Merleau-Ponty and political philosophy Diana Coole responds to Merleau-Ponty's critics, chiefly Levinas, who claim that the metaphor of the handshake is ethically defective because it privileges continuity over discontinuity, sameness over difference. She writes, "Merleau-Ponty is surely using the handshake to advance an ontological rather than an ethical claim and he does so in order to disclose the very possibility of ethical (and political) relations."[269] If Coole is right, and Levinas's charge holds, then Merleau-Ponty has misread a basic (ontological) difference at the heart of intercorporeity. But Merleau-Ponty does not see the handshake as an event of congruity, but one of *écart*, or separation, and so Levinas's criticism falters.[270] Merleau-Ponty retains the language of reversibility and is thereby left to account for the discontinuous continuity between the bodies exchanging the handshake. Is this continuity merely phenomenal? If not, what is the metaphysical mechanism of its *écart*? His life cut short, Merleau-Ponty never had time to provide an adequate reply to these questions.

The experience of the handshake illustrates how intercorporeal touching is fundamentally different from self-touching. The handshake exhibits an *exchange* of sensations that is not present in the case of self-touching. When I shift my attention and convert my touched hand into the hand doing the touching, as in the case of self-touching, there is no exchange of sensation, but rather a shift in attention, a reversal of intentionality. As Stawarska writes, "What distinguishes the intercorporeal relation from the intracorporeal one is that the passivity of my hand touched by the other—unlike the passivity of my hand that I touch—*cannot reverse into an activity (of touching) for me*, even though I can respond to the other touching me by touching them in turn."[271] The idea that two bodies stand in a relation of reversibility assumes that any passive relation is potentially convertible into an active relation, even if this reversal is impossible, as in cases of domination, oppression, torture, or murder.[272] The supposition of reversibility effectively neglects a fundamental feature of violence: the inequality of the sensations exchanged. This is precisely what makes intercorporeity irreversible.

The Reality of Violence

Rewriting the Cartesian cogito, Merleau-Ponty argues that the subject is an "I can" ["*je peux*"] before it is an "I think" (PP 137/160). But this formulation is only partially true. Is the subject not equally an "I can't," a perpetually constrained actor whose abilities cannot be privileged over its inabilities? The body's orientation is always a mixture of abilities and disabilities, and some orientations, as Ahmed and Fanon suggest, are more accommodating than others. Ahmed writes:

> If classical phenomenology is about "motility," expressed in the hopefulness of the utterance "I can," Fanon's phenomenology of the black body would be better described in terms of the bodily and social experience of restriction, uncertainty and blockage, or perhaps even in terms of the despair of the utterance "I cannot." … To be black in "the white world" is to turn back towards itself, to become an object, which means not only not being extended by the contours of the world, but being diminished as an effect of the bodily extensions of others.[273]

Nowhere is corporeal constraint more evident than in the threatened or disabled body. To say nothing, of course, of the corpse. If the subject, on Merleau-Ponty's model, is to be identified with the body in all of its materiality (not just the body insofar as it is animated by an intentional consciousness or mind, that is, the lived body), then each of the body's manifestations must be taken into consideration when embodied subjectivity is in question. Furthermore, the intercorporeal relation cannot just be the site where perception is born. It must also serve as the site where perception disintegrates or vanishes altogether.

Merleau-Ponty does not completely neglect the reality of violence, however. Coole has shown that he acknowledges its reality in his political studies, refusing to reduce it to a metaphor. As she writes, "His emphasis on the body brings home the vulnerability and mortality of the flesh. His actors find themselves suspended between the violence of the visceral and the potential violence of the structural, where even peaceful aims can have violent repercussions."[274] It is true that he recognizes the inherent vulnerability of the body in the face of the other. Not unlike Sartre, who theorizes the gaze of the other as an instrument of objectification or seizure, Merleau-Ponty considers how the presence of the other entails a conflict of interpretations where the truth of the object is at stake, where the body's hold on the world is contested by others (PrP 18/53). Just like me, the other fixes his or her grip on objects and appropriates them in the system of holds that make up his or her own practical horizon. My own body, too, can be seized by perception, as Sartre, Fanon, Yancy and others have demonstrated. Merleau-Ponty speaks of a "passive vision ... as in the case of a dazzling light," wherein perception is rendered incapable of making sense of what is seen (PP 315/364). He recognizes the impact of pain and fatigue on our capacity for action (PP 441/504; SB 189/204). Ultimately, he defines the freedom of the body negatively as a "tolerance" of institutional and physical forces, thus eschewing the ideal of a pure subject who remains invulnerable to material forces (PP 454/518). What Merleau-Ponty does not provide us with is an ontological explanation for how real violence is possible, how the reversibility of the flesh is suspended, violated, or overridden. Unfortunately, it is not enough just to emphasize that subjectivity is embodied or that pain occurs in fact.

In order accurately to portray intercorporeal encounters, and the violent in particular, a robust notion of irreversibility or alterity must be provided. This does not mean that reciprocity between bodies should be deemed impossible (which is implied in Levinas's ontology, as we will see in the next chapter). What we need is a model that acknowledges the distance between bodies, but also enables them to exchange a common currency and participate in a common experiential economy. I suggest we consider sensation as providing the currency and the aesthetic as the common economy. To be fair, I think Merleau-Ponty notices, but does not pursue, this possibility. It is present in his recognition of sensation as the past that never presents itself to perception; it is there in his acknowledgement of the affective quality of sensing; and it is implied in his ontology of the flesh (PP 53/65). These moments of divergence and diachrony are where Merleau-Ponty troubles the happy alliance of body and world while simultaneously recognizing an element shared by embodied beings. The dehiscence of the flesh, or what Hass calls the "constitutive difference in the fabric of experience," offers another moment of divergence.[275] But the mechanics of the involution of the sensible—how the flesh generates individual bodies—remains a metaphysical mystery for phenomenology. In *Phenomenology of Perception* it is temporality that drives the dehiscence of being, but time is conceived there anthropocentrically as "born of my relation with things" (PP 412, 426/471, 487, translation modified). Merleau-Ponty's later philosophy does not provide us with a non-anthropocentric conception of time or a metaphysical explanation of dehiscence or an adequate account of how bodies individuate themselves from the singular flesh of being, and eventually get destroyed.[276] This is not a failure of Merleau-Ponty, but work he left for us to accomplish.

The gap (is it real or apparent?) between entities never reaches closure; reversibility is always deferred. Nevertheless, Merleau-Ponty's analyses most often suggest the possibility of convergence: the subject is always on the way to a better understanding of its object; the left hand is always on the verge of touching instead of being touched; perception is perpetually on its way to a maximally clear expression.[277] His faith in reversibility, once again, effectively misrepresents the intercorporeal relation by attenuating the volatility introduced by the transcendence of the other qua sensible. Levinas would say that Merleau-Ponty's ontology ultimately reduces the other to the same and that reversibility denotes a relation whose "terms are indifferently read from left to right and from right to left" and which has been reduced to a "simple correlation" (TI 35/5).

Levinas's charge is a bit hyperbolic in the case of Merleau-Ponty since the latter's treatment of intersubjectivity cannot be reduced to a simple self-other duality and, indeed, actively strives to overcome such a reduction.

He does, however, tend to subordinate what Levinas calls the "enigma of sensation-feeling [*l'énigme sensation-sentiment*]" to the competent grasp [*prise*] of perception.[278] As Merleau-Ponty writes,

> my body, as the system of holds on the world, founds the unity of the objects which I perceive, in the same way the body of the other ... tears itself away from being one of my phenomena, offers me the task of true communication, and confers on my objects the new dimension of intersubjective being or, in other words, of objectivity. (PrP 18/53)

The world is not first what eludes my grasp, but what offers me things to grab; the other is not what threatens my subjectivity, but what offers to communicate with me. Others and objects offer possibilities for being and doing because they belong to the phenomenal field open before me and essentially synchronized with my body's practical horizon. Between seeing body and seen other there is "an intimacy as close as between the sea and the strand" (VI 130-131/173).[279]

The ideal of reversibility fails to notice that sensation, even in Merleau-Ponty's own terms, is precisely what cannot become phenomenal if phenomenality is the mode of expression proper to perception. Sensation remains forever out of step with the unfolding of perception; it is the dark side of visibility and ideality, what gives birth to perception and, perhaps, what accounts for its disintegration.

Carnal Sensibility

If we wish to talk about the centrality of the body, then it is necessary to attend to every aspect of its environmental sensitivity, the physiological as well as the phenomenal, insofar as this sensitivity gives rise to the corporeal structures that inform the contours of our perceptual and practical engagements. A neglect of the autonomy of sensation, by which I mean the sensible events which take place below the level of intentional consciousness and which remain "unstable, and alien,"[280] can only hinder a philosophy that seeks to overcome the conceit of an idealism which refuses to recognize the corporeal dimension of subjectivity, freedom, and responsibility. Regardless of whether sensation is a viable phenomenological concept, it is necessary to provide a complete picture of embodiment. And we risk misconception when we overemphasize the constitutive activity of the subject, or when we downplay its susceptibility, incompetence, disintegration, and mechanical or autonomic responses.[281]

Even though his philosophy of the body is sensitive to the constitutive function of the aesthetic dimension, Merleau-Ponty's privileging of perception entails a misrepresentation of how the body's identity is informed and sculpted by its aesthetic environment. He endorses the dialogical notion of aesthetic identity offered by Cézanne. Though instructive, this view does not do justice to the irreversibility of sensation. The pixelated images of the Impressionists, as already suggested, may offer us a better representation. Impressionism gives something like a snapshot of sensation; it captures the sensory event which, "strictly speaking," is "the first, last and only one of its kind, is a birth and death." These images ring false from a phenomenological perspective, but only because phenomenology distrusts and eschews speculation, preferring to derive its ontology from what is given to experience. For a philosopher like Merleau-Ponty and unlike, say, Hume the chaos of sensation can only be hypothesized from the more coherent world of perception. This is why he favors Cézanne over the Impressionists. But once again, Cézanne is a painter of reversibility, of sensing taken as an amicable dialogue. He jettisons the immediacy of sensation in favor of the world figured, or at least figurable.

One of the problems left here is to theorize the discontinuity between bodies without succumbing to the allure of absolute transcendence, as Levinas does, and without casting intercorporeity as purely continuous. To be sure, failure to concede the continuity or immanence of the intercorporeal realm results in a failure to see that sensory demands are communicated directly to the subject by the aesthetic environment. An account of the environment's immanent aesthetic directives is crucial to understanding the emergence of the body's competence and integrity. This is because there are provocations issued by the environment that the body *must respond to* in order to effectively adapt, ways in which the body is determined by its sensory milieu. These determinants are therefore more than optional solicitations: they are *imperatives*.[282] Sometimes these provocations are pleasurable, sometimes they are painful or even excruciating. They can end in bodily obliteration, which is an extreme form of incompetence but a form of responsiveness nonetheless. Merleau-Ponty appreciates this to some degree, but he consistently downplays the imperceptible quality of sensation, its objective power, and as a result pathologizes the vulnerability of the body. The tension between sensation and perception, which is clearly evinced in excessive or limit situations that threaten the coherence of perception and the organizational capacity of the body's schemata, is passed over in favor of a more sympathetic reciprocity or the ideal of "maximum clarity"/"optimum balance" in perception (PP 318/367).[283]

Merleau-Ponty's philosophy has the virtue of being grounded in the carnality of existence, and it does so without submitting to physicalism. Indeed, the depth of his phenomenological descriptions are borne of the concrete practices of the self as it engages other bodies, both human and nonhuman. The ontogenetic narrative Merleau-Ponty tells about the subject's embodiment, which is first and foremost a story of the body's anonymity and passivity, is grounded in the sensitivity of the body, or what we could call its *carnal sensibility*. This sensibility is at work in the sensuous communion of subject and object in *Phenomenology of Perception*; it is at the heart of *The Visible and the Invisible*'s notions of flesh, chiasm, and *écart*; and it is crucial to the psychogenesis of the child in "The Child's Relations with Others" as well as his analyses of Cézanne's theory of painting. In short, there is for me an inscrutable ambivalence at the heart of Merleau-Ponty's work. The problem we are left with is how to disengage the idea of carnal sensibility, which anonymously produces the body's organizational capacity, from the intentional structure of perception and the synchronic ontology of the flesh. Only after the diachrony of sensibility is disengaged from perception can we understand both the passivity of the body and its non-intentional responsiveness to sensations, that is, its obedience to the immanent directives embedded in the aesthetic environment.

Traces of Ambiguity

Reading Merleau-Ponty it is easy to get the impression that the body operates as a tool or prosthesis of consciousness, rather than a substitute for the Cartesian ego. This is because he sometimes speaks of perception and consciousness as though they were not functions *of* the body:

"Consciousness is being-towards-the-thing through the intermediary of the body" (PP 138-139/161). In his more radical formulations we *are* our bodies, nothing more. Establishing a non-reductive version of this identification of self and body is the most promising prospect of working through Merleau-Ponty's ontology.

To overcome modern dualism it is necessary that Merleau-Ponty collapse consciousness and body. If we are to avoid conceiving the body as merely a vessel for the mind or consciousness or perception, there cannot be any mysterious elements of subjectivity or suspicious unbridgeable gaps between subject and world. This means emptying absolute transcendence from ontology, something Merleau-Ponty only begins to accomplish in his unfinished later work. The challenge is formulated by Deleuze in *Pure Immanence* when he says that "consciousness becomes a fact only when a subject is produced at the same time as its object, both being outside the field and appearing as 'transcendents'."[284] In other words, a truly immanent ontology, like the one promised by the primacy of perception thesis or the ontology of the flesh, has to embrace an impersonal transcendental field, one free from the syntheses of a subject, the configuration of intentionality, and the prejudice of correlationism.

Merleau-Ponty's treatment of sensing in *Phenomenology of Perception* is the most promising concept upon which to develop an immanent conception of embodiment. Here we find a concept of sensibility that reverses the formal Kantian view of the subject's aesthetic faculty. Merleau-Ponty provides us with the means to envision sensibility as a kind of material transcendental. Recasting the continuities and discontinuities of the intercorporeal relation in terms of sensations and affects, rather than perception and flesh, recasts many of the problems raised by Merleau-Ponty's carnal ontology. Indeed, his reversibility thesis becomes more persuasive when we distinguish the sensible and perceptual life of the body, then restrict reversibility to the level of perception while assigning an irreducible alterity (irreversibility) to sensing.

The relation between perception and sensation has a double character. On the one hand, these two activities are coextensive; on the other hand, perception is the product of sensation, the latter serving as the "rudimentary" content of the former (PP 241/279). A tension between the impersonal, imperceptible layer of experience (sensation) and the personal, intentional (perception) arises at this point. If perception is given primacy in this tension, then experience must be always regarded as organized by the *telos* of our intentional arc. By the same token, if sensation is cast as the most basic form of perception, it can only appear as phenomenal and, in some sense, coordinated by the subject-object dialogue. But certainly there are sensations received by the body (what Leibniz would call *petites perceptions*)[285] that are never elevated to the level of consciousness and remain forever at the level of proprioceptive information.[286] Merleau-Ponty holds that every perception has something anonymous about it, and that this is linked to the body's habits and schemata as well its "unsophisticated" (read: sensory) life (PP 238/275). Therefore, to delimit the sensory life of the body and see how it functions transcendentally for perception, it is necessary to remain open to speculation about the aesthetic life of the "impersonal 'One'." This is the lesson that emerges when we inhabit the ambiguity surrounding Merleau-Ponty's work on sensibility.

Chapter 4

Sensibility, Susceptibility, and the Genesis of Individuals

> Even when unformed, or deformed, by knowing, sensible intuition can revert to its own meaning.
>
> Levinas, *Otherwise than Being*

Levinas's philosophy of the body contains an explicit commitment to the primacy of sensation, one that remains only implicit in Merleau-Ponty. Levinas's analyses of embodiment display a marked interest in the materiality of the subject. This is most evident in his remarks about sensation and the affective life of the self (the "I"), as well as in his critique of intentionality and his occasional criticism of phenomenological method. In his early texts *Existence and Existents*, *Time and the Other*, and *Totality and Infinity* this materialism appears through an ontogenetic account of the emergence of subjectivity; later, in *Otherwise than Being*, it is through novel accounts of sensibility and vulnerability that we find Levinas defending a materialist ontology. It is in the later work that Levinas's emphasis on the vulnerability of the body—that is, its susceptibility to wounding or its openness to the outside—goes too far in its appreciation of the reality of violence. The enabling aspects of the body-world relation are overshadowed by the exigency of violence that Levinas sees as basic to intersubjectivity. This chapter will not rehearse the drama of the same and the Other (*autrui*)[287] which dominates Levinas's ethics. It will instead reinscribe Levinas's phenomenology into the discourse of ontology and focus on the significance of sensation in his account of subjectivity. This is admittedly an heretical reading of Levinas, but one that is not forced upon him. The purpose of this reading is to supplement Merleau-Ponty's treatment of sensation, and to assemble from their texts an account of embodied subjectivity that is present in neither thinker considered independently of the other.

Corporeal Ontology

Levinas is not usually the first person invoked when the philosophy of the body is up for discussion. His exploration of embodiment is not as broad as Merleau-Ponty's; it is certainly less direct. To unpack Levinas's corporeal ontology the theme must be approached obliquely through his fascinating treatment of concepts like sensibility, alimentation, fecundity, living from, and enjoyment. This constellation of concepts, along with some others, represents Levinas's acute concern with affectivity as an individuating phenomenon. The same goes for sensation: with more candor than Merleau-Ponty, Levinas affirms sensation as basic to embodiment and the constitution of subjectivity. He goes further than Merleau-Ponty in pursuing sensation as a transcendental phenomenon. His analyses of sensation and sensibility try to fully appreciate the primacy of sensation and, in particular, its materiality.[288]

Claiming that Levinas is engaged in ontology is contentious among commentators because so much of the force of his philosophy operates as an evasion of ontology. In general he regards the desire for systematicity in ontology as inherently violent toward beings in their singularity. Ontology, in this respect, is Procrustean. Instead of approaching beings as unique individuals, ontology subsumes, or "totalizes" their uniqueness under a general system, thus reducing their otherness. To avoid violence of this kind Levinas consistently argues that ethics, rather than ontology, is first philosophy. In one sense this means that every individual maintains a peaceful, responsible, and heteronomous relation to the Other, one which is prior to any representation or understanding of him or her. Civil discourse among individuals forms the basis of the community of knowers, and therefore is the condition of possibility of any theory of being or epistemology (TI 72-77/44-49).[289] A certain intersubjective stability, a responsiveness to and responsibility for the other, is necessary for epistemological and ontological reflection to occur. So, ethics first, then ontology.

Levinas's critique of ontology, Heidegger's ontology in particular, often conflates "ontology" with "knowledge of Being" in order to argue for the priority of ethics. This conflation reduces being, or existence in general, to what can be known about being. This is a familiar move in the Levinas literature.[290] It is symptomatic of the view that ontology cannot get outside the subject-object correlation, and therefore cannot accommodate the alterity (the Other) that transcends the correlation. Only metaphysics of the Levinasian variety can prepare such accommodation because Levinasian metaphysics is in actuality an ethics dedicated to hospitality toward the Other, not a theory of what exists or the basic structure of reality. It resists absolutely any attempt to subordinate the singularity of the Other to the generality of Being. He writes in *Totality and Infinity* about how ontology "reduces the other to the same" by making the Other appear through a "third term, a neutral term, which is itself not a being" (TI 42/12). This third term, through which the "shock of the encounter of the same with the other is deadened" is the theory of being, or ontology understood as a system of knowledge of beings.

Prior to any conceptualization of the Other, Levinas argues, is the "calling into question of my spontaneity by the presence of the Other," or ethics (TI 43/13). But is not this calling into question an event that requires an understanding of its conditions and terms? That is, is it not necessary for us to comprehend the constitution of the subject and the Other in order to realize the force of ethics? Ontology seems to come before ethics. There is a sense, however, in which neither enjoys priority, in which *aesthetics that is first philosophy*. This thesis, which was suggested in previous chapters, will be deepened here and in the remaining chapters.

If Heidegger's ontology represents a form of correlationism—it would seem that this is how Levinas understands it, although the point is contentious—then Levinasian metaphysics challenges correlationism in the name of an infinity which exceeds the subject-object relation. The challenge operates as a response to what Levinas perceives as the inability of Heideggerian ontology to accommodate otherness, infinity, alterity—that is, to think beyond being. This may not be a failure of ontology in general, however, but a failure only of correlationist ontology. An ontology that surpasses correlationism might not meet the usual Levinasian criticism. Indeed, what Levinas provides, I think, is a non-correlationist ontology, although he is reluctant to call it ontology for fear that his work will be read too closely to Heidegger's. Putting this worry aside, we may surmise that ontology is not intrinsically reductive, violent, or unethical.

Levinas's critique of ontology is strongest, I think, when it is seen as an internal critique of correlationist (including phenomenological) ontology, rather than as a wholesale rejection of ontology. Moreover, it seems that Levinas's position would be strengthened if he allowed that what he calls ethics is actually grounded in ontology. On this reading our understanding of ourselves, others, and intersubjectivity would be seen as equiprimordial with (if not prior to) ethical responsibility.[291] The ontological reading of Levinas gains traction, I would argue, when we consider that it is not possible to see what is "called into question" by the Other until we have laid bare the constitution of the egocentric subject, or the individual who cultivates a life of enjoyment and material security.

A grasp of the ontology informing Levinas's account of the subject is essential for contrasting Levinasian and Kantian ethics.[292] It is through a rejection of the Kantian subject as immaterial agent that Levinas is able to make his case for the eminent vulnerability of the subject and, consequently, the ethical responsibility entailed by that vulnerability. Levinas argues in *Existence and Existents* that the Kantian subject, the transcendental ego, always stands at a safe distance from the effects of the world. As that which allows things to appear and be apprehended by cognition, but which does not act in the world, the Kantian ego presents "a way of relating to events while still being able to not be caught up in them. To be a [Kantian] subject is to be a power of unending withdrawal, an ability always to find oneself behind what happens to one" (EE 42/77). The Levinasian subject, by contrast, is caught up in, *produced* as an "ontological event" by the world. Indeed, the entirety of *Existence and Existents* can be read as the tale of the subject's emergence from bare existence, the assumption or actualization of a "position" out of what Levinas calls the "there is"—the *il y a* (EE 66-67, 88/120, 149; TI 175/149). This positioning is the material substantialization, or "separation," of the subject from anonymous existence, a process which is recounted in *Totality and Infinity* in terms of the body which enjoys, nourishes, and "lives from" (*vivre de*) the surrounding world:

> Enjoyment accomplishes the atheist separation: it *deformalizes* the notion of separation, which is not a cleavage made in the abstract, but the existence at home with itself as an autochthonous I. The soul ... dwells in what is not itself, but it acquires its own identity by this dwelling in the "other." (TI 115/88, italics added)

At bottom it is the invulnerability of the Kantian subject in the face of external affection, which is to say, the untraversable distance separating subject and world, that Levinas objects to.[293] It is in this context that Levinas foregrounds the affectivity, and ultimately the a priori vulnerability, of the subject.

Individuation; or, the Enjoyment of Immanence

The story of the emergence of the embodied subject, especially in *Totality and Infinity*, but in other texts as well, is guided by the concept of enjoyment (*jouissance*). It is precisely the being that enjoys life that is summoned by the Other to respond, and one responds with offerings of what one enjoys. But which comes first, the enjoyment or the individual who enjoys? Enjoyment, it would seem, must either produce individuation or enjoyment must take place in an already-existing individual. In Levinas's view, however, these events—enjoyment, individuation—are co-constitutive. They generate and reinforce one another, and there is an ontological story to be told about the process. And, arguably, this process must have occurred for there to be a responsive agent who can answer, adequately or inadequately, the call of the Other. Agency must be accomplished before it can assume responsibility for its genesis, otherwise what, exactly, is called into question?

What does it mean to be generated by enjoyment? The Levinasian analysis of enjoyment is packaged with companion concepts like living from, nourishment, alimentation, and need. These concepts possess physiological and phenomenological senses, both of which Levinas attends to, often collapsing their distinction. The scope of enjoyment is not restricted to what can be consumed, nor is it interpreted as a phenomenon exclusively attached to the practice of living, using, and doing. Levinas gives enjoyment a more expansive sense, identifying it as the affect that effects our separation and makes possible our manipulation of things; it thus conditions the economic/practical life that Heidegger sees as primordial to human existence.[294] The content of this individuation, this independence, is primarily affective and self-sustaining:

> One does not only exist one's pain or one's joy; one exists from pains and joys. Enjoyment is precisely this way the act nourishes itself with its own activity. To live from bread is therefore neither to represent bread to oneself nor to act on it nor to act by means of it. To be sure, it is necessary to earn one's bread, and it is necessary to nourish oneself in order to earn one's bread; thus the bread I eat is also that with which I earn my bread and my life. But if I eat my bread in order to labor and to live, I live *from* my labor and *from* my bread. (TI 111/83)

Enjoyment is not just about taking in and taking pleasure in taking in. This passage suggests that Sallis is too quick to reduce enjoyment to the consumptive aspect of alimentation when he characterizes enjoyment in the following way: "the determination by which to comport oneself to an object is to appropriate the object, that is, to cancel its otherness and affirm its sameness with oneself. As in eating."[295] This construal of enjoyment not only overlooks our affective engagements with what could never be consumed (the elemental, the ungraspable), it too narrowly restricts the meaning of the Levinasian alimentary. As we will see, alimentation has a much richer and more nuanced sense than that captured by "consumption."

To be sure, enjoyment is a phenomenon analogous to desire in that it feeds upon and produces itself, unlike need which is satisfied once its lack has been filled.[296] Hunger, for instance, results from a privation of food, and when I eat my hunger subsides. Even if the food is unsavory, my body takes pleasure in the sustenance. The structure of nourishment which is displayed by enjoyment is of a different order than my satiable hunger, however. Levinas's treatment of enjoyment belongs to his phenomenology of alimentation and his exposition of the concrete features of the interiority, or economy, of subjectivity.[297]

> Nourishment, as a means of invigoration, is the transmutation of the other into the same, which is in the essence of enjoyment: an energy that is other, recognized as other, recognized ... as sustaining the very act that is directed upon it, becomes, in enjoyment, my own energy, my strength, me. All enjoyment is in this sense alimentation. (TI 111/83)

To live is to savor life and to have that life nourished by the acts which make up living: sensing, knowing, imagining, wishing, resting, and so on. Each of these brings an immediate joy that feeds the egoism at the core of life (TI 112/84). And it is in this enjoyment that the "very pulsation" of the I occurs (TI 113/85). "Subjectivity originates in the independence and sovereignty of enjoyment," says Levinas (TI 114/86). Enjoyment makes no appeal to the absolute transcendence often cited by Levinas as the condition of possibility for subjective individuation. It is, after all, a product of immanence. It is no less significant for the genesis of subjectivity than the encounter with the Other, however.

Correlative with Levinas's emphasis on the irreducible and absolute transcendence of the Other is an attempt to think the immanent production of subjectivity. This is evident in the language he employs to describe the becoming of the subject in enjoyment. He speaks of individuation as a "coiling" (*enroulement*), "folding back" (*repli*), as "spiral" (*spirale*) and "involution" (*involution*) (TI 118/91; EE 81/138; OB 73/92). Enjoyment is denoted as the "eddy of the same" (*le remous même du Même*) (TI 115/88). The imagery here suggests that Levinas is trying to conceive individuation without recourse to some external, individuating agent or cause, but as an autoaffective process.[298] That is, he seems to want an immanent principle of animation. It is true that the call to responsibility commanded by the Other singles me out, or individuates me as an *ethical* agent, but this can only occur once I have become someone capable of responding—that is, become a subject who can be subjected to moral commands. Levinas often speaks of the encounter with the face of the Other as that which *accomplishes* my subjectivity *as* an ethical subject. For instance: "It is only in approaching the Other that I attend to myself." And:

> The face I welcome makes me pass from phenomenon to being in another sense: in discourse I expose myself to the questioning of the Other, and this urgency of the response—acuteness of the present—engenders me for responsibility; as responsible I am brought to my final reality. (TI 178/153)

It is true that for Levinas we are always already discursive, responsible beings; but he also implies that there is a form of subjectivity—incomplete, to be sure—which precedes our subjection to the Other. The material subject, the embodied I, must emerge into a position before it can be called to account for itself, its possessions, and its enjoyment.

For the subject to be responsible and capable of substituting itself in the place of the Other, which is precisely what Levinas wants to affirm of each of us, must not the subject already have something to give? Must it not be a singular individual, some actual person with actual resources? If not, would not Levinas be advocating a formal notion of responsibility, one which responds with empty hands? And would this not be the most abstract and general form of ethics, an ethics empty of content and on the verge of effacing the materiality of suffering, inequality, need, and vulnerability? A non-formal notion of responsibility seems to require a subject that has not only emerged as an individual, but one who has also already acquired possessions which it can offer to the destitute Other, before it can be designated as a responsible/responsive agent. There must be some form of subjectivity in Levinas's thinking which is not merely envisaged as formal subjection to the Other, but as actual, concrete existing.

Levinas is grappling with the problem of immanent individuation in *Otherwise than Being* when he writes that

> Matter "materializes" in satisfaction, which, over and beyond any intentional relationship of cognition or possession, of "taking in one's hands," means "biting into...." It is irreducible to a taking in one's hands, for it is already an absorption of a "within" including the ambiguity of two inwardnesses: that of a recipient of spatial forms, and that of an ego assimilating the other in its identity, and coiling in over itself. (OB 73/92)

And a little further along, he remarks how "there is enjoying of enjoyment before any reflection, but enjoyment does not turn toward enjoyment as sight turns toward the seen. Beyond the multiplication of the visible in images, enjoyment is the singularization of an ego in its coiling back [*enroulement*] upon itself" (OB 73/93). What Levinas calls the "advent" of the subject from out of the anonymity of existence is not a movement of transcendence, but the taking up of a position through effort, labor, and the consequent enjoyment which results from these acts. Enjoyment multiplies, folding back upon itself and wresting the I free, generating a substantial subject (EE 81/138). The substance of this subject is rooted in the thickness or viscosity of its affective life.[299]

Sensibility and the Elements of Representation

Levinas's apology for the primacy of affectivity and the sensuous embodiment of the subject operates as a response to a perceived deficiency in the phenomenological method devised by Husserl, in particular its doctrine of objectifying intentionality. It also continues his critique of the Kantian subject sketched above. Against Kant and Husserl he envisages the subject as a material event instead of as a transcendental ego that serves as the condition of possibility for representing or giving meaning to objects and events. Insofar as his philosophy attempts to supplant the privileged place of intentionality in phenomenology; as it attempts to install affectivity, alterity, and the like at the base of experience, Levinas's philosophy works against phenomenology in the name of a quasi-materialist metaphysics. His interest in phenomenology is driven less by a desire to contribute to a science of phenomena than by a desire to give a non-reductive metaphysical account of events that could otherwise be explained by the physical sciences or recuperated by a representationalist epistemology. In a strong sense Levinas's critique of intentionality is an allergic reaction to what he sees as the hegemony of representation in phenomenological accounts of otherness (TI 122-127/95-100).

Levinas's objection to phenomenological method is straightforward: if the objectifying acts of theoretical consciousness, what Husserl calls meaning-giving (*Sinngebung*) acts, are our primary mode of access to things, then those things can only appear to us as representations whose content is predetermined by the representing subject. In short, phenomenology becomes a modified transcendental idealism, its ontology correlationist. The problem is that this kind of transcendental philosophy leaves no room for the radical passivity Levinasian ethics requires, and it fails to appreciate the ambiguity of the given as well as its capacity to surprise (TI 123, 125/96, 97). "The 'act' of representation discovers, properly speaking, nothing before itself" (TI 125/97). From the practical perspective, the subject who constitutes the content of the world through representations retains an identity that persists throughout all of its experiences. It is not properly shaped by its world because it is not fully *exposed* to the world. The spontaneity of its freedom to represent is never compromised by the objects it represents. As Levinas says, "in representation the I precisely loses its opposition to its object; the opposition fades, bringing out the identity of the I despite the multiplicity of its objects, that is, precisely the unalterable character of the I. To remain the same is to represent to oneself" (TI 126/99). Representation is the ruin of alterity.

Levinas supplants objectifying acts of consciousness and installs sensation as the ground of experience. An analogous move is made by Merleau-Ponty when he (tentatively) places *le sentir* before both operative intentionality and intentionality of act. Levinas's move is more radical, however, because it unequivocally asserts that sensation is discontinuous with perception and cognition. He recognizes the content of sensibility as prior to intentionality of any form. This means that the subject's sensuous contact with what is exterior remains forever anterior to its perception and representational acts. Its sensuous contact with the Other, as well as with matter and the sensible as such (the diminutive other), thus comprises the transcendental field in Levinas's philosophy. John Drabinski writes of this field:

> The sensible surrounds and structures the movement toward the object and thereby structures the very possibility of the noematic horizons that form the field of transcendental exposition. The sensible is transcendental, not in the sense that it is already an ideality, but rather that it is a presupposed condition of all reflective life.[300]

That the sensible is "presupposed" signals Levinas's transgression of phenomenological principles, as well as his willingness to speculate about the ontogenesis of subjectivity. This does not mean that Levinas must break completely with phenomenology in order to rediscover the force of sensation—on the contrary, he finds that "intentionality rehabilitates the sensible [*réhabilite le sensible*]."[301] How so? He points to the tacit dimension of intentional acts, or that which "consciousness sees without seeing."[302] The tacit dimension of seeing is not just the unintended horizon of unfulfilled intentions which accompany explicit intentions, but represents the very excess of intentionality which "is incontestably akin to the modern conceptions of the unconscious and the depths." There is a reciprocal constitution at play in intentionality, whereby the object, which is supposedly constituted by consciousness, proves to contain more than its explicit constitution, and this "more than" reveals itself as always already conditioning thought. "A new ontology begins: being is posited not only as correlative to a thought, but as already founding the very thought that nonetheless constitutes it."[303]

Levinas's new ontology locates a fundamental excess at the heart of intentional consciousness, signaling the "ruin of representation" and the destabilization of the Kantian (and Husserlian) subject. If Kant's schema requires an imperceptible layer of content that lies below the level of representation, but one that is beyond the reach of transcendental idealism, then Levinas shows how this layer threatens to disrupt the stability of the subject of representation. Kant's transcendental method admits the existence of this layer of content, but effectively neutralizes its volatility. As Levinas writes in "The Ruin for Representation":

> The idea of a necessary implication that is absolutely imperceptible to the subject directed on the object, only discovered *after the fact* upon reflection, thus not produced in the present, that is, produced *unbeknownst to me*, puts an end to the ideal of representation and the subject's sovereignty, as well as to the idealism according to which nothing could enter into me surreptitiously. A deep-seated *passion* is thus revealed in thought.[304]

As the transcendental support of representation the sensible and its qualities constitute the milieu in which the subject perceives. *Totality and Infinity* gives a lengthy description of this ungraspable milieu, referring to it as "the element." The element has no profiles; it is a pure quality that we enjoy before we make any categorical judgments about it (TI 131-133/104-107). As Sallis characterizes it, the element is "irreducible to a system of operational references" and "has its own thickness and density.... And unlike the things that come to us in the medium, the medium itself is nonpossessable." Sallis continues: "The depth of the element does not, as with a thing, conceal a series of other profiles that could be offered to various perspectives."[305] The element is that which surrounds us, like climate or atmospheric temperature or the aesthetic.

Lover of ambiguity that he is, and despite the fact that he uses the term to describe the flesh, the element as Levinas understands it appears to be missing in Merleau-Ponty.[306] For Levinas the element is the very locus of ambiguity and what resists categorical judgment. This is its unique mode of being, what enables it to support the things that inhabit it without appearing as one of those things. And yet, it is not simply the horizon or background of an intentional act. It exceeds every such act. The elemental/sensuous milieu "is privileged, because within it that ambiguity of constitution, whereby the noema conditions and shelters the noesis that constitutes it, is played out."[307] Levinas notes that Husserl wanted to designate the sensuous as objective, that is, as independent of subjective constitution, but his adherence to the primacy of intentionality prevented him from doing so. This is because intentionality "plays the role of an apprehension with regard to those contents upon which it bestows an objective meaning and which it animates or inspires."[308] By contrast, Levinas insists that we *live through* the objectivity of sensations. Even Husserl recognized this. It is then more accurate to say that the "materiality of sensations [*matérialité des sensations*]" is, borrowing Levinas's own expression, *lived from* or enjoyed, never intended, apprehended or grasped by the intellect or perception.[309]

In addition to acting as a resistance to representational thinking sensation provides the aliment that gives birth to any subject capable of representing. Sensation, then, would not be just an effect of the objective on the subject, but a "complicity" between the materiality of subject and object:

"the corporeity of consciousness is in exact proportion to this participation of consciousness in the world it constitutes, but this corporeity is *produced* [*produit*] in sensation."[310] In *Otherwise than Being* this complicity is developed in Levinas's analysis of sensibility and in terms of "contact" with otherness, and contributes to Levinas's transcendental aesthetic of embodiment.[311] It is notable that emphasis in both texts is on the productive aspect of sensation, its capacity to generate the consciousness of the lived body.

The ensuous complicity of subject and object recalls Merleau-Ponty's idea of sensing as communion. The key difference between the two thinkers, however, is that Merleau-Ponty sees this communion as synchronous, whereas Levinas recognizes it as the locus of a diachrony which entails the very instability of the body-world relation. Also lacking in Merleau-Ponty's understanding is the idea that corporeity itself is produced materially by sensations, that sensations conspire with affects to produce singular subjects. In Merleau-Ponty's subject-object dialogue it is the movement of perception and the posture of the body (but not its materiality) that is affected by sensation, whereas for Levinas sensation actually produces the body qua living, sensing, enjoying being. The difference may be more palpable if Levinas's position is rendered in neuroscientific discourse, which regards "the conversion of what is felt into nervous material [as] nonstop," as Bernard Andrieu notes.[312] For Levinas, sensations and affects are converted—and this he tries to account for phenomenologically—into the content of life, or the feeling of living. Insofar as we live from this feeling and gain a desire to continue living, we can say that sensations are converted into material life. In biology there is a name for this process—*metabolism*.[313] Sensing, for Levinas, is a metabolic event. But it is also an intimate kind of transaction, beyond mere commerce or exchange, one that is felt and enjoyed by the being that metabolizes.

There is a distinct shift of emphasis between the analyses of sensibility given in *Totality and Infinity* and *Otherwise than Being*. In the earlier text Levinas concentrates his narrative of subject-constitution on the enabling features of sensibility and the dependence of the body on the material environment. In the later text he tends to cast sensibility as that which leaves the subject precariously exposed to the outside and vulnerable to wounding. That is, a non-reciprocity comes to mark the relation between the body and the other: the Levinasian body ultimately becomes a *susceptible* body, where susceptibility is understood as the radical passivity which arises from the diachrony of sensibility. In both texts sensibility is given a pre-reflective and pre-representational role, and it is clear that Levinas sees it as prior to the emergence of objectifying consciousness.

Levinas affirms, following Descartes, the irrationality and ambiguity of sensation. Like Kant, he separates sensibility from the understanding and relegates sensible "matter" to a place beyond "the synthetic power of representation" (TI 135-136/109). Nevertheless, Levinas maintains that a phenomenology of sensation is possible. I will try to adduce in the remainder of this chapter Levinas's "phenomenology of the sensible" (TI 136/109) and his unique perspective on sensibility.

The Phenomenology of Sensation

Totality and Infinity ties sensibility to enjoyment, calling enjoyment the "essence" of sensibility. Conversely, sensibility is determined as the "*mode* of enjoyment" (TI 134, 135/107, 108). Sensibility is therefore determined as a mode of affectivity or point of access for pleasurable and painful encounters. If, as we saw earlier, enjoyment is responsible for the genesis of the self, then sensibility must also have something to do with how the self is generated.

Sensibility's modality is undirected and sufficient unto itself (TI 135/108-109), which means that it does not belong to the order of instrumentality that Levinas assigns to the economy of possession—the hand that grasps objects as tools/implements (as in Heidegger or Merleau-Ponty) or the mind which grasps objects as concepts (as in Hegel) or assigns phenomena their meaning (as in Husserl).[314] Sensibility is neither "a means to…" nor "in the service of…," despite being basic to labor, work, effort, dwelling, and so on. Above all, it is a direct encounter with the otherness that is given through sensation and material life, which is not for Levinas simply a question of resistance to action or opposition: sensibility establishes our relation to the elemental through our corporeal enjoyment of aesthetic qualities (TI 136/109). This enjoyment is discontinuous with the synthetic acts of consciousness. It is not a stage toward representation, but the fleeting affective rhythm of the I. It is, as Merleau-Ponty has put it, a mode in which the subject is born and dies as each instant (TI 136, 143/109-110, 117; PP 216/250).

Silvia Benso illustrates this process with an analysis of breathing. Breathing is a twofold process, inspiration and expiration. Inspiration and expiration, which are structurally equivalent to birth and death, animate the subject with the element of air. "Such an animation does not occur at the level of cognition, theory, or intentionality, claims Levinas. Rather, it is only possible at the level of the body, through an incarnation."[315] This interpretation of living disengages the body from its reliance on the soul by localizing the animation of subjectivity in the intercorporeal, rather than spiritual, realm. The problem of the interaction of body and soul drops off in favor of a phenomenology of corporeal life and its reliance on the elemental. "The body thus is retrieved from its confinement in that Cartesian ... order of materiality for which the body and the soul 'have no common space where they can touch'."[316] The significance of breathing is not merely physiological, as Levinas makes clear. It yields a transcendental interpretation that locates the conditions of possibility at the border between body and environment, that is, in sensibility.

The pulsation of the I is supported by the sensible, while the sensible itself remains groundless, anarchic. The insecurity entailed in this anarchy is not exactly a material threat, but a question of the temporality of the sensible. The sensible world "precedes me as an absolute of an unrepresentable antiquity" that is perhaps only apprehensible by imagining the total destruction of the world—an impossible thought experiment (TI 137/111; EE 51/93). We cannot know from whence it comes or whether it will continue in the future. Its promise is precarious, without guarantee that it will continue to sustain life.

It is true that we always access the sensible in the present and, affective and abstract encounters notwithstanding, via representations. Merleau-Ponty points to Cézanne's painting; Deleuze, Francis Bacon's. Digital imaging of the autonomic nervous system offers a high-tech representation of the sensing body. This does not mean that the totality of the sensible is given *in* representations, for "the represented, the present, is a *fact*, already belonging to a past" (TI 130/103). Representations are laced with an anteriority that cannot endure the formal exigencies of the present. To represent the sensible as such would be analogous to encountering the *il y a* in pure form, bare existence, in its absolute formlessness. It would be an actualization in the present of the absolute past, the *apeiron* whence everything comes. Despite the impossibility of this event—we are always already caught up in a world of thought, language, perception—Levinas assures us that we do in fact come face to face with formless phenomena (TI 139/112). In *Totality and Infinity* he speaks of how our identities are haunted by the elemental and the insecurity this brings us, while in *Existence and Existents* he speaks of the horror of the *il y a* that we experience in the night.[317] But how are these formless phenomena revealed, that is, accessed phenomenologically?

Building an Identity

Existence and Existents traces the genesis of the individual existent from out of the anonymity of pure existence, being qua being. This anonymity, although not temporally prior to individuation, maintains an ontological priority over the subject who thinks, acts, and feels as a singular ego or person. On Levinas's account the existent breaks free from anonymity by taking up a position or assuming an identity, exerting itself against the indeterminacy of being and feeling itself alive in its efforts. It is only when we make an effort through labor that a rift is created in being and the present is allowed to open up: "Effort is the very effecting of a present," says Levinas (EE 23/48), because the fatigue which results from effort dislocates the existent from its synchrony with the uninterrupted duration of bare existence.[318] The same is said by Rousseau in the *Discourse on the Origin of Inequality*, in which it is work and the subsequent circumscription of property that extricates human being from the infantile and innocent realm of sensibility.[319] What Jean Starobinski calls the "struggle to overcome natural obstacles" with the application of tools is what gives rise to the psychological transformations that institute a critical reflective distance between humans and their environment.[320] Work, in short, conditions reflection and leads eventually to the inequalities of society. For Levinas, work introduces more than a psychological rift and more than social inequality: work tears pure being and time apart. Work produces subjects. Whereas the process of individuation, and the opposition of self and other entailed in it, is for Rousseau psychological, for Levinas it is basically affective. And this affectivity performs a transcendental function that is not found in Rousseau's speculative anthropology. As an affective, rather than reflective, event the retroactive movement of work on the partitioning of being awakens us to our interminable contract with existence. Despite appearances, work is not an escape from existence: "Fatigue is to be sure not a cancellation of one's contact with being. The delay it involves is nonetheless an inscription in existence..." (EE 25/51).

Our inescapable attachment to existence is dramatized in the experience of insomnia. The insomniac not only feels herself alive in her fatigue, she suffers existence in a much more menacing form. She faces the insufferability of pure existence as she seeks, through what Levinas calls "vigilance," to tear herself free from the indeterminacy of the night which watches over her, holds her hostage to her wakefulness.[321] Particularly in *Existence and Existents* the night figures as the experiential form of the *il y a*, or pure being. In the night, Levinas tells us, things lose their form and the dark matter of existence encroaches upon us. Being takes on a menacing aspect through which we are confronted with the anonymity of our own existence. Insomnia reminds us that we are not completely in control of our being.[322]

The insomniac experiences a wakefulness at night that contests the spontaneity of her will, that challenges the authority she claims over her position in existence. She wants and wills sleep, but sleep will not come. And it eventually seems that it is the night itself which withholds sleep from her. The sense of being alive that comes with fatigue transforms into a restless horror. She finds herself at the mercy of being. Instead of fatigue giving way to sleep, "One watches on when there is nothing to watch and despite the absence of any reason for remaining watchful" (EE 61/109). It is as though, in the grip of the night, the restlessness of the insomniac's body has extinguished the freedom of the ego and rendered the ego a prisoner of the night. "I am, one might say, the object rather than the subject of an anonymous thought" (EE 63/111). And this, says Levinas, is a horrifying condition (EE 55/98).[323]

The horror of existence is articulated with the insecurity bestowed upon our bodies by our sensibility, a condition which is warded off (for a time) in dwelling (TI 137/110-111). In dwelling we shelter ourselves from the elements, and this sheltering offers the nourishment of enjoyment. The enjoyment of warmth, security, comfort. We shelter ourselves because we are incapable of getting a hold on or containing the elements that, beyond a certain threshold, begin to destroy instead of sustain us. The air we breathe is the same air that freezes our flesh. The themes of fatigue and effort found in *Existence and Existents* recur in the narrative regarding dwelling and possession contained in *Totality and Infinity*. The phenomenon of dwelling is elaborated against the backdrop of enjoyment, on the one hand, and the insecurity buried in the depths of enjoyment, on the other. Dwelling is an ambivalent affair.

Dwelling gives rise to the representation and, ultimately, possession of objects. But dwelling is not only an activity in which consumption and possession occur, it is itself an event of alimentation. There are multiple kinds of alimentation involved in dwelling, some affective and others consumptive. In the home the subject takes up a position of refuge. Only after this position is established can labor commence, and it is this labor, for Levinas, that gives form to matter and produces the world of graspable/consumable things—possessions (TI 156, 157, 159/130, 131, 133).[324] "A subject does not exist before the event of its position. The act of taking a position does not unfold in some dimension from which it could take its origin; it arises at the very point at which it acts" (EE 81/138). Taking a position is a condition of laboring, and yet it is not yet acting. Acting is a movement of transcendence, whereas laboring is a movement of immanence. Assuming a position belongs to the involuntary movement of effort and fatigue, of enjoyment and living from.... Positioning and dwelling are the concrete modes through which the subject comes to be situated in the objective world. They lend bodies the support needed to come to terms with the elemental through labor (TI 158/131). Yet, this is the kind of support that must be constantly taken up, rebuilt, and maintained—a Sisyphean labor.

Labor leads to possession and is guided by the final causality of the hand. The hand takes hold of things, masters them, comprehends them. It takes them up and puts them to use. "Possession is accomplished in taking-possession or labor, the destiny of the hand" (TI 159/132). Possession is contrasted with the enjoyment of sensibility, which is precisely determined by its non-possession: "The hand *comprehends* the thing not because it touches it on all sides at the same time … but because it is no longer a sense-organ, pure enjoyment, pure sensibility, but is mastery, domination, disposition—which do not belong to the order of sensibility" (TI 161/135). Levinas aims to designate possession as a practico-ontological affair, one that assuages the insecurity brought on by our exposure to the elemental: "Possession masters, suspends, postpones the unforeseeable future of the element—its independence, its being" (TI 158/132). Despite its attachment to ontology, however, Levinas refuses here to call labor a violence. This is because "it is applied to what is faceless, to the resistance of nothingness" (TI 160/134).

All of this—from individuation to dwelling to labor—involves and influences the genesis of the body of the subject who dwells and labors. First, the hand substantializes things, outlines their contours and draws them out of the pure quality of the element. Things are not first there, waiting to give themselves to consciousness.[325] Second, Levinas argues that the subject is originally influenced by its affective commerce with the element. It is "the product of the medium." The lived body is no more active than it is passive, no less affective than perceptive. This is not an endorsement of the duality of the body (lived body/objective body), but of its "ambiguous" nature, which Levinas identifies with consciousness (TI 165/139). Consciousness, he says, is not an incarnation, but a "disincarnation," a "positioning of the corporeity of the body" which emerges in the "concreteness of dwelling and labor" (TI 165-166/140). Consciousness, then, arises out of the body's pulsations in labor. The rhythm of labor, and the tension involved therein, give rise to consciousness. He thus provides an account—part phenomenological, part speculative—of the birth of subjectivity in the body. One is reminded here of Nietzsche's remarks on the origin of consciousness in *On the Genealogy of Morality*, where the inhibition of physical human activity gives birth, in a folding back upon oneself, to the "*internalizing* of man"—conscious reflection.[326] Only after the fact of embodiment do reflective and representational activity become possible. Appreciating the ambiguity of the body's relation to the other, Levinas writes:

> In its deep-seated fear life attests this ever possible inversion of the body-master into body-slave, of health and sickness. *To be a body* is on the one hand *to stand* [*se tenir*], to be master of oneself, and, on the other hand, to stand on the earth, to be in the *other*, and thus to be encumbered by one's body. But—we repeat—this encumberment is not produced as a pure dependence; it forms the happiness of him who enjoys it.
> (TI 164/138)

The body's capacity to work on things acts as a consolation for its inability to rend itself from being to enjoy a degree of autonomy and accumulate a stock of resources that may be shared with the needful Other. Consciousness relieves the body—gives respite, allows it to stand out—from the physical realm, helping to postpone the disintegration and death proper to material life. At the same time the body remains prey to the Other who "paralyzes possession" (TI 170, 171/145).

The Rhythm of Sensation

Levinas's prioritizing of sensibility over the grasp and comprehension works as a critique of Merleau-Ponty, in particular the latter's insistence that our basic modus operandi involves an initial hold on things that increasingly converges upon an even better hold. While Levinas certainly appreciates that our practical relations with things, our treatment of them as implements, is our primary means of handling the world, he insists that below the equipmental and perceptual levels lies the inscrutable level of sensation. Sensation is not part of perception. Perception belongs to the intentional sphere, the realm of consciousness, whereas sensation anonymously haunts the edges of perception. The affectivity of sensation functions transcendentally; it is virtually real. Perception actualizes representations.[327] "The very distinction between representational and affective content is tantamount to a recognition that enjoyment is endowed with a dynamism other than that of perception," writes Levinas (TI 187/161). He realizes that such claims stretch the limits of phenomenology, but he aspires to a phenomenology of sensation nonetheless.

Levinas's entire ontology of the sensible is built on the claim that the pure quality of existence is independent of us, anarchic, and ungraspable—and yet, it is given. No reversibility can exist between us and the purely sensible because it is in the nature of the sensible to exceed our representational and practical capacities; it is impossible to "get a grip" on it. This leaves us vulnerable to its precarious future. At the heart of sensibility is a diachrony, or dehiscence, that interrupts the synchrony of body and world just as a caress of the skin defers the immediacy of contact indefinitely. "In a caress, what is there is sought as though it were not there, as though the skin were the trace of its own withdrawal, a languor still seeking, like an absence which, however, could not be more there. The caress is the not coinciding proper to contact" (OB 90/114).[328]

In "Reality and Its Shadow," one of his most sustained treatments of aesthetics and art, Levinas explicitly argues for the diachrony of aesthetic experience. Here he is close to Deleuze in at least one respect: both thinkers see the effects of aesthetic "rhythm" as constitutive of aesthetic experience and, consequently, the integrity of the embodied subject. For Levinas rhythm is the means by which we are affected, against our will, by the work of art. This is how the work hits us. This affection, however, is different from that undergone when someone is faced with the *il y a*, which "lacks rhythm" (EE 62/111), suggesting that the pure encounter with being is outside aesthetics. Rhythm conducts the passive moment of sensing, the moment in which our active representation is converted into a passive reception:

> Rhythm represents a unique situation where we cannot speak of consent, assumption, initiative or freedom, because the subject is caught up and carried away by it. The subject is part of its own representation. It is so not even despite itself, for in rhythm there is no longer a oneself, but rather a sort of passage from oneself to anonymity.[329]

This is applicable not only to music, but to poetry and painting as well. Rhythm is precisely that sensible form/content that detaches itself from the artwork and seizes upon sensibility, bypassing consciousness, folding the subject into the aesthetic event.[330]

> To insist on the musicality of every image is to see in an image its detachment from an object, that independence from the

category of substance which the analysis of our textbooks ascribe to pure sensation not yet converted into perception (sensation as an adjective), which for empirical psychology remains a limit case, a purely hypothetical given.[331]

Embedded in the figure and form of representational content lies the sensory content which informs the rhythm of the aesthetic. Granted, we may not always apprehend the rhythm of sensation phenomenologically, but that is just the point: the function of sensation is to affect sensibility directly and render the viewer/listener captive. This is why Levinas says that sensibility is "realized only by the imagination."[332] Only the imagination of the painter, poet, musician, for example, can represent the aesthetic event with which sensibility comes into contact, that is, pure sensation detached from representation. The audience can attempt the same.

Sensation is an interpellation, a kind of imperative that cannot be dodged because its subtle force operates immediately on the body, below the level of both perception and apperception. Insofar as it engages us simultaneously at the level of perception and sensation, indirectly and directly on the body, the aesthetic dimension operates diachronically. It is, in short, out of step with the correlation of thought and being.[333] Since the sensory event is always happening behind the scenes, animating the present representation but never rising to the level of representation, it remains forever in the past.[334]

Rhythm affects sensibility as a "distinct ontological event," according to Levinas.[335] Deleuze has argued a similar point about the effect of some painting, specifically Francis Bacon's. For Deleuze rhythm is fundamental to the "logic" of sensation; it is what animates/unifies the senses and their discrete content.[336] This logic does not belong to the physiological layout of the organic body, but rather it operates on the body "at the point where rhythm plunges into chaos, into the night, at the point where the differences of level are perpetually and violently mixed."[337] Because the body is not just an organized set of organs, but also an event ("at one and the same time I *become* in the sensation and something *happens* through the sensation…")[338] whose integrity is constituted by thresholds and limits, the body becomes organized by the sensations it receives or gives off.

It is not the stable form of the body that Bacon paints, but what sensation does to the body, the body as sensory event: "what is painted on the canvas is the body, not insofar as it is represented as an object, but insofar as it is experienced as sustaining *this* sensation," argues Deleuze.[339] As Panagia frames the problem: "Bacon is thus not painting figures, nor are his paintings merely grotesque; he is, rather, making invisible forces palpable; for Deleuze, Bacon confronts the central problem of painting, the problem of rendering invisible forces."[340] In a sense what Bacon paints is the "accumulation" of forces that makes up the identity of the body—its sensory fingerprint or signature, so to speak. This identity is, however, never fixed or properly personal: it belongs to the anonymous rhythm of the sensible and is always prone to the "violence" or "disfiguration" of sensations emitted by other bodies.[341] It just happens.

Deleuze gives us a more radical expression of what sensation does than Levinas, although I think they are effectively on the same page about what sensation is. Although the two philosophers have many differences, taken together Levinas's and Deleuze's analyses of aesthetic rhythm allow us to glimpse a dynamic, and somewhat paradoxical, conception of aesthetic identity. On this model identity is constituted by the imperceptible exchange of sensations between bodies in direct communication. Sensations accumulate in the body, giving it a particular figure or disfiguring it. Bodies are thus determined by the sensations they offer and receive from other bodies. They are, as Spinoza has it, capacities to affect and be affected aesthetically. Or, as Hume might have said, I am nothing more than the sensations which pass across and territorialize my body. I am little more than the sounds, scents, colors, textures, and tastes emitted from my body. I am a *conspiracy of sensations*.

Alimentation and Susceptibility

The significance of this conception of bodily identity is ramified in Levinas's work because he regards sensation as foundational to both experience and selfhood. Levinas's brief discussion of the "transcendental function" of sensation circles us back to the analysis of enjoyment and the immanent constitution of the subject by the other.[342] We must always keep in mind that sensation, for Levinas as for Deleuze, is never just a matter of the "ambivalence" of feeling.[343] With the explicit affirmation of its transcendental function we see Levinas appreciating the force of sensation significantly more than Merleau-Ponty, who, in Levinas's view, overlooks the deep ambiguity and passivity of sensation.[344] To achieve this appreciation Levinas must venture outside of phenomenology and into speculative metaphysics, affirming the reality of sensation not only as something that provides the content of cognition, but also as something that directly shapes the structural integrity of the subject. Sensation, then, names a fundamental, if not radical, passivity of the subject.[345] The subject, as embodied, finds itself from the start in a heteronomous position—affected and nourished by what is other than itself. Its first receptivity is its sensibility; it lives from sensations which provide the alimentary content of its representations. This alimentary layer of sensation "recovers a 'reality' when we see in it not the subjective counterpart of objective qualities, but an enjoyment 'anterior' to the crystallization of consciousness, I and non-I, into subject and object" (TI 188/162).[346] Sensation here names the experience of the body in immanence, but an immanence which is constantly broken up by a double temporality: the temporality of the represented and the temporality of the sensed.

No one has appreciated the alimentary or enabling dimension of sensation more than Alphonso Lingis. In fact, Lingis goes so far as to defend the ethical valence of the force of sensation. Prior to any formal imperative imposed on the intellect by reason is the imperative the body receives from the environment, which orders the body to adapt itself to the contour of the land, the shape of the tool taken up in our work, or the elements which envelop it.[347] This contact with things is directly received as sensations which are assimilated into the posture of the body and its body schema. Or, to put it more radically, the body *is* schematized by the sensuous environment which accumulates in its flesh. Sensation and schematization name an identical process:

> The imperative in our environment is received, not on our understanding in conflict with our sensuality, but on our postural schema which integrates our sensibility and mobilizes our motor forces. It is received on our sensory-motor bodies as bodies we have to center upon things that orient our movements, bodies we have to anchor on the levels down which our vision, our touch, our listening move, on which we

station ourselves and move in the heart of reality. It orders our competence.[348]

Of course, we always negotiate with the layout of the environment as we make our way through it. But there is a sense in which our bodies are *made* to move in certain non-negotiable, imperative ways: reflexes and other autonomic responses, debilitating and incapacitating ways necessitated by our materiality. Levinas speaks of how the face of the Other does not compel me to accept its solicitation after I have considered it, but before: "In the proximity of the face, the subjection precedes the reasoned decision to assume the order that it bears."[349] Lingis finds this kind of subjection in sensation writ large, not just in the aesthetics of the human face.

Imperative responses cut straight to our sensibility and *would be* apprehended as pure sensations if perception did not filter them through figured representations and the figure-ground structure. This is a speculative point, but one worth risking. We live from these responses because they enable our bodies to move through and work competently in the material world. However, we do not constitute them. They are the medium through which the world communicates to us. This is possible because our bodies are immanent to, and in many respects dependent upon, other bodies like and unlike our own. Radios, daffodils, street signs, and neighborhoods impress us and invest us with their diverse sensuous content. This is what it means to belong to an ecological community and to be a member of what Vivian Sobchack calls the "interobjective" realm. Interobjectivity describes the anonymous community in which our bodies, otherwise consciously, "exist with the common matter and potential of materiality that is mutually shared not only by intentional subjects but also by *nonintentional objects*."[350] The passions we undergo in the interobjective realm inform us of what it means to be "not only an *objective subject* but also a *subjective object* whose intentionality and alterity can be sensed from *without*." And, continues Sobchack, it is in the passionate suffering of interobjectivity that we gain "an enhanced awareness of what it is *to be material*" and an appreciation for "the material foundation of our *aesthetic* behavior toward the world and others."[351] To feel oneself as a material being that suffers and makes others suffer is to recognize at once that the aesthetic foundation of action is likewise the basis of the ethical. Ecological life is not just about flowers, furry critters, conservation, and cooperative living.[352] There are darker sides of relational life that harbor their own power, as we will see later on.

In Levinas's later work, *Otherwise than Being*, immanence takes on a grave tenor. As Stella Sandford notes, "Both stress the corporeality of the subject as sensibility, but in *Totality and Infinity* the emphasis falls on pleasure, while in *Otherwise than Being* the keynote is suffering."[353] The heteroaffection of sensibility becomes a transcendental vulnerability and the animation of the subject is cast as the "body exposed to the other" (OB 69/87).[354] The alimentary function of sensation, which is apparent throughout Levinas's exploration of dwelling and enjoyment in *Totality and Infinity*, is displaced by a desire to articulate the way in which sensibility leads to the break up of identity, and is the means by which the subject is subjected to the diachrony of the sensible (OB 14-15/17-19).[355] Levinas goes so far as to identify subjectivity with the vulnerability of sensibility (OB 15, 50, 54/18, 65-66, 70). This vulnerability is given a carnal form, the skin, and a phenomenological interpretation that will serve to reground his theory of ethical responsibility.

Levinas once again points to labor, fatigue, and effort to reprise the embodied aspect of subjectivity. But the affection of the subject is interpreted now more emphatically as obsession, pain, and the interruption of enjoyment. Corporeality "is the pain of effort, the original adversity of fatigue, which arises in the upsurge of movement and in the energy involved in labor" (OB 54/70). Levinas has replaced the originary enjoyment of labor with an originary suffering: "As a passivity in the paining of the pain felt, sensibility is a vulnerability, for pain comes to interrupt an enjoyment in its very isolation, and thus tears me from myself" (OB 55/71). It is difficult to discern whether enjoyment or pain takes precedence now, or whether they are equiprimordial modes of existence. For instance, Levinas says that, "It is with savoring and enjoyment that the analysis of sensibility will have to begin" (OB 56/72), but this does not mean that sensibility is originally savoring and enjoyment. Nor does this statement outweigh what he says in defense of the primacy of pain in *Otherwise than Being*. Dennis King Keenan points out a similar ambiguity regarding Levinas's position on sensibility. It is not clear, says Keenan, whether enjoyment of sensibility is an exposure to the other or a singularizing involution, or if our relationship with the other should "be characterized as enjoyment, menace/necessity, or responsibility, all of which are singularizing *and exposure*. Despite Levinas's attempts in *Totality and Infinity* to establish and maintain a rigid distinction, there is blurring."[356] What is clear is that pain and enjoyment both belong to sensibility, which in either case provides the body's first opening onto its other.

Immediacy and materiality lend sensibility its constitutive susceptibility. Levinas writes of how matter "materializes" in enjoyment and satisfaction, which is first and foremost a seizing and a consuming (OB 73/92). The materiality of enjoyment is then correlated with the excess of meaning involved in alimentation, an excess that "conditions the very thought that would think it as condition" (TI 128/101; see also, TO 62-64/45-49). But, at the same time and paradoxically (not unlike Derrida's *pharmakon*, if you like), what nourishes us is also what threatens the stability or integrity of our bodies. The material we come into contact with through sensibility contains a basic ambivalence: it enables us, but remains perpetually capable of disabling us. Sensibility, as a form of contact, is the reversion of our grasp on things into our being grasped by them, a situation which is described by Levinas "in the ambiguity of a kiss" (OB 75/94). This ambiguity is not equivalent to the reversibility that Merleau-Ponty sees in the handshake, because, in Levinas's view, the supposed imminence of reversibility is precisely what remains in question and precarious, even if his diachronic structure of self and other is analogous to Merleau-Ponty's.[357] It is as though the ambiguity of the kiss, or the handshake, is what short-circuits or prevents reversibility, thus undermining Merleau-Ponty's image of the flesh by installing an image of irreversibility. One never knows whether the encounter is reciprocal or oppositional; both are viable possibilities. "[Sensibility]" writes Levinas, "reverts from the activity of being a hunter of images to the passivity of being prey, from being aim to being wound, from being an intellectual act of apprehension to apprehension as an obsession by another who does not manifest himself" (OB 75/95).

Contact has a technical sense for Levinas; it names a precise situation. It is basic to the embodied subject and describes the absolute "proximity of the other" as "the immediate opening up for the other of the immediacy of enjoyment, the immediacy of taste, materialization of matter" (OB 74/94).

Contact likewise describes the original exposure of sensibility to the other, that is, the transcendental aspect of heteroaffection. The subject who enjoys and is born from enjoyment is always already enjoying the other as element, sensation, matter. Subjects live from the other, hence their responsibility for the other. Levinas gives contact/proximity a carnal signification:

> Sensibility—the proximity, immediacy and restlessness which signify in it—is not constituted out of some apperception putting consciousness into relationship with a body. Incarnation is not a transcendental operation of a subject that is situated in the midst of a world it represents to itself; the sensible experience of the body is already and from the start incarnate. The sensible ... binds the node of incarnation into a plot larger than the apperception of the self. In this plot I am bound to others before being tied to my body. (OB 76/96)

Proximity, then, is prior to the emergence of the subject who represents or whose body is an "I can." It opens the subject to the approach of the other, which arrives "as though from an immemorial past, which was never present, began in no freedom" (OB 88/112). Our contact with the transcendental past is embodied in the skin, which Levinas, echoing Merleau-Ponty, calls "the divergency [*l'écart*] between the visible and the invisible" (OB 89/113). The skin is not a flesh in which each one of us participates, but a surface that at once keeps us separated and touching, substances who exist in themselves yet nevertheless relate. Sandford captures the carnality of proximity, and recalls Benso's remarks on breathing, when she writes:

> It is the respiration of the skin prior to any intention, a being turned to the Other as a being turned inside out, a going beyond the skin, to the underside of the skin, a getting underneath the skin, an obsession, a nakedness more naked than any excoriation (*dépouillement*). This is proximity.[358]

The skin is a liminal site, "the gap [*décalage*] between approach and approached" where alterity is produced (OB 90/114; TI 26-27/xiv-xv). In *Totality and Infinity* (26-27/xiv-xv) Levinas explains that the idea of infinity—which is synonymous with the revelation of the Other—is *produced* in me, "in the improbable feat whereby a separated being fixed in its identity, the same, the I, nonetheless contains in itself what it can neither contain nor receive solely by virtue of its own identity." It seems to me that the skin, insofar as it is receptive to an influx of sensory material which it could never hope to process completely, is the site where the depths of things—their matter, according to Levinas—is produced/revealed. That is, the skin is the surface where our objectifying representations find their limit.

The skin is naturally vulnerable because of its permeability. As Rudolf Bernet explains,

> Even a tight and thick skin has small and large holes that one can adequately call "openings." There are natural openings as well as artificial or forced openings called "wounds." Natural openings are still subject, however, to being forced and wounded. The natural openings allowing for a passage and exchange between the inside and the outside of a body cannot prevent the violence of a traumatic intrusion or expulsion.[359]

Levinas must have something like this in mind when he argues that sensibility *is* vulnerability and exposure to the other. Bernet points out that the singular nature of the skins involved in a particular instance of contact lend their quality to the intersubjective encounter, and help to determine whether the encounter is friendly or violent.[360] This means that the skin, or contact/proximity, cannot be deemed violent a priori. And if we are going to allow Levinas to say that the sensitivity of the skin—sensibility generally—is susceptibility, then this condition must be understood as ambivalent. Above all it should be maintained that my exposure to the other equally enables and disables, figures and disfigures my body. A priori this exposure is neither painful nor pleasurable.

Hopefully it is becoming clearer how and why the aesthetic dimension of existence is basic to Levinas's ontology of the body. In fact, we could go so far as to affirm that aesthetics—understood as the ontology of *aisthesis*—must be first philosophy for Levinas.[361] The subject's primary opening onto the other is the body's sensibility—that is, its capacity to sense and be affected by the material it lives and dies from. Sensibility is the condition of possibility for enjoyment, discomfort, and pain, and therefore a condition of possibility for ipseity, or selfhood. It is this ipseity which is interpellated by the Other and called into question. But this ipseity must first be won through effort and labor before it can answer responsibly the call of the Other.

We have seen that for Levinas sensation has an affective dimension, as is connoted in the French *sentir*, and also names a distinct ontological event. This event involves the passivity of the subject, on the one hand, and the objectivity ("transcendence") of the sensations which direct sensibility, on the other. Levinas's disqualification of the view that sensation is purely subjective, something that happens inside the mind or only as a correlate of consciousness, commits him to a form of ontological realism. Unlike Kant or Husserl, whose methodological commitments should prevent them from speaking about what lies beyond the bounds of the phenomenal, Levinas breaks free from phenomenology to make metaphysical claims about the non-intentional/transcendental realm of sensation. In fact, he openly admits that these claims are metaphysical and beyond the purview of phenomenological method. They are, however, not unintelligible: "This is the whole point," says Sandford, of Levinas's method:

> Levinas's philosophical method therefore consists in a series of metaphysical declarations apparently extrapolated from and further supported by phenomenological evidences. Metaphysical truths are revealed through phenomenology, both in the sense that phenomenology allows one to encounter them and that it functions verificationally after the event of disclosure. In this way, the strong claim for the intelligibility of transcendence is apparently based on, revealed through or justified by the appeal to the phenomenology of the ethics of affect.[362]

It is precisely because sensations come from *outside* that Levinas can characterize sensibility as vulnerability. Indeed, he requires the externality of sensation, and the corporeal vulnerability this implies, in order to prioritize ethics over any other branch of philosophy. Or, as David Michael Levin has said, "The embodiment of the categorical imperative cannot be understood … until our way of thinking about the body undergoes a radical revision."[363] If the *ambivalence* of sensibility is recognized—as I have argued—then the exigency of ethics becomes bound to the ontology of the body, and it becomes less clear which branch of philosophy enjoys primacy. Levinas would have us believe that our bodies are constantly under attack from the outside, and at times it seems as though he were arguing that intercorporeal encounters are *essentially* violent. He speaks of our openness to exteriority as "the vulnerability of the skin exposed, in wounds and outrage" and of sensibility as

> a nakedness more naked than that of the skin which, as form and beauty, inspires the plastic arts, the nakedness of a skin presented to contact, to the caress, which *always*—even, equivocally, in voluptuousness—is suffering for the suffering of the other. Uncovered, open like a city declared open upon the approach of the enemy, the sensibility, *prior to* all will, action, declaration, all taking up of positions, is vulnerability itself.[364]

Like a faithful phenomenologist, Levinas notes that this susceptibility is not reducible to the physiological body's causal relations. No, this susceptibility is a passivity "more passive than every passivity," which is to say, a radical transcendental passivity. "It is the aptitude … 'to be beaten', 'to receive blows'. … In vulnerability there then lies a *relationship with the other* which causality does not exhaust, a relationship antecedent to being affected by a stimulus."[365]

It is one of the virtues of Levinas's analyses that they fully appreciate the reality of violence. He keenly recognizes that an adequate account of alterity is needed in order to render this reality intelligible. A conception of alterity which acknowledges that some of our experiences do not submit to our representational capacities, that some experiences resist what we can know or think about them, is required to explain the inevitable encroachment of bodily degeneration and death, for instance. Death comes from elsewhere, and too quickly to register its face. Levinas writes in *Totality and Infinity* (224/199-200):

> The notion of a mortal but temporal being, apprehended in the will … differs fundamentally from every causality leading to the idea of the *causa sui*. Such a being is exposed, but also opposed to violence. Violence does not befall it as an accident that befalls a sovereign freedom. The hold that

violence has over this being—the mortality of this being—is the primordial fact.³⁶⁶

There is no need, however, to accept the susceptibility of the body as a fundamental vulnerability. Of course, it is that too. But it is also a capacity to be affected with joy or pleasure and to have the body enabled, in its posture and kinaesthetic responses, by the sensations it receives from the other. It is a capacity to be challenged by the outside, incited to exceed its limits and gather strength or power. In short, the sensitivity of the body is ambivalent a priori.

Our bodies are simultaneously constituted by ambivalence and alterity. This lesson is in Levinas as well as Merleau-Ponty. "Merleau-Ponty," writes Dan Zahavi, "can describe embodied self-awareness as a presentiment of the Other—the Other appears on the horizon of this self-experience—and the experience of the Other as an echo of one's own bodily constitution." For Merleau-Ponty, the Other can be received as such because its exteriority mirrors my own exteriority. "The reason I can experience Others is because I am never so close to myself that the Other is completely and radically foreign and inaccessible. I am always already a stranger to myself and therefore open to Others."³⁶⁷ It is not necessary for alterity to be a matter of pure transcendence—a transcendence, it must be said, whose alignment with humanism, anthropocentrism, and a particular religious tradition excludes the nonhuman from ethical consideration³⁶⁸—for it to command ethical consideration. That our relation with otherness is ambivalent, and that we can be enabled as well as disabled by that which we rely upon for our very being, is enough to give us pause.

It is true that Levinas gives a richer, more complex description of alterity than Merleau-Ponty. As well, he does much, contra Cartesian and Kantian forms of subjectivity, to give a corporeal form to the self and, consequently, the ethical imperative. Moreover, he gives us an account of the immanent genesis of the subject that rivals that of Deleuze. But in the process he sacrifices the actually ambivalent experience of embodiment in the name of a transcendental responsibility whose hyperbolic foundation leads to extreme claims about the vulnerability of the subject. This hyperbole respects the reality of sensation while at the same time betraying the plasticity of our sensibility. To avoid the ethical exclusivity of Levinas's anthropocentrism, which is most pronounced in the moral privilege he grants to human others, and to remain true to the ambivalence of our sensuous existence, it is advisable for us to develop a more mundane and faithful immanent form of the imperative, situating its force in the sensuous economy in which existents, objects, elements, and environments interact.[369] For this we need a conception of embodiment that avoids the excesses of both Merleau-Ponty and Levinas. That is, we need an adequate account of the plasticity of the body.

Chapter 5

On Aesthetic Plasticity

> ...we should try to discover how it is that subjects are gradually, progressively, really and materially constituted through a multiplicity of organisms, forces, energies, materials, desires, thoughts, etc.
>
> Foucault, "Two Lectures"

> ...sensation is the master of deformations, the agent of bodily deformations.
>
> Deleuze, *Francis Bacon*

The argument so far has followed two general, intertwined trajectories: one critical, the other constructive. The critical thread has argued that the two visions of embodiment offered by Merleau-Ponty and Levinas are inadequate for thinking how our bodies actually interact with the material world. The constructive thread has assembled evidence which suggests that both phenomenologists were cognizant of the function that sensation plays in the constitution of experience and identity. The nature and function of sensation, along with its difference from perception, has been adduced. In this chapter I build upon the analyses of sensation and sensing given by

Merleau-Ponty and Levinas in order to develop an account of embodiment that reconciles the extremes of their respective views. Instead of reversibility and susceptibility, my view features the *plasticity* of the body and argues that the dynamism of plasticity is more true to the aesthetic dimension of existence and the transactional nature of intercorporeal encounters.

Methodologically speaking, there is more than one way to defend the body's plasticity. Because the notion of plasticity is tacitly at work in poststructuralist philosophers like Foucault and Deleuze, and increasingly visible in the work of embodied cognition theorists, a wholesale assault on the phenomenological body could be launched from a number of non-phenomenological camps. An antagonism of this sort could be construed as a clash between modern and postmodern views of the body.[370] Such a neat division, however, does not do justice to the degree of overlap which obtains between phenomenological and non-phenomenological accounts of embodiment. This is why I have chosen for my defense of plasticity to synthesize the insights of Merleau-Ponty and Levinas with a number of non-phenomenologists, from Spinoza, James, and Dewey to Mark Johnson, Manuel DeLanda, and Catherine Malabou. It should also be noted that what I find most productive in the phenomenologists is not always what they produce from a phenomenological perspective. In fact, as I have noted in earlier chapters, it is often the phenomenological method itself which constrains some of the most fertile insights stumbled upon by Merleau-Ponty and Levinas, and what troubles any attempt to synthesize phenomenology with other approaches to embodiment. Oftentimes it is when these two thinkers are on the verge of transgressing the strictures of phenomenology that their thinking takes off in metaphysically daring directions.

The Meaning of Plasticity I

What does it mean for a body to be plastic and why is it necessary to conceive the body in this way? The term has a popular aesthetic meaning, as when we talk about "plastic surgery" or the "plastic arts." But I am not specifically concerned with either of these meanings. When I speak about plasticity I intend the meaning that is now common currency in the discourse of contemporary neuroscience, as well as cognitive and evolutionary theory. I first ran across the term in a text closer to my home discipline, that is, while reading the philosophical psychology of William James, who writes in *The Principles of Psychology* that plasticity broadly "means the possession of a structure weak enough to yield to an influence, but strong enough not to yield all at once. Each relatively stable phase of equilibrium in such a structure is marked by what we may call a new set of habits."[371] Plasticity in James's sense not only provides a useful means of imagining the dynamics of brain and body, it also offers a way to think the dynamic structural integrity of the embodied subject. When I use the term "integrity" I do not mean it in the moral sense, but as someone who says, "The integrity of the building has been compromised by the earthquake." The analogy between bodies and buildings is deliberate here. It is meant to suggest the reciprocal determination of body and building, and the structural homology of individual and environment.

Assuming with Merleau-Ponty that we simply *are* our bodies, we are absolved from positing a self-identical core of subjectivity which would remain untouched throughout any and all intercorporeal engagements, be they social, physical, or cultural. Plasticity helps us work through many of the questions that arise when we identify the subject with the body. In the end the plastic body gives us a fully immanent version of subjectivity without compelling us to grant the body an indeterminate fluidity that would make it difficult to explain how stability emerges and is maintained.

There are empirical and practical reasons for favoring plasticity over reversibility or susceptibility as the defining feature of the body. First, the body disintegrates, decays, and dies. Its relation to other bodies—and sometimes to itself, as in the case of autoimmune disorders—is often violent, as I have argued. Innumerable examples of irreversible situations can be given. These are defined by the powerlessness of human beings in the face of a materiality which burdens or exceeds them. As Ronald Bruzina expresses it, "human powerlessness is fundamentally that of being subject to structures around and within itself that are not of a human individual's own doing."[372] A piano is pushed out a window and crushes someone on the sidewalk below. An airplane plunges into the ocean and is obliterated along with all of its passengers. These are situations wherein the bodies involved are not on the verge of reversal: the person on the sidewalk has no chance of becoming the crusher, nor will the piano become the crushed, although it will suffer some damage upon impact. Perhaps only the sidewalk will suffer negligible harm, its capacity for resistance being greater than the unfortunate bystander or instrument. The airline passengers will have their perceptual capacities extinguished, and in a sense their bodies will die, but the material reality which destroyed them will remain. Perhaps the perceptual situation is reversible, but asymmetrical physical contact between bodies powerful and powerless is certainly not. Our bodies, I would contend, sense this asymmetry in themselves and build upon it when forming bonds with other bodies.[373]

Now, I am not so foolish as to think that the images of falling pianos and plunging airplanes alone stand as refutations of constructivist idealism or correlationism. They are offered here, in one respect, as a metaphor of the intractability of the material world. Additionally, they work to unsettle our comfort with an idealism or phenomenology whose conventional images portray an inquisitive observer gazing intently on some medium-sized domestic object. Objects, however, are not always so wieldy. And if Meillassoux's argument for the necessity of contingency holds, neither are the very laws governing the existence of these objects.[374] In short, we have reason to distrust the stability of appearance and the synchrony of body and world.

Considered from a different angle the body is indeed a resilient thing. It resists disintegration by nourishing itself, defends itself from assault, and deftly assembles resources which help it postpone death. It fashions clothes and designs shelters, devises means of repairing itself when wounded, and takes measures to prevent further wounding. It gathers these resources from its environment and from others; it is enabled by otherness just as much as it can be disabled by it. It is certainly true that tragedy may befall the body at any moment, so it is indeed a susceptible entity. But given the extraordinary nature of tragedy, the threat of violence cannot be the ground upon which the body is defined as a body. It is much more than a passivity: it preserves itself and pushes itself to become more powerful; it adapts and evolves, yes, but it also destroys and imposes form. These are Nietzsche's lessons.[375] That the body is threatened by violence and prone to disintegration, but at the same time enabled by what resists its efforts and movement, leads us necessarily to consider the ethics and politics of plasticity.

A body whose integrity is plastic is definable by its thresholds. This means, as we saw with Merleau-Ponty's notion of style, that its identity is constantly shifting and constituted by an indefinite and fragile disposition. This disposition will either display typical effects, or the potential for these effects will be virtually present, harbored in the body and actualizable under the right conditions.[376] Shifts in identity or the compromising of bodily integrity will be induced by a breakdown in the body's own maintenance or by pressures exerted on its constitution by an external force. In both cases what gets compromised is an alliance maintained between a collective of bodies functioning together as a singular body (a friendship, political demonstration, or soccer team) and conspiring together to reciprocally determine each individual body's identity. Such a view of identity obliges us to imagine the substance of identity as fleeting and dependent rather than enduring and self-sufficient. Individuals enjoy only a transitory autonomy, a limited immunity from degeneration. As Mach asserts, "The ego is as little absolutely permanent as are bodies. That which we so much dread in death, the annihilation of our permanency, actually occurs in life in abundant measure."[377] The meaning of death is likewise reoriented by this definition of identity, which is why the hypothetical victims of the plane crash example can be said to die only "in a sense." One may die without actually becoming a corpse, but one may become a corpse without technically dying.[378]

Composite Bodies

Spinoza employs the term *ratio* to describe the dynamic alliance that composes corporeal identities. He speaks of identity thresholds as ratios of motion and rest, speed and slowness.[379] The body is not merely a figure or style, but a system of relations governed by a specific principle of relating, or ratio. Following on his heels Deleuze and Guattari elaborate the Spinozan conception of bodily identity with concepts like assemblage, machine, multiplicity, and body without organs. These concepts provide an understanding of bodily identity that makes no appeal to an immutable organic (biological, physiological, neuronal) structure; they leave the body fully open to deformation and reconstitution, and therefore to the aleatory and to alterity. Spinoza begins to build the plastic body, while Deleuze and Guattari draw out its complexity.

A body, for Spinoza, is never purely individual in an atomistic sense, for an individual is always a composite or collective of bodies. What individuates a body from the single substance (God, or Nature) in his monistic ontology is the body's effects, which are determined by its singularity. Spinoza defines a singular thing as a thing that has a finite, determinate existence. "If several things concur in one act in such a way as to be all together the simultaneous cause of one effect, I consider them all, in that respect, as one individual."[380] In short, an individual *is* a singularity. A body, then, is individuated as *this* body by what it can do or what it can effectuate materially (efficient causes), psychologically (affects), politically (uprisings, policings), and so forth. The capacity of the body to create a singular effect, or what we can call the body's power, is always variable and vulnerable to disintegration because this power only subsists as long as the collective of bodies working together to create a singular effect maintain their particular ratio of motion and rest. Spinoza writes:

> When a number of bodies of the same or different magnitude form close contact with one another through the pressure of other bodies upon them, or if they are moving at the same or different rates of speed so as to preserve an unvarying relation of movement among themselves, these bodies are said to be united with one another and all together to form one body or individual thing, which is distinguished from other things through this union of bodies.[381]

Now, this ratio is not precise: it is plastic, which is to say its identity is marked by a precarious formal variability, or threshold of integrity.[382] The form is not what determines the body ultimately, it is the kinetics of the body's composition that constitutes its individuality. "The important thing," Deleuze tells us, is to see individuality "as a complex relation between differential velocities, between deceleration and acceleration of particles." This is what Deleuze calls Spinoza's "kinetic proposition."[383] Let's call it the *ecological account of bodies*.

Deleuze distills the Spinozan problematic of bodies into the question, *What is a body capable of?* He poses the problem in this way in order to suggest two things: (1) to know what a body does is to know what it is; and (2) the power of the body is unknown to us, so we are far from fathoming the possibilities for action, change, and enhancement that new technologies and new modes of collective existence have in store for us. I am thinking in particular of human-machine interfaces, participatory art, prostheses, genetic manipulation, and the whole range of what Deleuze and Guattari call "unnatural participations."[384] Deleuze's question also pinpoints another ontological claim advanced by Spinoza: bodies just are their capacity to affect and be affected. Deleuze writes, "a body affects other bodies, or is affected by other bodies; it is this capacity for affecting and being affected that also defines a body in its individuality."[385] This notion of individuality yields a new method of classifying things, one whose principle of differentiation is produced immanently. What a body is becomes less important than what it can do.[386]

This new method prefers a genetic or evolutionary conception of form to the ancient hylomorphism. It regards the genesis of form as initiated by contact between heterogeneous material elements, which results in multiplicities that endogenously give rise to singular bodies.[387] In this ontology the "structure and genesis [of the body] are in principle indiscernible."[388] Dewey's definition of aesthetic form is representative here: "Form may then be defined as the operation of forces that carry the experience of an event, object, scene, and situation to its own integral fulfillment."[389] It is crucial that this formulation acknowledges the priority of circumstance over teleology in the determination of structure, and locates its genesis in the materials and energies that compose an aesthetic event. The event, at bottom, is rhythmic.[390] Similarly, Deleuze writes of how

> relations of speed and slowness are realized according to circumstances, and the way in which these capacities for being affected are filled. For they always are, but in different ways, depending on whether the present affects threaten the thing (diminish its power, slow it down, reduce it to the minimum), or strengthen, accelerate, and increase it: poison or food?— with all the complications, since a poison can be a food for part of the thing considered.[391]

The point here is that the maintenance of corporeal identity is not only a matter of intersubjective/intercorporeal relations. Identity is also dependent on environmental conditions and the nourishment they provide (or fail to provide)—the ambivalence of the environment is recognized as fundamental to corporeal power and action.

One of the advantages of working with the Spinozan definition of bodies endorsed by Deleuze is that it frees us from entrenched binaries like artificial/natural, animate/inanimate, organic/inorganic, sentient/insentient. For Spinoza and Deleuze all bodies belong to the same ontological plane and can be evaluated in terms that do not force us to distinguish between, say, the human and nonhuman or living and nonliving. This is the advantage of a "flat ontology" of bodies.[392] As a consequence of undoing old binaries we are free to imagine new composite bodies and, therefore, new possibilities for collective experience and bodily identity. Hybridity and community become the norm. As Elizabeth Grosz puts it,

> [Deleuze and Guattari] provide an altogether different way of understanding the body in its connections with other bodies, both human and nonhuman, animate and inanimate, linking organs and biological processes to material objects and social practices while refusing to subordinate the body to a unity or a homogeneity of the kind provided by the body's subordination to consciousness or to biological organization. Following Spinoza, the body is regarded as neither a locus for a consciousness nor an organically determined entity; it is understood more in terms of what it can do, the things it can perform, the linkages it establishes, the transformations and becomings it undergoes, and the machinic connections it forms with other bodies, what it can link with, how it can proliferate its capacities....[393]

The model of embodiment described by Grosz regards the body, in Deleuze and Guattari's language, as a "machinic assemblage." This concept is democratic insofar as it counts a wide range of phenomena as bodies and refrains from privileging one kind of body or relation over another. There is nothing special about a naturally occurring body; human bodies are not elevated above their vegetal counterparts. Any body type can join forces with a different body type and initiate new identities, new effects. Corporeal difference is a matter of degrees of complexity; what matters most is the effects and affects produced by the body, irrespective of its compositional heritage. The concept of assemblage has far-reaching consequences for ecological thinking.

Assemblages and Machines

There is an assemblage theory of bodies available in the literature on embodied/enactive cognition. Take the work of Andy Clark. In *Being There* Clark develops the concept of "scaffolding" in order to demonstrate that our minds are not locked in our heads, but extended throughout the interobjective environment. The external environment provides support, scaffolding, for the body in countless forms, from simple implements like pencils, paper, and photographs to languages and digital storage devices. This way of thinking is common to the "extended mind" hypothesis. As Clark argues, "these external structures function so as to complement our individual cognitive profiles and to diffuse human reason across wider and wider social and physical networks whose collective computations exhibit their own special dynamics and properties."[394] Noë includes a helpful discussion of *virtual* representation that relies on something like scaffolding when he writes, "Off-loading internal processing onto the world simplifies our cognitive lives and makes good engineering and evolutionary sense."[395] Scaffolding serves as the network within which individuals work out solutions to problems, but from what we have said so far, it would be misleading to regard it as "external" to the body. And this is Clark's point: individuals cannot be understood as standing apart from the scaffolding that supports their behavior—they are extended throughout, and in a real sense emerge out of or *are* the scaffolding of their environment.[396] The extended mind's plasticity is what allows the body to adaptively integrate and design scaffolding that aids in problem-solving. Understanding how our brains design and inhabit the vast assemblage of networks, institutions, societies, and myriad dynamic systems in society is the present task of cognitive science.[397]

The assemblage theory of bodies forms the basis of what Jane Bennett calls "distributive" or "confederate" agency. In her view agency in an assemblage is "distributed across an ontologically heterogeneous field, rather than being a capacity localized in a human body or in a collective produced (only) by human efforts."[398] Agency is here equivalent to efficacy. Any efficacious thing qualifies as an agent, which means that any thing whatsoever that makes a difference in the world possesses agency, even if that thing cannot be cited as the source of its agency. Since every thing makes some difference, however small, every thing bears the mark of agency.[399] Bennett writes in *Vibrant Matter*:

> This understanding of agency does not deny the existence of that thrust called intentionality, but it does see it as less definitive of outcomes. It loosens the connections between efficacy and the moral subject, bringing efficacy closer to the idea of the power to make a difference that calls for response. And this power, I contend along with Spinoza and others, is a power possessed by nonhuman bodies too.[400]

This radically democratic theory of bodies disintegrates the plausibility of classical liberal autonomy and disperses responsibility across the entire field of being.

Assemblages are essentially multiplicities whose identity is determined by the unified effects they produce. Their identity is in their plurality. If bodies are assemblages, then they are less like fixed structures and more like heterogeneous events that derive their consistency/integrity from a certain threshold for change. This threshold is governed by the active conjunctions which make up the assemblage. Assemblages are always provisional, non-hierarchical, and precariously organized.[401] They subsist only as long as they actively maintain their constitutive ratio of motion and rest, that is, their intensity.[402] Following my unorthodox reading of Levinas in the last chapter I would insist that this process occurs at the level of sensibility. An intensity is a bodily event—a passion, affection, sensation—directly related to the "*capacity* to enter into relations of movement and rest," as Massumi puts it.[403] Intensity differentiates the body's power, makes it stand out, and allows it to take up a position. Intensity can be generated in myriad ways and with a variety of inorganic and organic components. Whatever accumulates can increase in intensity. Think of a wolf pack or a school of fish darting through the sea. These are natural events, and as such would seem to be understandable only as governed by fixed natural law. As assemblages, however, this is not necessarily the case. Assemblages are dynamic unities, immanently organized and constructed ad hoc—*haecceities*.

Deleuze and Guattari conscript the medieval concept of haecceity because it allows them to think identity and individuation in terms of events, intensities, and becoming. A haecceity, in short, is a specific "accidental form."[404] That is, it is a historically emergent and singular form. It contrasts clearly with the notion of substance, substantial form, person, subject, thing, and so forth, each of which is held to be self-contained and in some sense necessary unto itself. Thinking along with Spinoza they explain how one defines the body as a haecceity, here presented in cartographic terms:

> A body is not defined by the form that determines it nor as a determinate substance or subject nor by the organs it possesses or the functions it fulfills. On the plane of consistency, *a body is defined only by a longitude and a latitude*: in other words the sum total of the material elements belonging to it under given relations of movement and rest, speed and slowness (longitude); the sum total of the intensive affects it is capable of at a given power or degree of potential (latitude). Nothing but affects and local movements, differential speeds.[405]

The concept of haecceity enables us to think of individuation, and therefore identity, as a completely contingent intercorporeity or event of plasticity. It helps us escape the substance-ontological view that sees historical emergence as inessential to identity. It also aids us in articulating a theory of identity which balances the fluid as well as (meta)stable elements of the body, and refers these elements to the immanence of cosmological, evolutionary, and human history.[406] Following Spinoza, Deleuze and Guattari provide a number of resources for thinking corporeal plasticity, although at times they push the fluidity of their notion of a "body without organs" to an untenable extreme. Even though the body can attempt to escape its organic constitution, it is never completely devoid of organization or, at least, a minimal set of habits. The body without organs remains an ideal.

Whether or not a body without organs is achievable, what we have seen open up so far in this chapter is the potential meaning of "individual" and "body." What a body *is*, as well as what it *can do*, all of a sudden become radically open questions. The body's power becomes free to proliferate, and the individual free to develop, but always under the precarious and singular ecological conditions regulating the assemblage of bodies. The practical consequences of conceiving the body in this way will become clearer as we progress.

Equally important to the Deleuzean/Guattarian development of the composite body, or assemblage, is its machinic feature. In *Anti-Oedipus* a machine is defined as what introduces interruptions into otherwise continuous flows of material (*hyle*): a machine is "a *system of interruptions* or breaks." The orifices of our bodies are machines because they interrupt the flow of air (mouth) and the flow of sound (ear) and the flow of feces (anus).[407] The sensory apparatus of our bodies can be seen as a complex machine insofar as the senses function as a multifaceted device for cutting up the manifold of sensory material flowing through the body. At the same time as it cuts the machinic body is apt to create new linkages, that is, new assemblages composed of intensive relations and affective transactions. Again, these linkages are ad hoc, a form of *bricolage* that potentially, if Clark is correct, opens our bodies to "episodes of deep and transformative restructuring, in which new equipment (both physical and 'mental') can become quite literally incorporated into the thinking and acting systems that we identify as minds and persons."[408]

In explicating his assemblage theory of society Manuel DeLanda includes a helpful illustration of the formation of personal identity. If territorialization denotes a process that increases the internal homogeneity of a person's corporeal identity, then identity "may be deterritorialized not only by loss of stability but also by augmentation of capacities." The following images bring to life the transformative potential of the machinic body:

> When a young child learns to swim or ride a bicycle, for example, a new world suddenly opens up for experience, filled with new impressions and ideas. The new skill is deterritorializing to the extent that it allows the child to break with past routine by venturing away from home in a new vehicle, or inhabiting previously forbidden spaces like

the ocean. New skills, in short, increase one's capacity to affect and be affected, or to put it differently, increase one's capacities to enter into novel assemblages, the assemblage that the human body forms with a bicycle, a piece of solid ground and a gravitational field, for example.[409]

Machines engage in transactions that assemble "disparate elements." This means that they carve into and interface with material from diverse ontological domains. Think of a soldier with a titanium prosthetic arm or a person with an online avatar. Think of a kid whose pleasure is generated by an imaginary friend or videogame. Think of a guy whose masochistic desires require leather or stone or plants for him to reach sexual satisfaction.[410] These people are machines; their identity, materially composite.

There is a certain technique or artisanship to the machinic process, one which the body already possesses insofar as it effortlessly hooks into environments that produce natural, artificial, physical, linguistic, imaginary, and abstract effects.[411] Since the body is never without a nourishing environment composed of disparate elements, or prostheses/tools, we could reasonably assert that it takes no stretch of the imagination to see that *the human body just is a complex machine*, if not in La Mettrie's sense, then definitely in Deleuze and Guattari's. Its machinic infrastructure is constructed by a team of physical, phenomenological, and ecological agents united by a principle of individuation proper to neither domain in particular. Although they recognize the machinic potential of the body, it seems to me that both Levinas and Merleau-Ponty refuse to endorse the view that the body is nothing more than a complex machine. Both phenomenologists recognize that subjects are partially constituted by their sociolinguistic, historical, and physical milieus, but the thesis affirming that the structure of the subject is completely dependent on a field of material forces that literally assemble the identity of the body is missing from their texts.[412]

The Meaning of Plasticity II

Before going any further I want to gather a fuller account of the meaning of plasticity and suggest some of its implications for embodiment and identity theory. This will enable us to understand the machinic body in its plasticity and see how the integration of body and environment is critical to understanding corporeal plasticity. Additionally, it will prepare us to see how the body's plasticity is determined by its aesthetic constitution, that is, the history of its sensory apparatus.

If it is at least plausible to claim that the modern account of embodiment is marked by the view that there is a substantial core or immutable structure to the body, whereas the postmodern account is characterized by a desire to see the body vanish into an anonymous field of desire, pleasure, and flux, then the concept of plasticity belongs to neither historical period.[413] Given this historical partition it would seem that Merleau-Ponty belongs in neither the modern nor postmodern camp, for he downplays bodily anonymity just as much as he contests the modernist's substance ontology. Regardless, he does not deliver us a plastic body. The dynamic of his reversible body is more akin to the mechanics of elasticity. Elasticity can be understood by considering a rubber band. The rubber band is flexible and deformable, but in the absence of resistance or external force it tends toward a specific formal state. Accordingly, elasticity does not properly describe a structure open to permanent deformation. Permanent deformation means breakage and the elimination of the precise disposition which constitutes the rubber band's elasticity. The disappearance of its elasticity is equivalent to death for the rubber band. In other words, its structure is not identical to its historical genesis. From the perspective of elasticity the band's structure is prescribed by the rubber band type. Similarly for Merleau-Ponty's lived body: its structure tends toward a certain coherence that is prescribed by the lived body type. Insofar as the lived body is flexible within certain normative limits, the Merleau-Pontyan body is best conceived on the model of elasticity.

Merleau-Ponty's lived body possesses a number of structural features which exhibit a dispositional elasticity, and whose absence would entail the impossibility of subjectivity. These include the features of consciousness (for instance: intentionality, perspectival perception), the body schema, the movement of transcendence or ability (the "I can," which effectively operates as a transcendental norm and therefore makes *dis*ability a derivative mode of comportment), and the general tendency toward convergence attributed to perception.[414] Throughout each of its engagements with the world, other bodies, alterity in general, the reversible body maintains its relative stability with a number of quasi-transcendent, admittedly malleable, structures. They are not indefinitely malleable, however, which would render them plastic. If anything, their malleability is always seeking to return to the equilibrium point which we defined earlier as body-world synchronization. Plasticity, on the other hand, pursues no such telos.

Merleau-Ponty's view of embodiment is accomplished only by quarantining the objective body and suspending the question of how its physiology and materiality interfere with, as well as support, the lived body's phenomenological world of perception. As I have been arguing, what threatens to undo or undermine the body's elasticity is the sensory field's immediate contact with the body's sensorium, along with the material composition of the body more generally. In other words, the anonymous aesthetic life of the body is the locus of deformation and disfiguration, or what Panagia calls a "zone of indistinction."[415] This is not to say that Merleau-Ponty lacks any notion of plasticity. On the contrary, both style and habit (perhaps the body schema, too?) display a marked plasticity. My point is that his text runs the risk of pathologizing plasticity and normalizing elasticity, and this in the interest of drawing a distinction—fundamental in his view—between the lived body and the objective body. We must take care to recognize the plasticity of the phenomenal, as well as the material, levels and not to regard these two levels as regulated by different ontological principles.

Plasticity contrasts, and is designed to replace, both infinite malleability and immutable substantiality. It is, at bottom, neither stability nor instability, but metastability. Remarking on current brain research, Catherine Malabou writes that

> the word *plasticity* has two basic senses: it means at once the capacity to *receive form* (clay is called "plastic," for example) and the capacity to *give form* (as in the plastic arts or in plastic surgery). Talking about the plasticity of the brain thus amounts to thinking of the brain as something modifiable, "formable," and formative at the same time.[416]

This conception of plasticity is not meant to suggest that the brain is merely flexible, for as Malabou goes on to show, the brain is at once prone to historical deformations and capable to effecting historical deformations.

> To be flexible is to receive a form or impression, to be able to fold oneself, to take the fold, not to give it. To be docile, to not explode. Indeed, what flexibility lacks is the resource of giving form, the power to create, to invent or even to erase an impression, the power to style. Flexibility is plasticity minus its genius.[417]

The brain is docile to a degree, but this docility is simultaneously tempered by tolerance and creation, taken together as a single trait: *creative tolerance*. Our brains are, to an extent, evolutionarily determined, but it is this inescapable determination that allows for "a possible margin of improvisation" that is at once singularly determined and historically singularizing.[418] Every body's experience will likewise be singular, which means that no two bodies are capable of the same encounters.

Plasticity describes the simultaneous determinacy and indeterminacy of morphogenesis. In other words, it names the potential of the body to have its initial determination transformed indefinitely.[419] Even if it is granted that the human brain displays a universal anatomy, or that its physical makeup is structurally invariable, learning and memory—history in general—guarantees that no two brains will be the same. In their history "repetition and habit play a considerable role, and this reveals that the response of a nervous circuit is never fixed. Plasticity thus adds the functions of artist and instructor in freedom and autonomy to its role as sculptor," argues Malabou.[420] The singular identity of an individual brain emerges from that gap opened up between freedom and determination, which is to say, in the space of history. The constitution of the individual is determined by how the body's mechanisms are transformed by the experiences it enacts or suffers. Plasticity is the "eventlike dimension of the mechanical," which

> between determinism and freedom, designates all the types of transformation deployed between the closed meaning of plasticity (the definitive character of form) and its open meaning (the malleability of form). It does this to such a degree that cerebral systems today appear as self-sculpted

> structures that, without being elastic or polymorphic, still
> tolerate constant self-reworking, differences in destiny, and the
> fashioning of a singular identity.[421]

Our brains are machines, but machines that repair themselves and reprogram themselves according to information they receive from their surroundings. The identities they achieve strike a balance between passivity and activity, infinite possibility and finite determination. At the end of the day, however, their constitution gives way to the exigencies of the material world, leaving only the trace of their singular destiny and returning to the anonymous material of being.

A similar line of thinking is pursued in Foucault's work on history and embodiment. He chooses "docility" to describe the body invested with power and disciplinary techniques, but the manner in which he thinks docility resonates with the concept of plasticity. The docile bodies populating *Discipline and Punish* seem, on the one hand, merely pliable, or "flexible" in Malabou's sense. They are *made* to take on a pre-programmed form, rendered automatic or mechanical (territorialized) by the machinations of state power or biopower. Foucault writes of how

> the soldier has become something that can be made; out
> of formless clay, an inapt body, the machine required can
> be constructed; posture is gradually corrected; a calculated
> constraint runs slowly through each part of the body,
> mastering it, making it pliable, ready at all times, turning
> silently into the automatism of habit.[422]

But this is only half the story. The body would not take on this apparent automatism were it not for its capacity to take on any number of historically determined forms. When Foucault says that the body has to be broken down and rearranged, he is acknowledging that disciplinary techniques must grapple with corporeal determinations that offer resistance and harbor their own power. Oksala has pointed out, against Butler and others, that it is the body *as formed* which offers its own resistances to reformation.[423] In Foucault's words, "Discipline increases the forces of the body ... and diminishes these same forces.... In short, it dissociates power from the body" and transforms the body into an "aptitude" or "capacity."[424] Recalling James's definition of plasticity, the disciplined body is given a structure strong enough to resist power, but weak enough to yield to a sufficiently technical and more intense power.

The event-like structure of the body is given further expression in "Nietzsche, Genealogy, History," where Foucault explicitly rejects the view that the body is an ahistorical, physiologically-determined entity: "The body is *molded* by a great many distinct regimes; it is broken down by the rhythms of work, rest, and holidays; it is poisoned by food or values, through eating habits or moral laws; it *constructs* resistances." Put negatively, its history is "without constants."[425] Formulated positively: the body is plastic. This does not mean that the body is reducible to a series of oppressive events, or that the forms it assumes do not constitute real dispositions or determinate capacities for action. It means that any particular disposition is contingent and susceptible to change, whereas dispositional plasticity is structurally basic to embodiment.[426]

Malabou's investigation of plasticity implicitly follows, in the philosophical tradition, the naturalistic insights of James and Dewey. She rarely, if ever, writes about either thinker. She discovers plasticity in Hegel; I have been arguing that it is basic to Spinozism too, a point she notes in *Ontology of the Accident*.[427] What she says about the brain can be profitably broadened to describe the constitution of the body. This does not lead to a reductive physicalism. Phenomenology, and the phenomenological sympathies of the pragmatists, help us avoid that course. For instance, Bernard Andrieu, following Francisco Varela and others, contributes to a program called "neurophenomenology," which focuses on the material genesis and plasticity of cognition while considering equally legitimate the phenomenological and neuroscientific descriptions of this process. Central to this "dynamic materialism" is an updated notion of Merleau-Ponty's concept of flesh, which Andrieu says "defines the historic construction of the nervous system through the interaction of the body with the world and the progressive embodiment of these incorporations."[428] The temporal dimension of the construction of the body is linked to the principle of plasticity, which says that the body "must first be understood as an interaction with its environment because it is itself the receptive matter both informed and informing."[429] Merleau-Ponty may not have been willing to subscribe to this materialist program for the flesh, but his thinking does exhibit sympathy for the kind of mutual formation described by Andrieu and Malabou. Once again, this is evident in his conception of habit.

Habit, Circuit, Territory

Recall that for Merleau-Ponty habits are like the body's original prostheses. The idea that habit is *first* nature is in fact a point found in James, although the American is not Merleau-Ponty's source. Habits offer a metastability to the body without fixing it absolutely. They render the body automatic to a degree, but this automatism is never complete. There is some room left for freedom, but what this freedom entails is left for discussion in the following chapter. The body is not born with a set of specific habits, but almost immediately adopts habits which endow it with a specific integrity and allow it to negotiate its situations with relative ease.

Habits belong among the historical a priori which condition perception and action; they arrange and rearrange the body schema, while leaving the body open to receive new habits.[430] Habits are not just passively received, however: they are projected out into the environment as actions whose repetition wears down the environment in specific ways. Conversely, repetition wears upon the actor. The possibilities for habituation are limited by the effects of habit introduced into the layout of the environment. As Casey writes, the "power of orientation" (Merleau-Ponty) we call our *habitus* is correlated to the kinaesthetic situation we call our habitat.[431] Now, I think a general conception of habit is essential for understanding corporeal plasticity. In fact, we might say that habit is emblematic of plasticity, but it is not sufficient to keep our discussion of habit at the level of perception, without serious consideration of its material aspect. Otherwise, habit becomes a structure of the body that deals with material conditions, while remaining immaterial itself. We saw in our earlier discussion that an account of habit is provided by the pragmatists and we turn to them now to consider habit from a naturalistic perspective, one which is not incompatible with, but rather supplemental to, the phenomenological.

In James's *The Principles of Psychology* habituation takes hold in the neural network of the brain. And it is precisely this network's plasticity that enables the body to acquire habits. The physics of plasticity, in this case, implies that the nervous system is susceptible to a series of habit sets which lend it its structure at a given historical point. Each successive phase of the system's development contains a specific integrity which resists alteration while at the same time remaining susceptible to environmental influence.[432] The influence of the body's sensory life carves pathways into its nervous system, predisposing it to particular patterns of behavior which correspond to these pathways.[433] We now know that these pathways are the locus of the body schema, which Clark describes as "a suite of neural settings that implicitly (and non-consciously) define a body in terms of its capabilities for action…."[434] The plasticity of the neural network is what enables the body schema to change over time as it genuinely *incorporates*, and not merely uses, the instruments that "dilate" (Merleau-Ponty's term) the body-subject's world.

Habits, then, exhibit internal/physiological and external/environmental aspects.[435] Neither of these can be reduced when considering the identity of the body. On the one hand, the neural pathways recorded in the material of the body physically determine the range of actions and passions the body is capable of at any given time. On the other hand, the range of behaviors the body exhibits at a specified point in its life determine its style and make it recognizable as the individual it is. The variability of this style—which may result from self-reflection or environmental changes, for instance—introduces a degree of indeterminacy that can effect an alteration of the body's habit set.

Allowing for the reality of creativity, we must not overestimate the power of the will to alter the body's habits. When the will is set against the force of habit as the agent of rehabituation—and this is even more the case when habit is localized in the brain—one runs the risk of reinforcing the dualism of master mind and servant body. Carlisle leans in this direction by suggesting "awareness" as the remedy for undesirable habits. She writes, "Habits carry a momentum that must be countered by an opposing medium."[436] Awareness involves attending to the transitive sensations left unremarked in habitual action. It contains "the power to *unconceal* habits, and so to weaken and eventually unravel them." But if sensations actually operate below the level of perception, or attention, then the possibility of bringing them to attention becomes suspect, if not impossible, as does the freedom to choose between awareness or obliviousness to "one's living, breathing experience."⁴³⁷ The covert nature of sensation leaves consciousness in a state of perpetual unawareness. The option of bringing sensation, and the habits informed by it, to consciousness is thereforecompromised.

Just as the neural network is a kind of circuit along which habits flow, the behavioral aspect of habits can also be regarded as a circuit. Doing so allows us to see how the habits each one of us adopts can come to constitute who we are at the most fundamental level.

Habits economize our actions by locking us into certain behavioral patterns, while also releasing our attention to explore new modes of action. James's description of habitual circuits of behavior is as mechanical as it is phenomenological. "In action grown habitual, what instigates each new muscular contraction to take place in its appointed order is not a thought or a perception, but the *sensation occasioned by the muscular contraction just finished.*"⁴³⁸ The idea here is that habits are chains of sensations and muscular responses, set in motion by a single impulse. The sensations occur below the level of conscious attention, but this does not mean that they are not registered by the body. Indeed, they are situated somewhere between the physiological and phenomenological: "that they are more than unconscious nerve-currents seems certain, for they catch our attention if they go wrong."⁴³⁹ Quoting a certain Schneider, James dubs habits "processes of inattentive feeling."⁴⁴⁰ We might call them circuits of inattention.

Favoring a more holistic representation of the habitual act, the phenomenologist will want to downplay the imperceptible and auto-reflexive elements of James's description of habit. Interestingly, it is the phenomenologist who would provide us with an expansive description of the series of sensations and muscular contractions which comprise a given habitual behavior. The key difference between the mechanical and phenomenological accounts of a circuit of behavior rests with the latter's insistence on the intentionality motivating the circuit and the former's insistence on sensation as the motor of action. There is no reason why we cannot regard habits as motivated by intentional aims but proceeding mechanically, however. To do so we must admit a certain autonomy— that is, a degree of unconscious activity—to the sensations propelling the mechanism.

James's account of habitual circuits leads us to see that our corporeal identities, insofar as they are comprised of sets of habits, are made up of a series of responses correlated with a series of sensations. In other words, our body's integrity is partially determined by the sensory circuits to which it responds. These circuits have aesthetic, phenomenological, affective, and unconscious elements. They constitute the largely anonymous substratum of our everyday lives. Of course we carve out some of our own circuits, but we just as often adopt them from the rituals and routines of culture. We may commute, dine, and shop like everyone else, but we might also invent, collaborate, and produce like no other. These rituals and routines find themselves recorded in the musculature of our bodies and driven by the mundane sensations of everyday life. These circuits coalesce into a system that subtracts from the abundance of incoming sensations and outgoing efforts required to sustain life. They make up what Schneider calls our "body's attitude"[441] and provide an analogue to what we have called proprioception. As Massumi shows, the "habitual autopilot" of our daily navigation is linked to the body's proprioception, and is predominantly a non-cognitive orienting.[442] Our body's attitude, individuality, orientation—in short, its very *animation*—emerges from its habitual economy. Everything hangs on whether the impetus of this economy is intentional, non-intentional, or a combination of both.

To better capture the complexity and diversity of our identities, the notion of circuit can be generalized and applied to all aspects of our existence. We can speak of political and moral circuits, for example, which might include the patterns of thought, action, and speech typical of a particular political ideology or moral framework.[443] These circuits, as plastic structures, display a relative stability. An analysis of any social circuit would have to include consideration of its sensory and affective content, for these are what regulate individuals and keeps them attached to the circuit, even when their attachments result from a diminished or indifferent concern for the circuit's value. It is arguable that, although we are quasi-automatically attached to our habits, we remain attached to them only insofar as they retain a degree of importance for us. Importance can come from the understanding, yes, but ultimately importance can only dictate our actions if we are *passionate* about it.[444] What we are passionate about is what gives our body incomparable pleasure and draws it near, or what infests our body with frustration, rage, or pain, thus repelling it. In short, our affective responses keep us locked into a circuit of behavior or induce us to switch to another circuit. Affects are a currency traded in the habitual economy.

In contrast with the phenomenological notion of an existential "field" we can think of the totality of the circuits which orient our individual lives as defining our *territory*, while considering each individual habit as a *milieu*.[445] These terms work in tandem and derive from the work of Deleuze and Guattari. A territory is roughly demarcated and abides by a specific set of laws; it is a stratified and policed assemblage. Habits are stratifications of the body, while its automatic aspects are symptomatic of its "territorialized" or "coded" disposition. As DeLanda explains, territorialization is a process which increases the internal homogeneity of an assemblage. It can be accomplished through exclusion, profiling, segregation, regulation, and so forth. Coding is a second reinforcement of homogenization and can be witnessed in our genes and in our language.[446] A milieu, by contrast, is defined by its instability and liminality: a milieu occurs between two clearly defined spaces, like a border or threshold, and maintains only a relative or fleeting stability. While dependent on the homogeneity of its environment, a habit is like a milieu in that it is susceptible to deformation or deterritorialization. Habits maintain their integrity by virtue of the stability of environmental conditions, but they are not fully determined by them.

Deleuze and Guattari consider milieus in terms of rhythm and haecceity, two concepts we have dealt with already. The unfamiliarity of the concept of milieu can be mitigated here by comparing it with Dewey's theories of form and growth. Together they give us a non-phenomenological way of understanding the sensory link between body and environment. Dewey's theory focuses on the qualitative and aesthetic dimensions of embodiment and, not unlike Levinas, offers an account of the alimentary function of sensation.

Considering how they invest the bodies populating them, we see that territories, or "territorialities (habitual constellations of affects and patterns of movement)," are not very different from what we have been calling circuits.[447] A territory lays down laws or codes which organize and render obedient the bodies inhabiting its space. The affective component of territoriality is, in John Protevi's words, "inherently political: bodies are part of an ecosocial matrix of other bodies, affecting them and being affected by them; affect is part of the basic constitution of bodies politic."[448] This is why we must always ask whether the affective circuits of territories (or bodies politic) increase or decrease the power of the bodies that inhabit them. What feels important inside the territory?

Territories gain strength when the qualities of a milieu, or its rhythm, are forced to express the marks/coordinates of the territory, when the *nomos* of the body politic is embodied in the *ethos* of those bodies which constitute it. This is a performative act, the signature of the territory.[449] Territorialization occurs when an otherwise non-signifying set of qualities (milieu) is made to signify or represent a particular style: "One puts one's signature on something just as one plants one's flag on a piece of land."[450] A birdsong, or refrain, works in this way. The birdsong delimits a territory by marking the sonic boundaries of the bird's property. This is accomplished by a "little tune" or "melodic formula" (a meme) whose performance enacts the territorialization. In the same way, our bodies come to function by innumerable cultural refrains, some of which we enact for ourselves, like the frightened child who, "gripped with fear, comforts himself by singing under his breath."[451] Like any body whose posture or gesture reproduces the body language of a particular cultural setting, the child builds a little space of comfort around him with a familiar sound. The sound shelters him from the indeterminacy haunting his imagination.

Despite the fixity of territory, bodies and spaces display characteristics which oppose and undo territorial codes. Improvisation, for instance. Improvisation, or any chance encounter, is made possible by the "cracks" in territories which Deleuze and Guattari call milieus. A milieu is like the unstable and indistinct, but not inconsistent, qualitative dimension of a territory. In a word, it is the territory's heterogeneity. Just as territorialization must enlist the qualities of milieus, milieus must rely upon territories for the formal expression of their individual styles. The dialectical relation here is not pure, however, because milieus take ontological priority over territories. "The territory is the product of a territorialization of milieus and rhythms."[452] Milieus bear within themselves rhythms which produce their identities. The rhythm of a milieu is its own code.[453] It must, however, be noted that—given what has been said about assemblages—this rhythm is never proper to a milieu, but resonates *between* two or more milieus. The rhythm is a haecceity, an intensive threshold which is constantly produced and reproduced—by a movement of involution—by the difference or in-between that constitutes the milieu. It is this "difference that is rhythmic, not the repetition, which nevertheless produces it."[454] Milieus present the transactional space or passage between two heterogeneously coded stabilities, "*the interior milieu of impulses and the exterior milieu of circumstances*,"[455] for instance. As a threshold between inside and outside, a body operates as a milieu and is prone to the same kinds of instability, determination, co-optation, and coding.

The "Precious Part of Plasticity"

The difficult conceptuality of Deleuze and Guattari can be substituted, at the risk of oversimplification, with the naturalistic presentation given in Dewey's work on habit. Following James, Dewey defines habit as a process that is, in a word, plastic. Dewey explicitly presents two phenomena that are for the most part only implied by the phenomenologists: material *dependence* and material *growth*. It is true that Levinas gets at these aspects of existence in his notion of living from..., but his analysis fails to consider dependence from the perspective of natural life and is virtually silent, as is Merleau-Ponty, on the growth of the body.[456]

In *Human Nature and Conduct* Dewey speaks about the "plasticity of impulse," whereas in *Democracy and Education* he considers growth in terms of plasticity as well as dependence. In the former text, plasticity prima facie denotes a state of complete indeterminacy, as though our impulses were an unrestrained chaos of drives waiting to be channeled into deliberate behavior. But we quickly learn that plasticity signifies for Dewey an "original modifiability" that is initially determined by its interactions with the environment. Plasticity, then, signifies neither pure novelty nor pure docility, neither activity nor passivity: "the most precious part of plasticity consists in ability to form habits" which are (1) flexible and (2) able to modify sedimented customs and institutions, which for Dewey are just embodied habits.[457] Impulses are creative in that they instigate the renewal of habit, which is itself an ability and an art.[458] Habits "are adjustments *of* the environment, not merely *to* it. At the same time, the environment is many, not one; hence will, disposition, is plural."[459] Our habits are as diverse as the environments to which they respond. Environments take on the dispositions we impart to them, while habits are symptomatic of how environments have compelled us to adapt.

Much of this sounds like Merleau-Ponty, and we might have to concede that some aspects of the lived body bear the mark of plasticity. Especially with regard to habit, style, and postural schema, there are traces of plasticity in Merleau-Ponty's body-subject. The growth and disintegration of the body in its materiality is not a focus of his study, however, and unless we want to institute a new dualism of objective and subjective corporeality, the structure of the lived body must be seen as fundamentally material, and therefore liable to generation and degeneration. Even in "The Child's Relations with Others" the body is presented as mature and capable. Its habitual relations are presented as regulated by "a single global phenomenon" (i.e., perception). As Merleau-Ponty writes, "the internal characteristics of the subject always intervene in his way of establishing his relations with what is outside him. It is never simply the outside which molds him; it is he himself who takes a position in the face of the external conditions" (Child 108/17). Put otherwise, the existential field solicits and suggests responsive behavior, it does not determine it. Absent here is the physical growth of the child, which determines the manner in which he or she receives and processes—or fails to do so—environmental information. And while it is true to say that this physical development is never simply a matter of the outside "molding" the inside, it must be admitted that the internal relation between subject and object entails, at least initially, an asymmetrical relation of dependence whereby the subject (child) is deeply susceptible to outside influence. This dependence signifies the need for growth as well as a state of immaturity. Neither of these terms should be interpreted negatively, however. Dependence and immaturity, as Dewey shows, assert their own productive forces.

Human bodies develop. After development, disintegration. Both stages can be given positive treatments, provided they are taken on their own terms rather than dialectically. The child's body is exemplary. Immaturity is not simply an absent or nascent maturity: immaturity is a power, the capacity to grow. This capacity is at once dependent and plastic for Dewey. Plasticity here indicates the "specific adaptability of an immature creature for growth." This is not equivalent to "a capacity to take on change of form in accord with external pressure," but means the "power to modify actions on the basis of the results of prior experiences, the power to *develop dispositions*. Without it, the acquisition of habits is impossible."[460] Dewey locates the subject's plasticity *below* the level of disposition and habit, thus assigning it a transcendental aspect. But this aspect is nothing more than the volatility of organic processes. It is not that biology is prior to culture, but that corporeal structures are emergent, resilient, and pliable. In other words, the condition of possibility for habit acquisition is experimentation, or the indeterminate determinacy of a socially embedded impulse and instinct.

Growth comes with the acquisition of habits, which enable independence and maturity. "Maturation," as Noë writes, "is not so much a process of self-individuation and detachment as it is one of growing comfortably into one's environmental situation."[461] Independence comes with increased control of the body, which includes integration and cultivation of the environment, as well as orientation within it. And it is only when our habits become mechanized routines, when we get locked into circuits of behavior or when our bodies become territorialized, that our plasticity is paralyzed. The tendency toward decreased plasticity, the dissolution of the power to grow, quickens with age. It is not just a matter of inattention, it is a physical necessity. This is why James instructs that, in education it is imperative that we "*make our nervous system our ally instead of our enemy.*" As the power to efficiently and effortlessly think and act decreases, the exigency of adaptation and habituation—"the effortless custody of automatism" – increases.[462]

Dewey explicitly links the habituation of the subject to its qualitative surroundings—the aesthetics of the environment. Our growth depends on the sensations our bodies exchange with others like and unlike our own. Like Levinas, Dewey holds that we live from our sensations. We are organisms whose habits serve to increase "susceptibility, sensitiveness, responsiveness." An individual's capacity to exist, or their power, is directly determined by the exchange of old habits for new sensations:

> Thus even if we think of habits as so many grooves, the power to acquire many and varied grooves denotes high sensitivity, explosiveness. Thereby an old habit, a fixed groove if one wishes to exaggerate, gets in the way of the process of forming a new habit while the tendency to form a new one cuts across some old habit. Hence instability, novelty, emergence of unexpected and unpredictable combinations. The more an organism learns—the more, that is, the former terms of a historic process are retained and integrated in this present phase—the more it has to learn, in order to keep itself going; otherwise death and catastrophe.[463]

Given that sensitivity here entails a capacity to take on and annihilate form, which is to say, indicates a certain plasticity, increased exposure to different sensory environments can lead to the sedimentation or explosion of an individual's ethos (habituated identity, the law of the individual). It is not so much that life itself is inherently explosive. It is the *power* of the organism that is explosive. This power is dictated by the disposition of the organism, including its set of habitual circuits, state of physical maturation, and possibilities for experimentation. It is fascinating to note that Dewey regards death here as the inability of an organism to continue learning. In other words, death is the extinction of growth, or the absolute slackening of plasticity. Life, by contrast, is the force which encourages novelty by learning how to replace old habits with new ones.

Aesthetic Animation

In *The Meaning of the Body* Johnson shows how important the aesthetic dimension is for the body to make sense of its environment. He argues that the aesthetic is usually downplayed in our discussions of experience. This happens because we take a certain limitation in our knowledge of qualitative experience to indicate a limitation of experience itself. Put otherwise, we disregard the qualitative dimension of experience because it belongs to the difficult-to-articulate affective register, rather than the less unruly perceptual and cognitive. The present rehabilitation of sensation is motivated by a desire to redraw the limits of experience. Even phenomenology, Johnson notes, "has a hard time with the qualitative dimension, for it is easier to describe the *structural* aspects of experience than it is to describe felt qualities. The tendency is thus always to look for the constituting structures of experience, at the expense of the actual experience of qualities."[464] Following Dewey, Johnson shows that qualities—as liminal events occurring between bodies, as milieus—are felt and, as such, allow the sentience of the body to discern immanently the meaning of events and objects. "Once we are struck, caught up, seized," writes Johnson, "only then can we discriminate elements within our present situation."[465] Sensations are responsible for instigating and giving meaning to the dialogue between subject and object.

What is it that discriminates? *Our bodies.* Their sensorimotor and neural makeup, both the products of material growth, "determine what stands out, for us, from a situation or scene. Therefore, how we 'take' objects would change if our bodies, brains, or environments changed in some radical way."[466] Rarely radical in act, our bodies are constantly adapting to the aesthetic provocations of their surroundings. Only upon this instigation (*sens*) are they moved to adapt and make sense of things. As Johnson concludes,

> we are living in and through a growing, changing situation that opens up toward new possibilities and that is transformed as it develops. That is the way human meaning works, and none of this happens without our bodies, or without our embodied interactions within environments that we inhabit and that change along with us.[467]

Our bodies take on the qualitative meanings of their environments. Their integrity depends on these meanings which first register on their sensibility. Sensibility regulates their capacity to be formed and deformed by the aesthetic dimension, for better or worse.

It must be noted that a similar idea is available in Casey's invaluable work on place. Casey writes of the disorienting effect of wild places or wilderness on the body. Built places, by contrast, serve to orient and sustain the properly human dimensions of the body.[468] Disorientation in wild or natural places is, he writes, "often radically independent of human corporeal intentionality, to the point of challenging and undermining this intentionality."[469] This point is precisely what we indicated as deficient in Merleau-Ponty's analyses, particularly with respect to his treatment of violence. What we realize in the wilderness, for Casey, is that body and world are only reversible in familiar, manageable places. Everyday places. And yet, the radical independence that wild places present to us is only radical as an excess of intentional content, as a surplus of meaning. That is, their independence is only relative to the reach of everyday phenomenological experience, which means that the source of their disorienting effect can only be inferred from within the subject-world correlation. Are they really wild, or do they just appear so? Wild places tell us that the intentional arc of our bodies does not constitute the world, but the phenomenology of wild place stops here. It fails to tell us what the excess of intentionality consists of, what savage power is capable of disorienting the intentional arc.[470] As we have seen, this excess is aesthetic, a surplus of sensations. But this is an excess that resides in even our most familiar places; we simply fail to notice, precisely because they are familiar. "Wilderness" is all around us.

Places are liable to orient us as much as disorient us. This is just as true of built places as wild ones, and it is precisely what makes architectural design so important, and why specialists are needed to carry out this design work. Otherwise, disorienting places are more likely to be constructed. My claim at this point is that disorientation as well as orientation spring from the sensory environment, not just the sphere of intentionality. Our bodies receive and respond to environmental directives that cannot become the object of intentionality. Or, if they can, it is only upon reflection. Because they contact the body's sensibility directly, they animate us automatically, and this animation—of which reflection is a part—is always one step ahead of our intentions. It is in this sense that they exceed the phenomena of perception and elude our volition. These directives, what Lingis calls *imperatives*, are ambivalent. They are volatile. Every place, I would argue, harbors a volatility because every place is constituted by an aesthetic dimension with the potential to affect us in ways that accommodate and/or diminish us.

Environmental Imperatives

Sensations are imperatives. Following Kant's distinction, we could ask: do sensuous imperatives command hypothetically or categorically?[471] As we pursue our practical aims environmental aesthetics offer numerous scenes, settings, and pathways, each with its own sensory atmosphere. In most cases I am able to choose from a finite set of routes to my destination. I leave my house to buy groceries. There is a busy street with cars, buses, and pedestrians that leads to the market; there is a quieter residential street that also leads to the market. I must take some street, but the specific one I choose is up to me. Or at least it seems that way. Perhaps I am lured in a particular direction by the promise of a singular set of sensations, so I choose it because of what it promises me? This is the hypothetical dimension. Now, once I am committed to a single route (is it one of my habitual circuits?) I find myself inserted in a sensory milieu that makes unique claims on my body's sensory apparatus. My body is commanded categorically by the sensations comprising the milieu because it cannot but receive and respond to these sensations, which are, in Lingis's words, "not reactions to physical causality nor adjustments to physical pressures, nor free and spontaneous impositions of order on amorphous data, but responses to directives."[472] Our carnal sensibility obeys environmental commands as they are given, but not necessarily as a form of subjection. Sensibility, because it is of the same environment to which it responds, is precisely what enables the body to get along in that environment. Sensibility is the body's freedom, but a freedom bestowed upon it from without.[473] The sensory imperative is a heteronomous imperative.

Elaborating on the imperative, Lingis takes up Merleau-Ponty's notion of the levels of perception. Lingis writes of

> the level of light which our gaze adjusts to and sees with as it looks at the illuminated contours that surface and intensify, the level of the sonority our hearing attunes to as it harkens to sounds and noises that rise out of it, the level of the tangible our posture finds as our limbs move across the contours and textures of tangible substances....[474]

What makes the levels different from the objects of perception is that the former are decidedly *ungraspable*. Their adumbrations cannot be explored or enumerated, for they have no profiles. Our bodies cannot pursue a better hold on them, cannot enter into a dialectical relation which slowly converges on their essence. To engage a level, the body "adjusts to it, is sustained by it, moves with it and according to it."[475] In a word, the body is animated by the aesthetic of the levels. A place, or the world taken as the totality of places, is composed of a nexus of levels. Its style is determined by this nexus which cannot be "survey[ed] from above." The style of a place is something our bodies "catch on to by moving with it." It is not given to us in perception, but engaged as an imperative whose force comes from the "sensorial patterns" which order intentionality.[476] If perception wants to perceive things, it must adjust itself to the levels in which things are situated. To pursue the profiles of objects, the body must subject itself to the shifting qualitative dimension of the levels. The levels are elemental and, therefore, a kind of depth in which the world is immersed. It is because we are immersed in this depth, not set over against it, that it cannot be grasped by perception, only yielded to or traversed.

From an aesthetic perspective we can conceive the identity of a place as composed of an indeterminate series of sensations, the nexus of levels that gives this series its specific dimensions, and the circuits of behavior they engender. The body's identity is susceptible to the imperative force of each of these environmental aspects. And insofar as these aspects are perpetually shifting and prone to a range of sensory variations, we could say that a place's sensory identity is never fixed in its form, but maintains the integrity of a haecceity—a metastable and coherent, yet precarious, aggregate of sensory qualities. Of course we can say that this aggregate points us toward a unified object, but does that not unnecessarily reduce the complexity of the sensory content to a simple substance or telos? Or rather, can we not think of the object as radiating its complex of qualities outward, and therefore as a multiplicity exploding its apparent unity? To imagine this would be to think from the perspective of the object, or to take an object-oriented approach to embodiment.

Given that the bodies that populate a place are partly responsible for that place's sensory content, whose directives command bodies to respond in particular ways, the identity of the bodies situated within a place will also have the character of a haecceity. The integrity and intensity of the place gets reflected in the body. Consequently, the range of sensations and affects the body is capable of gets determined by the range of sensations and affects it receives from its environment. At any given time the singular constitution or dispositionality of a body is made possible by its plasticity.

Metabolism

The critical takeaway here can be illustrated with an appeal to the biological concept of *metabolism*. In our consideration of the aesthetics of place, the identity of bodies, and the alimentary aspect of sensation, we have worked toward a philosophical encounter with metabolism. Biologically speaking, metabolism is a fact. Ontologically, it describes the genesis of form and exemplifies the plastic nature of bodies, both organic and inorganic. Organic bodies are aggregates of matter and void, "void mostly, crisscrossed by the geometry of force," as Jonas puts it.[477] Through the metabolic process the organic body trades its matter with the matter of its surroundings. This exchange gives rise to a "living form" whose matter is never the same from one moment to the next. No identical core persists through the metabolic process, which means that an organism is not the same as a machine understood in the usual sense. As Jonas says, "Metabolism thus is the constant becoming of the machine itself—and this becoming itself is a performance of the machine: but for such performance there is no analogue in the world of machines."[478] Writing of the body-world interface, Andrieu strikes a similar note about the non-mechanical individuation of the metabolic process:

> As an interface, the body doesn't remain passive: it doesn't obey the orders of the nervous system in a servile manner, neither is it an objective reflection of the world. Failing to be this recording chamber, according to the mechanical metaphor, the human body is the way in and out, through which the inside communicates with the outside (and vice-versa). This crossing is subjectifying in the sense that the matter of the body is the result of this building up interaction.

> By "subjectifying" I mean the movement which singularizes each human body by successive incorporations. Subjectivity is a result, in continuous movement, of adaptation and regulation.[479]

From the perspective of biological metabolism the organism is a material event, a function of metabolism, not the converse.[480] From the ontological perspective metabolism offers us a conception of identity as active self-integration and renewal, as the integration of a fluctuating multiplicity.

On the one hand, the material exchange that bodies conduct with the world replenishes their form. On the other hand, our perceptual dialogue enables us to maintain our balance in the phenomenal world; it helps keep the world intact, manageable. The individual on this materialist view—which Andrieu describes as "dynamic" and Bennett calls "vital"—develops a certain degree of freedom in its form, but it remains bound to the environment by and for its matter. In Jonas's words, the individual is "needfully free."[481] Our freedom is our ability to negotiate the determinate indeterminacy offered by the world.

The biological concept of metabolism applies only to organic, living beings. It need not be so limited in application, however. The concept can be profitably co-opted by the carnal ontology under development here, and extended so as to describe inorganic relations. As Bennett writes,

> The activity of metabolization, whereby the outside and inside mingle and recombine, renders more plausible the idea of a vital materiality. It reveals the swarm of activity subsisting below and within formed bodies and recalcitrant things, a vitality obscured by our conceptual habit of dividing the world into inorganic and organic life.[482]

To illustrate the aberrant materialism exemplified by this metabolic process, we turn to Yukio Mishima's autobiographical meditation on identity, *Sun and Steel*, a text which allegorizes the plasticity of the body. *Sun and Steel* recounts Mishima's turn away from words and toward the body, namely, his initiation into the world of bodybuilding.

Mishima recognizes the human tendency toward automatism of mind and body. But he also sees that habits are not destinies: they can be molded and redirected, not just intentionally but also materially. We are not actually automata. As Bergson has shown, following Félix Ravaisson, habits link us into the mechanisms of nature and often act as efficient responses to the directives contained therein.[483] The sun provides a directive for Mishima.[484] Its rays are absorbed into his body and incorporated into the surface of his skin. In a similar fashion the steel of the weights he lifts gets incorporated into his musculature. These are not metaphors. Mishima writes: "Little by little ... the properties of my muscles came increasingly to resemble those of the steel. This slow development, I found, was remarkably similar to the process of education, which remodels the brain intellectually by feeding it with progressively more difficult matter."[485] Mishima does not literally ingest steel, although his body certainly does take in the vitamins provided by the sunlight. Nevertheless, Mishima's body lives from, metabolizes the steel no less than the sun. His body engages organic and inorganic matter and, enacting an unnatural participation, converts both into muscle. According to Lingis's description,

> In the coupling of organism with steel, the vital substance with the extreme condensation of night and death, there was not competent intentional force shaping inert substance into implements, but *transference of properties*. The properties that came to compose the excess musculature came from the steel and were its own properties. In the contact with the substance of steel, Mishima found a body become ferric substance.[486]

This muscle not only gives him strength, it provides his form as well. The form emerges from the circuitous relation which obtains between body and milieu, both of which must be regarded as organic/inorganic composites.[487]

The idea that Mishima metabolizes sun and steel is more than metaphor. His body is sculpted and polished by repetitive exposure to metal and solar energy. Sun and steel territorialize his body and augment his vitality. He exchanges for this his sweat, vitamins, calories, pallor. In his words, he transforms "the silence of death into the eloquence of life."[488] His writer's body, with its distinctive habits and traits, is molded into the body of a weightlifter and begins to signify differently, in the code of the bodybuilder. This signification is transmitted through a new set of sensations. The bodybuilder's circuit of training lends Mishima's body its stability, its integrity—its power. The circuit enables him to cut into certain material flows and generate a new form. Mishima is a machine, but not in the mechanical sense. The organic/inorganic metabolism of Mishima's body demonstrates the machinic process, described by Deleuze and Guattari, and allows us to see that insofar as each one of us metabolizes materials from the natural and social environment—including affects and sensations, signs and gestures, rituals and mannerisms—our corporeal identity is literally formed by what we inhabit. Metabolism exemplifies plasticity just as well as any other process.[489]

Bodies/Buildings

Some architectural theorists think about body/building relations in a similar way. They consider the sensory design of a building as fundamental to the experience of place precisely because the body's sensibility is susceptible to the qualities endemic to a particular building. There is both an aesthetics and an ethics of design at work in sentiments of this kind. In *Atmospheres* the architect Peter Zumthor writes about how the "atmosphere" of a building is its rhythm, which we pick up "through our emotional sensibility."[490] He elaborates a series of points about how to generate atmosphere, which include sensory and material considerations:

> It's like our own bodies with their anatomy and things we can't see and skin covering us—that's what architecture means to me and that's how I try to think about it. As a bodily mass, a membrane, a fabric, a kind of covering, cloth, velvet, silk, all around me. The body! Not the idea of the body—the body itself! A body that can touch me.[491]

> In his meditation on atmosphere, he exhibits a distinct sense of how the body is immediately affected by the building it inhabits, and how the body demands certain architectural qualities for its well-being. He considers temperature: "It is well-known that materials more or less extract the warmth from our bodies."[492] Atmosphere, I would argue, is just another name for the singular sensory structure of a space.

Juhani Pallasmaa writes in "An Architecture of the Seven Senses" about how our bodies adopt the structure of buildings in their skeletal structure and bodily sensations.[493] He argues that "Every touching experience of architecture is multi-sensory; qualities of matter, space, and scale are measured equally by the eye, ear, nose, skin, tongue, skeleton and muscle. Architecture involves seven realms of sensory experience which interact and infuse each other."[494] The identity of a space is distinct and can be apprehended by the senses. Hollow spaces resonate with emptiness, whereas furnished spaces will have an aural identity specific to the arrangement, quantity, and quality of the furnishings.[495] He summarizes how the identity of architect and building merge in the design process, and how this identity is passed on to the building's patrons:

> an architect internalizes a building in his body; movement, balance, distance and scale are felt unconsciously through the body as tension in the muscular system and in the positions of the skeleton and inner organs. As the work interacts with the body of the observer the experience mirrors these bodily sensations of the maker. Consequently, architecture is communication from the body of the architect directly to the body of the inhabitant.[496]

Pallasmaa's phenomenological convictions win the day, however, and he concludes that while sensations engage the physical body, "the generative force lies in the intentions."[497] I would contend that while intentions do indeed propel our engagement with places, it is the directives embedded in places—built and natural—that initially strike the body. It is strange that Pallasmaa does not concede this point, for his analysis emphasizes the role of the skin in the experience of architecture. The skin, it seems to me, only takes on an intentional aspect when it directly contacts some object, not when it senses an atmosphere. And even then it is questionable whether or not it is intentional in the sense that vision or imagination is. I would claim, following Levinas, that the skin is precisely that sense organ which testifies to the primacy of sensation over perception because it is constantly processing environmental information that never rises to the level of conscious representation.

Our bodies are of the environment, but not identical to it. Merleau-Ponty says the same thing about the flesh, but his exposition leaves us wanting a fuller account of how bodies are individuated from and eventually annihilated by the flesh's general element. The concepts of metabolism and growth offer us a picture of the individual as at once attached to and independent of its environment. This is not a relation of reversibility, but one of volatile transaction. The transaction can go off well or it can go badly. The individual is not fully determined by its situation, although it is fundamentally enabled by it. Who is this individual? It is the body which refers to itself as "I" and understands itself as a singular locus of sensations, passions, and actions, and which feels itself limited by and attached to a particular set of material, cultural, and linguistic circumstances.

Following up this view of individuation, we can conceive the body as a singular locus of sensations (haecceities), or as a specific conspiracy of environmental impressions which define an exact position, a longitude and a latitude.[498] A body can be anything, but it will always be defined or mapped according to the ratio governing it as a composite of simple bodies and the affective, anonymous forces traversing the composite at a given moment.[499] On this reading sensations are neither mere epiphenomena produced in the mind nor content merely inferred from perception. They are productive of clearly demarcated bodily responses, what we might call, with Dewey, experiences: "An experience has a unity that gives it its name, *that* meal, that storm, that rupture of friendship. The existence of this unity is constituted by a single *quality* that pervades the entire experience in spite of variation of its constituent parts."[500] This quality need not be simple. Indeed, most experiences are differentiated by a multiplicity of qualities that we identify as a singularity. That bodies undergo or suffer experiences implies that experiences are objectively given and generate their own form. That we metabolize the qualities which pervade experiences—that experiences shape who we are and what we can do—means that we become who we are along with our experiences. Subjectivity is produced as this qualitative becoming.[501]

Qualities are neither atomistic nor indeterminate. They do not derive their form from a thing or lose their autonomy just because they are "attached" to a thing, but rather they give rise to the form and qualitative identity of the thing as an assemblage of potential sensations. This idea is found in Mach as well as James: "Thing, body, matter, are nothing apart from the combinations of elements—the colors, sounds, and so forth—nothing apart from their so-called attributes."[502] The same can be said of space, as well as the bodies that populate that space. As James writes, "Space *means* but the aggregate of all our possible sensations."[503] Consequently, the body becomes the site of these sensations, each and every one of which leaves a trace that makes it impossible for the body to undergo the same impression twice.[504] Its disposition is constantly changing with its environment. In this way bodies are at every moment individual aesthetic events whose power to produce sensible effects is constituted by the aesthetic experiences they suffer. Power, then, is a *plastic disposition*—autonomous in effect but relational in constitution. Death, on this view, is simply the exhaustion of the individual's power, or the transgression of the threshold that defines the individual's power at a particular moment. When your body ceases to produce the sensations that define you, you have become something else. You begin to produce new sensations, engender a new power, however enfeebled or strengthened. Your matter continues, reincarnated, in an infinite succession of new metabolic events. This is your immortality.

The Principle of Aesthetic Individuation

There is no reductionism involved here. What I have attempted is to render life and individuality in aesthetic terms, and to do so according to a corporeal ontology that avoids, if I have succeeded at all, both transcendent principles and anthropocentrism. This is not in the interest of homogenizing the diversity of life, but in affirming the singular complexity of each individual and flattening the field of being. One of the primary benefits of shifting the discourse of embodiment to the aesthetic level is that it allows us to displace the problems of environmental philosophy—in particular the animality/humanity, artificial/natural, and nature/culture debates—onto a different plane. This opens new non-anthropocentric avenues for interrogation and new possibilities for solving old problems. It might be objected that such a shift of emphasis leads to a reduction of the complexities of our experience and is an attempt to translate the myriad qualitative aspects of life into quanta of stimuli. On the contrary, it *affirms* the complexity found in every corner of material life and challenges the hierarchical ontologies that anxiously defend the sanctity of only one form of life—the human. It also affirms that sensing is not at all a mechanical process.

Toward these ends I have adduced a theory of corporeal plasticity which is both phenomenological and materialist, and derived from this theory an immanent form of the imperative as well as a principle for valuing the diversity of aesthetic experiences. We can call this the *principle of aesthetic individuation*, which runs as follows: since a body's sensory identity is determined by the sensory blueprint of its environment, that body's power to affect and be affected will only be as complex as the totality of its aesthetic experiences. Since this principle has relied on an unorthodox conception of sensation (which I have developed piecemeal in each of my chapters), I would like to reprise sensation's several aspects.[505]

Aspects of Sensation

First, sensations are *objective*. An object, for instance, is recognizable as an aggregate of qualities apprehensible by our senses. We imagine that even when we are not there to apprehend it the object retains a real power (or disposition) to produce roughly the same aggregate of sensations. In some cases—pain, for instance—we feel ourselves attacked from outside by sensations. They lead an autonomous life; this autonomy is evinced in the resistant aspect of a plastic body, its capacity to hold a form, even if only for a moment. Autonomy derives from the form assumed by sensations conspiring to produce bodies and bodies conspiring to produce complex corporeal systems like dust clouds, forests, traffic patterns, schools, and flocks—however fleeting or precarious these conspiracies may be—for it is their form that allows them to stand out from, stand up to, connect with, and attract other objects. The objective (autonomous) aspect is needed to explain where disruptive and violent sensations come from, or how, as Levinas puts it, sensation breaks up a system.

Second, sensations are *relational*. They only affect, or make sense, when they come into contact with bodies. Their effects are a matter of contrast, as James notes.[506] Put otherwise, we could say that the meaning of a sensation is diacritical; its effectiveness depends on the field of sensations it is embedded in. As diacritical, a sensation's effect will be neither intrinsically nor extrinsically determined. Its effect will be determined between subject and object, or object and object. This leads us to a more democratic view of bodies, one that maintains that sensations are traded between any and all bodies (inanimate as well as animate). The odd idea that two inanimate bodies can exchange sensations is not unprecedented. As Heller-Roazen explains:

> Even in Greek psychological writings, the meaning of the term [*aisthesis*] was fluid, and it could stray very far from the field of human perception. At times, it was even employed to mark the affections of the inanimate, in punctual opposition to the animate: a fifth-century treatise in the Hippocratic corpus, for example, has the verb *aisthanesthai* characterize the effects of the wind on lifeless things."[507] This is a conception of sensation that is not available in Aristotle, for whom even plants—let alone inanimate objects—cannot sense because they lack the sensitive part of the soul. That is, they lack *aisthesis*. I wish to retain the Hippocratic idea that all things are moved by sensation, and this because sensation does not happen *in* the sensing being, but rather *on* them, and is not restricted exclusively to beings with souls.[508]

Third, since sensations harbor the potential to enable or disable bodies, they are said to be *ambivalent*. This aspect has particular import for the ethics of embodiment. The volatility of sensations must be taken into consideration when designing buildings and public spaces, or when considering the preservation or destruction of a natural environment, for example.[509] An ethics based on the plasticity of the body as I have described it will necessarily be a kind of environmental ethics. It will pay specific attention to the aesthetic scaffolding of the environment and the way in which aesthetics fosters and diminishes our body's power to exist. Generally, it will be concerned with the sensory aspect of places, although a theory of art could also be envisaged. Above all, given how the body's composition relies on the composition of its environment, the concept of integrity will be central. The principle of aesthetic individuation dictates this.

Fourth: sensations are *alimentary*. We live from our sensations, but we also die by them. Since they are also ambivalent, they need to be regarded as both nourishment and poison. Their intensity and affectivity will determine whether they enable or disable our bodies. Our corporeal plasticity remains needfully vulnerable to them.

Fifth, sensations belong to nothing and no one: their liminality, objectivity, and ambivalence entail a certain detachment or *anonymity*. When we say that we "have" sensations, what we describe is a particular bodily response *to* a sensation. The response operates below the perceptual level which would determine it as "mine," as personal. Once we have noticed it, the sensation has already seized us. When we project sensations from our bodies, they can be attributed to us only to a degree. Try as we might, we cannot regulate completely our own aesthetic signification. And insofar as our bodies are a composite of sensations, and we are nothing more than our bodies, there is no substantial "person" to which the sensations attach as properties. Sensations affect *a* body; they produce *this* body. Never is this body or its aesthetic properly one's own.

Finally, sensation *belongs to the past*. Although they are actualized in the present, their presentation is always delayed. And this delay is absolute. The body's receptivity always lags behind the efficacy of sensation. The body, once it takes notice of its sensory input, has already had its plasticity activated. If sensation can be said to exist or reside anywhere, it is in the past which has never been present, the virtual past.

I have here presented an image of the body as plastic and adduced evidence for preferring it over the theories of embodiment offered by Merleau-Ponty (reversibility) and Levinas (susceptibility). This image could not have taken shape without certain insights ascertained by the phenomenologists, however. I take my efforts to have balanced their perspective with supplemental evidence from non-phenomenological theorists, and to have outlined a new theory of sensation that may serve as a program for future work on sensation. My purpose in the final chapter is to draw some of the practical consequences of the theory of corporeal plasticity.

Conclusion

Plasticity and Power

> The palace is the body of the king. Your body sends you mysterious messages, which you receive with fear, with anxiety. In an unknown part of this body, a menace is lurking, your death is already stationed there; the signals that reach you warn you perhaps of a danger buried in your own interior. The body seated askew on the throne is no longer yours, you have been deprived of its use ever since the crown encircled your head; now your person is spread out through this dark, alien residence that speaks to you in riddles. But has anything really changed? Even before, you knew little or nothing about what you were. And you were afraid of it, as you are now.
>
> Calvino, "A King Listens"

Assemblage, fold, eddy, haecceity; sensory, behavioral, and habitual circuits... Throughout this book an entire vocabulary has accumulated to describe and defend the immanence of the body so that, in spite of Paul Klee's epitaph, the body is indeed "caught in immanence" (EM 188/87). But what about transcendence? What about freedom? To be sure, the phenomenologists never leave these questions out of their equation. So it would not be unfair to object that the foregoing account of embodiment is slanted to the extent that it suppresses the dimension of transcendence operative in Merleau-Ponty and, crucially, in Levinas. It has, as a result, said relatively little about the freedom afforded by transcendence.

Post-Dualist Freedom

If I have passed over freedom in silence, it is because I think freedom is something only the committed dualist has to worry about. Post-dualists have turned to the body precisely to discard such concerns. Or, put differently, what the post-dualist means by freedom may be difficult for the dualist to recognize *as* freedom. But just because we have evacuated the interiority of the subject (classical locus of free will) and given up on liberal individualism, however, does not mean that we must resign ourselves to some vulgar determinism. That much should be apparent at this point. The challenge to be met by philosophies of immanence is to account for the "freedom" of the body in terms of "corporeal surfaces, in terms of rotations, convolutions, inflections, and torsions of the body itself," as Grosz puts it.[510] In other words, to transcribe the freedom of the lived body into the power of the body as a dynamic materiality. Toward this end it is worth unpacking (with the aid of Spinoza) the following lesson from Merleau-Ponty: *the power of the body is an expression of the system of appearances it encounters*. Put otherwise, the body is—not unlike the electrified Rugendas of Aira's novella of the landscape painter—the radiant center of a sensory economy.[511]

Along the way I have sometimes drawn a distinction between the ontological and practical power of the body, implying that there is a real difference between what the body is and what it can do. Against Levinas I suggested that ontology is, indeed, prior to ethics. Here I want to plainly assert that this only a nominal distinction. The power of the body to exist and the power of the body to act are in fact metaphysically equivalent. This principle I adopt from Spinoza, who writes in the *Ethics* that "the power or conatus by which [a thing] endeavors to persist in its own being, is nothing but the given, or actual, essence of the thing." Furthermore: "since the ability to exist is power, it follows that the greater the degree of reality that belongs to the nature of a thing, the greater amount of force [*vis*] it has from itself for existence."[512] A thing's essence is its internal necessity, the law ordering its nature, which is always composed of a number of bodies acting together as an individual. In the language I have developed here, the power of the body is equal to the disposition of its plasticity. To see how this might be borne out in Merleau-Ponty we must distinguish between his theory of freedom and his theory of power.

The phenomenological portrayal of freedom makes up the entire closing chapter of *Phenomenology of Perception*. True to form, Merleau-Ponty's interrogation of the nature of freedom splits the difference between absolute determinism and absolute freedom. To discard the former he affirms that it is evident through reflection that I am not a thing; I do not find myself objectified by a situation, I take a position in it, so I must therefore be more than a thing. I am a consciousness too. Sympathetic to Sartre's Kantian defense of the absolute freedom of the ego, Merleau-Ponty identifies consciousness as our "power of escape" from the causal relations which obtain between mere things (PP 434, 435/496, 497). From one angle we find that the limitations placed on action are self-imposed by the projects we choose to undertake. As Merleau-Ponty puts it, "there are no obstacles in themselves" (PP 441/503). A fallen tree blocking the street is only an obstacle if I desire to travel down that street. What I can and cannot do is dictated by the synchrony achieved between my practical intentions and the existential field opened up by those intentions. Unlike things, I possess the power of transcendence. That is, I am free to move beyond the given. Things, for lack of consciousness, are condemned to immanence.

The practical intentions I seek to fulfill can only come to fruition within a field of behavior inflected by social, historical, physical, cultural forces. My conscious body is invested with these forces, and must make sense of them, in order to act. Freedom depends upon this field for its meaning and, therefore, its possibilities. The field is instrumentally necessary to the movement of transcendence enacted by freedom, but it is also what gets transcended by consciousness. Conscious action generates its own obstacle course, although it does not completely control it. The autonomy of the course is revealed by the fact that my body suffers intentions it does not choose (PP 440/502). Descartes, Berkeley, and others used a similar argument to prove that sense experience is produced by something other than the sensing subject, that the world is not merely my illusion, but ruled by something other.

The "autochthonous significance" of the existential environment presents a system of appearances that the body must adapt itself to in order to thrive. To be free is to be able to confront competently the obstacles engendered by one's projects and to understand how intentional action squares with the resistances of the given. "Our freedom does not destroy our situation, but gears itself to it: as long as we are alive, our situation is open, which implies both that it calls up specially favoured modes of resolution, and also that it is powerless [*impuissante*] to bring one into being by itself" (PP 442/505). The immanence of the subject does not restrict freedom; rather, it obliges the subject to garner adequate sets of habits and styles of living that will allow it to escape from immanence and recreate its horizon of action (PP 443-444/505-507). An able body acquires its freedom through a dialogue with the existential field. A balance of creation and conformity determines the nature of this freedom:

> What then is freedom? To be born is both to be born of the world and to be born into the world. The world is already constituted, but also never completely constituted; in the first case we are acted upon, in the second we are open to an infinite number of possibilities. But this analysis is still abstract, for we exist in both ways *at once*. There is, therefore, never determinism and never absolute choice, I am never a thing and never bare consciousness. (PP 453/517)

The subject's identity is decidedly not given; it is achieved. Partly a matter of facticity, partly a matter of coping, its genuinely indeterminate possibilities are open, yet limited.

One of the key problems with the exoteric account of freedom found in the *Phenomenology* is its faith in body-world synchronization (reversibility), which was criticized in chapters two and three. This kind of faith contains remnants of a liberal individualism, as Dewey points out.[513] However, when we consider that Merleau-Ponty regards freedom also as a matter of *tolerating* the environmental conditions that determine what it can and cannot accomplish, the residual individualism begins to fade away. "Taken concretely, freedom is always a meeting of inner and outer ... and it shrinks without ever disappearing altogether in direct proportion to the lessening of the *tolerance* allowed by the bodily and institutional data of our lives" (PP 454/518). By shifting our attention away from how the subject overcomes his or her situation, and concentrating on how this situation imposes itself, resists or does violence to the subject, we come to see the power of embodiment in terms of determination instead of freedom. The advantage of this shift in perspective is that it allows us to abandon the language of inner and outer, consciousness and transcendence, without succumbing to absolute determinism. That is, it allows us to think the immanence of body and environment without completely giving up the notion of freedom, which is arguably what Merleau-Ponty aspired to when he gave up the dualism of his early text for the monistic ontology of the flesh.

How can we understand freedom as tolerance? One strategy would be to recast the weakness or vulnerability of the body as its power.[514] Another would be to extol the virtues of resignation and acceptance. These two options are ontologically and morally unattractive, precisely because we really want to figure out what our bodies can become, not just what they are. What then is the virtue of tolerance? In a word, *necessity*. Since an embodied subject never exists outside of an entanglement of bodies, understanding and affirming how these bodies enable and/or disable it is tantamount to realizing its freedom. The composition of a collective body, as we have seen, informs the disposition of each individual body involved in it. And it is the disposition of a body, or the specific state of its plasticity, that defines the range of what it can tolerate and accomplish in that state. Tolerance is thus governed by a threshold of power which expresses the dispositional plasticity of the body. For Merleau-Ponty this threshold is delimited by the body's habituation to environmental aesthetics.

To draw the practical consequences of this point let us now consider tolerance from the perspective of aesthetics, or what I have called the principle of aesthetic individuation. I will argue that the body's capacity to suffer and respond to appearances is closely tied to the diversity and intensity of appearances comprising its aesthetic environment, along with the habits it has accumulated in response to these appearances.

The Spinozist aspect of Merleau-Ponty's notion of freedom is scattered throughout the *Phenomenology*'s analyses of space, sensing, and things.

It is not quite esoteric, but it is less visible than his phenomenological account. It accompanies his remarks on appearances [*apparences*] and is contained in his discussion of how to view objectively an object or painting. Phenomenologically speaking, it is the case that the true identity of a painting appears to the viewer when he or she achieves the "privileged perception" necessitated by the painting—the point at which the painting reveals a maximum of clarity and richness. Articulated in spatial terms, "For each object, as for each picture in an art gallery, there is an optimum distance from which it requires to be seen" (PP 302/348). There is an imperative here: the viewer *must* situate herself in a specific location, dictated by the painting or object in question, if she is going to acquire "the power [*puissance*] of achieving a certain spectacle." Power in this scenario is determined by, writes Merleau-Ponty, "a certain kinaesthetic situation" to be negotiated by the body, which is permanently and constantly "enveloped" by a set of appearances that direct it to get a hold on the world (PP 303/349). Now, since the body is an object and a perceptual phenomenon as well, what is said here about how objects and paintings are to be rightly viewed and identified pertains as much to the body, insofar as the body is itself a work of art, or a collection of sensations commanding its own perceptibility (PP 150, 451/176, 514; CD 16/27).

Attempting to open up new avenues for ethical thinking, Foucault eventually asked about how we might fashion our own lives as works of art. "But couldn't everyone's life become a work of art? Why should the lamp or the house be an art object but not our life?," he asks.[515] As always, Foucault's question aims at discerning the limits of disciplinary regimes and the experiential prospects of disciplined bodies. Imagining Foucault's problem from the environmental angle, Merleau-Ponty prompts us to envisage the emancipatory potential of aesthetics, where the practical purpose of aesthetics would be to promote experiences that sculpt our sensibility and intensify the body's capacity to act. The *Phenomenology* consistently equates this capacity with our ability to negotiate the appearances that populate the environment. At many places in the text Merleau-Ponty denotes this capacity as our power (*pouvoir*, *puissance*), leaving us to distinguish the power of aesthetics as well as the aesthetics of power entailed in his metaphor of the body as work of art.

The question of corporeal power is necessarily a question of performance. The body acquires tools and prostheses, learns adaptive skills and behaviors, arranges and rearranges its repertoire of actions in order to act efficiently in and expand its world. Since I am my body, I am this performance, and my identity is glimpsed in the spectacle I stage. Just as my gait can be deciphered by a friend too far away to make out my face but close enough to see me walking, my bodily kinaesthetics betray who I am. In large measure this results from the cultivation of habit and, consequently, the arrangement and rearrangement of the body schema. Each rearrangement better equips the body with the "power [*pouvoir*] to respond" to the general field of action. This is not a power of understanding achieved through intellectual synthesis: it is a correlation of the habituated form of the body with the corporeal significance of the field of action (PP 142-144/166-169).

Tools and implements enrich our power to act by expanding the range of our technique and increasing our range of action. Habit is the general tool that allows us to enter into relations with the people, animals, cooking utensils, and vehicles that comprise the assemblages to which we belong. "Habit expresses our power [*pouvoir*] of dilating our being in the world, or changing our existence by appropriating fresh instruments" (PP 143/168).

Merleau-Ponty is articulating what Bennett, after Spinoza, calls "distributive agency." Distributive agency is the expression of a heterogeneous confederation of animate and inanimate bodies, supported by a network of scaffolding or infrastructure. A distributed agency gathers its power from sources local and distant, and concentrates this power into a singular effect.[516] Power here, once again, names the body's capacity to produce effects, to do what it is capable of doing. For Spinoza this capacity is equivalent to the singularity of bodily composition determined by the ratio of "motion and rest, quickness and slowness" a body maintains with other bodies, whether near or far.[517] The freedom of the body, then, is an expression of how it is (ontologically) determined within an assemblage or distributed agency.

The body's senses hold a power of their own. This power results from the sensations the senses take in and determines how they will tolerate future sensations. Colors, qualities, figures, and so forth present themselves to the power (*puissance*) of the senses, soliciting from the body a "type of behaviour" that is conditioned by habit and sediments into a habitus. These qualities come in from everywhere, all the time. The aesthetic is never turned off. It is worth recalling here an earlier citation: "The subject of sensation is neither a thinker who takes note of a quality, nor an inert setting which is affected or changed by it, it is a power [*puissance*] which is born into, and simultaneously with, a certain existential environment, or is synchronized with it" (PP 211/245). The subject is produced by a singular set of perspectives taken in from the aesthetic environment. It is likewise produced as a singular set of perspectives that it gives back to the environment. This metabolic process is reflected in the practical competence the body uses to orient itself in its habitat.

A competent body is one that knows how appearances will determine or affect its disposition as *this* body at *this* location (PP 302/348). A powerful body is one that can and will, additionally, fashion its habitat to intensify its habitus. Power synthesizes stability and productivity into creative tolerance. It is in this sense that the body is a work of art, that is, a unified composition that radiates a singular set of sensations and necessitates a particular perspective for its identity is to be apprehended. In Merleau-Ponty's words, the body is a "mosaic of given sensations" (PP 249/288). In the same way, Deleuze and Guattari, insisting on the autonomy of the work of art, cast the work of art (the thing and the body) as "*a bloc of sensations, that is to say, a compound of percepts and affects.*"[518] Under this definition the integrity of the body admits of a set of aesthetic and affective limits that cannot be transgressed if it is to remain the particular body it is; beyond these limits it becomes an altogether different body. Its aesthetic variability and the appearances it stages admit of no underlying agency, just a vital materiality that I am calling the plastic body.

An Explosive Form?

From her inquiry into brain plasticity Malabou sketches a number of political implications, some of which I have alluded to already. Among them, three call for commentary. First, the identity of an individual is to be situated somewhere between the twin processes of taking on form and annihilating form.[519] This is basically the definition of plasticity we have been working with all along. Second, individuals are to some degree capable of "self-fashioning" their identity. This is possible, on the one hand, because plasticity no longer subscribes to a substantial conception of the self and, on the other, because

> the plasticity of the self, which supposes that it simultaneously receives and gives itself its own form, implies a necessary split and the search for an equilibrium between the preservation of constancy (or, basically, the autobiographical self) and the exposure of this constancy to accidents, to the outside, to otherness in general (identity, in order to endure, ought paradoxically to alter itself or accidentalize itself).[520]

The autoconstitutive function of the subject is caught between its creative and adaptive impulses. It feeds off of the contradiction embodied in its simultaneous resistance to conformity and its desire to maintain itself by reproducing the norms of culture and remaining "flexible" to the demands of labor, citizenship, and so forth.[521] Malabou's paradoxical idea of exposure, which we also met very briefly in Foucault's notion of limit experiences, is critical to drawing the political consequences of plasticity.

Plasticity, however, is not flexibility. Flexibility is plasticity evacuated of its vitality and reduced to pure adaptation. The third point Malabou makes is that the vitality of plasticity entails the detonation of form, explosiveness. Plasticity is naturally explosive, and it is this explosiveness that transforms nature into freedom. She writes:

> On the one hand, the coincidence between formation and disappearance of form is diachronic: a past form cedes place to a new form, and one thus changes identity of "self" in the course of time. On the other hand, form is synchronic: the threat of the explosion of form structurally inhabits every form. All current identity maintains itself only at the cost of a struggle against its autodestruction: it is in this sense that identity is dialectical in nature.[522]

The dialectic of formation and explosion is meant, it seems to me, to salvage a conception of agency that respects the gap existing between the homeostatic impulse (self-preservation) and the creative impulse (self-production).[523] I hesitate to endorse the idea of explosiveness because it seems to me that, while plastic explosives are, of course, designed to blow things up, this does not mean that explosiveness is implicated in the concept of plasticity itself. At least, I would not wish to implicate it. I would instead prefer to avoid the problem of how a plastic body would reach the point of destroying its own form—what Malabou calls autodestruction—by ascribing the destructive force to the other. Her analyses of brain damage and the loss of identity that accompanies it seems to point us in this direction, but she also seems to be committed to the idea that plasticity is *inherently* capable of autodestruction.

Habits and body schemata, in the absence of violence, work to stabilize the integrity of the body. Radical transformation does not belong to plasticity as such, which is why it seems that Malabou's autodestruction requires further (psychoanalytic) elaboration.[524] This is not to say that plasticity tends naturally toward fixity or suspension, rather than creativity, but rather to assert that the material conditions of identity require that a number of disparate forces, foreign and domestic, must conspire for change to occur. Plasticity should therefore not be regarded as an impulse of any kind, creative or destructive, but instead as the generalized disposition of material bodies such as ours. A remark in *Plasticity at the Dusk of Writing* better captures the temperance of plasticity. "Plasticity," writes Malabou, "characterizes a regime of systematic self-organization that is based on the ability of an organism to integrate the modifications that it experiences and to modify them in return."[525] These modifications are germane to intercorporeity. Now, it is true that Nietzsche said, "I am no man, I am dynamite."[526] But saying that the nature of life is to discharge its power, as Nietzsche does here, is not the same as saying that life seeks to annihilate itself—unless what Malabou means by autodestruction is analogous to what Freud meant by the death drive, in which case the power of self-destruction lies not in the plasticity of the brain but in something else inside us.

Malabou's incorporation of explosiveness into her theory of plasticity responds to a worry, rightly voiced by Weiss, that the deterministic dimension of plasticity does not leave enough room for novelty and radical change, particularly the kind involved when unforeseen events compel us to revise our habitual circuits.[527] There are actually two concerns involved here.

The first is general: Weiss is unable to see how a deterministic ontology can account for the perceived novelty of experience. This supposes, of course, that genuine novelty exists. The second, more specific, concern judges that the Jamesian version of plasticity "makes it difficult to see how significant individual and social change can ever really occur once the character of the individual or of a particular social class has been firmly established."[528] For my part, I admit to skepticism about the kind of spontaneous, radical change invoked by Weiss. Or rather, if there is radical change, it is not spontaneous; it is always, at least in part, a yielding to what Michel Serres calls the "inconstancies and deviations" produced by "the agency of the storm that is the other."[529] In fact, if our condition as embodied beings is characterized by a fundamental plasticity, then spontaneous action would always be tempered by the material resistance of social and natural habits.[530] Which is not to say that there is no phenomenological evidence for the reality of chance or indetermination. Instead, it is to contend that "radical change or spontaneous innovation," if it exists, must be accounted for at the ontological level in a way that plasticity does not.[531] Otherwise, we need not assume that it actually exists.

Weiss is no doubt right to be on guard against plasticity's tendency toward fixity. While theoretically open to infinite permutations, our habits often do seem to become rigid or, at the limit, petrified. Our desire for organization and functional efficiency promote this social danger.[532] The power of plasticity faces the constant threat of fixity, homeostasis, sedimentation, conservatism, dogmatism, intolerance. Even though it does lend a necessary degree of stability to our corporeal disposition, fixity also signals the arrest of plasticity's capacity to yield to influences. Another name for this arrest is death. When the body can no longer tolerate transformation, whether because of illness, trauma, or structural disintegration, it has ceased to live. The challenge for the model of plasticity I am defending is to first conceive the plastic body's ontology, its structure and prospects for alteration; and, second, to exhibit some of the practical measures available for preserving the suppleness of plasticity and increasing the body's power to exist. The greater part of my effort has addressed the first prong of this challenge. Let us now distill some practical principles.

In Praise of Suppleness: Censorship and the Virtue of Exposure

The body is an aesthetic phenomenon. Its aesthetic composition is arranged according to the sensations it metabolizes from the environment. In order to maintain a suppleness of composition, the body must not only avoid circuits of experience that arrest its plasticity, it must actively *expose* itself to percepts and affects that intensify its power by bolstering its tolerance, that enable it to radiate new sensations and pleasurable affects.[533] This principle of exposure offers a counterargument to the defense of censorship inaugurated by Plato's expulsion of artists from the Kallipolis, and his disparagement of mimesis on both epistemological and pedagogical grounds. Aesthetic exposure offers the antithesis of censorship and an antidote to intolerance.

Censorship is enforced sensory deprivation. It is deliberate resistance to aesthetic exposure, enforced upon one individual who does not yet know what she can become, by another individual who already does know, but fears or rejects this potential. What gets censored is typically cited as painful, dangerous, or socially unsavory. The intention here might be admirable, especially when children are involved. But in order to be effective the censor must always presume to know what bodies can and will do. And yet, this is precisely the question which remains indefinitely open for each one of us. When we say that children are "impressionable," we mean to say that they are easily influenced, that influences can stick, and therefore that we must think twice about exposing them to "explicit" material. In this we both recognize and fear the maximally supple plasticity which, as infants, *requires* environmental and interpersonal stimulation for the child to adequately connect and grow with its surroundings.[534]

Given the advances of technology, evolutionary theory and genetic enhancement, as well as our posthuman aspirations and the pervasive desire to multiply the dimensions of the real, there is no precise way to calculate the possible transmutations of the body. The potential of the child is not a predetermined or natural fate, although it can be contrived to be so. The child possesses an internal force that Dewey identifies doubly as immaturity and plasticity, or the power to grow and develop dispositions that will enable the acquisition of new habits and, therefore, new powers to exist.[535] The vitality concentrated in the body of the child horrifies us, not because it is autodestructive, but because we cannot fathom what it may convert its impressions, explicit or otherwise, into. We cite its vulnerability to justify reinforcing our "regimes of perception," when we could instead encourage its plasticity to unleash its unimaginable power to grow through education and experimentation.[536]

Because we are ignorant of the future of our bodies, there is no telling which individual, social, or ecological compositions will enhance our power. Our ignorance should compel us to remain open to whichever aesthetics our bodies can tolerate, not just the fine, innocuous, beautiful, or sublime, but also the sinister, gruesome, disgusting, horrific—the totality of the real. When the identity of individuals necessarily depends on a panoply of local and foreign populations, then political fights—for media exposure, for arts endowments and education, for environmental protection, for ergonomic working conditions—are inherently ecological. Our ecological life is an assemblage of objects, humans, animals, energies, elements, and dark forces beyond our ken. The alterity that summons our responsibility, our responsiveness, lurks immanently in the very plasticity of this ecology. "*Plasticity*," writes Malabou, "designates the form of a world without any exteriority, a world in which the other appears as utterly other precisely because she is not someone else."[537] This world is not simply uncanny, it is eminently strange.

Embracing the principle of exposure requires a double affirmation. First, a Dionysian affirmation of "all that appears."[538] Second, an affirmation of chance encounters, of accidents that may or may not disrupt our tendencies toward fixity and intolerance. There is a pragmatic reason to face the obvious risks of exposure. We cannot know what encounters will yield, or what will become of us when faced with aesthetic forces that threaten to dismantle or reassemble our identity.[539] Even if we could attune our perception to the minute intricacies of the aesthetic, we would still be incapable of comprehending the impact sensations have on our capacity to act and be acted upon. They are forever anterior to perception; they strike straight at the center of the body, like lightning. As Deleuze and Levinas have taught us, the body is immediately seized by the rhythm of sensation and forced to participate in its own representation. Aesthetic experience produces a "unique situation where we cannot speak of consent, assumption, initiative or freedom, because the subject is caught up and carried away by it."[540] The aesthetic produces affects, and these affects individuate, but they do so anonymously and at the risk of disfiguration/deformation. Such is the diachronic and dissensual nature of sensation.[541]

If our aesthetic responses remain, from this perspective, aleatory and anonymous affairs, then we cannot know what aesthetics can do for us—or, better put, what it can do *to* us. We can only experiment to find out what works and where it takes us. This may come through self-fashioning, pushing the avant-garde, or constructing new environments and preserving the extant unique.[542] The options are diverse and should focus as much on the everyday as the extraordinary, since, as Paul Duncum argues, "ordinary, everyday aesthetic experiences are more significant than experiences of high art in forming and informing one's identity and view of the world beyond personal experience."[543] Experimentation keeps our plasticity supple, open to influences that can intensify our tolerance. It is *amor fati*, education by chance. As Dewey argues, the purpose of experimentation is to allow freedom to grow; education's purpose is to exercise our plasticity and thereby position us to democratize our social organization.[544] As goes the institution, so goes its subjects.

The principle of exposure should not be cast in a conservative light. It is not advocating that we, in the name of tolerance, expose ourselves to exotic experiences or new cultures or foreign agents merely for the sake of understanding the other. Nor is it echoing the humanistic ideal of exposing oneself to artwork in the name of moral edification. Its aspirations are more radical. When we expose our bodies to the entire domain of the aesthetic we effectively expose ourselves to deformation and welcome the possibility of reconfiguration, perhaps beyond recognition. And it is precisely our plasticity that would facilitate this potential deformation. The aesthetic harbors the potential to increase or decrease our power, or to transform us into something else altogether.

Diversification and annihilation compose the life of the environment. Some aesthetic experiences bring joy and pleasure, other pain and sadness. Trauma is a real possibility, but so is ecstasy. When we are affected our power is modified for better or worse. In either case affects exceed us at the same time as they individuate us, according to the dynamic nature of our corporeal disposition.⁵⁴⁵ "Affects are no longer feelings or affections; they go beyond the strength of those who undergo them," write Deleuze and Guattari.⁵⁴⁶ The paradox of exposure is that in order for a finite plastic body to stave off the inevitable compromise of its integrity (fixity or breakage), that body must risk exposure to deformation or death. It must be pushed to the outer limits of its threshold in order to figure out what it is and what it might accomplish. In Serres' words:

> If you want to save yourself, take risks. If you want to save your soul, do not hesitate, here and now, to entrust it to the variable storm. An inconstant aurora borealis burst forth in the night. It spreads, blazing and bleeding, like those footlights that never stop blinking, whether they are switched on or off. It either passes or doesn't, but flows elsewhere in a rainbow-coloured stream. You will not change if you do not yield to these inconstancies and deviations. More importantly, you will not know.⁵⁴⁷

Freedom is nothing other than the *dispositional necessity* of the body, or the capacity of the body to exist and act according to the law organizing its dynamic constitution. This necessity, which at once individuates the body as *this* singular individual with *this* singular threshold of power, is precisely what Spinoza calls the virtue and right of the body.⁵⁴⁸ As Balibar explains, "the individual's right includes all that he is effectively able to do and to think in a given set of conditions."⁵⁴⁹ As such, the power of an individual is necessarily limited by ecological factors: internally by the other bodies in the assemblage (friends), externally by those assemblages acting according to a different ratio of motion and rest (enemies). The freedom I call mine is a transient power, susceptible to the health and disease, joy and sadness, of the totality of animate and inanimate bodies with which I interact at any given time.

To be free is to understand as much as possible the myriad ways in which one's body is acted upon, restricted or enabled, by the bodies composing it as an individual—in other words, how individuals are determined. In Deleuze's terms, our power is mapped along the lines of longitude and latitude, intensities (affects) and extensities (components) that intersect our body.⁵⁵⁰

> We know nothing about a body until we know what it can do, in other words, what its affects are, how they can or cannot enter into composition with other affects, with the affects of another body, either to destroy that body or to be destroyed by it, either to exchange actions and passions with it or join with it in composing a more powerful body.[551]

Where Kant would offer a practical rationality immune to the contingencies of the corporeal world and its natural laws, Spinoza gives us a body whose freedom is necessitated by the field of causal encounters that engender its singularity. Insofar as we can diagram and negotiate these encounters—*which could not have been otherwise than they are*—we are said to be free.[552]

At any given moment we do not know what a body can do, or which encounters will intensify its capacity to affect and be affected. As Spinoza reminds us, "nobody as yet has determined the limits of the body's capabilities; that is, nobody as yet has learned from experience what the body can and cannot do, without being determined by the mind, solely from the laws of its own nature insofar as it is considered as corporeal."[553] One way to approach the transgression of these limits is to diagram all of the ways in which the body is etched, chiseled, painted, and polished by the aesthetic environment, and then to build and preserve sites that will work on us differently. Foucault named this work of emancipation the "critical ontology of ourselves," which he advocated as "an attitude, an ethics, a philosophical life in which the critique of what we are is at one and the same time the historical analysis of the limits that are imposed on us and an experiment with the possibility of going beyond them."[554] There is no telling how a particular aesthetic will strike us or how our senses will react to its stimuli. Despite this uncertainty, if we desire to do more than simply dwell in environments that reveal to us what we already know about ourselves, or reinforce the complex of habits that automate our habitus, then we will find ourselves compelled to speculate about and produce aesthetics that enable our bodies to realize unimaginable performances.

Notes

Foreword

1. Maurice Merleau-Ponty, *Phenomenology of Perception*, trans. Colin Smith (London: Routledge, 1962), 132.
2. Merleau-Ponty, *Phenomenology of Perception*, 131, 132.
3. Merleau-Ponty, *Phenomenology of Perception*, 141.
4. Merleau-Ponty, *Phenomenology of Perception*, 107-108.
5. Emmanuel Levinas, *Otherwise than Being*, trans. Alphonso Lingis (Pittsburgh: Duquesne University Press, 1974), 90.
6. Emmanuel Levinas, *Totality and Infinity*, trans. Alphonso Lingis (Pittsburgh: Duquesne University Press, 1969), 155.
7. Levinas, *Totality and Infinity*, 198.
8. Levinas, *Otherwise than Being*, 90, translation modified.
9. Levinas, *Totality and Infinity*, 50-51.
10. Levinas, *Totality and Infinity*, 65-66, italics omitted.

Chapter 1

11. Glen A. Mazis, *Earthbodies: Rediscovering Our Planetary Senses* (Albany: State University of New York Press, 2002), 3.
12. César Aira, *An Episode in the Life of a Landscape Painter*, trans. Chris Andrews (New York: New Directions, 2006), 32-33.
13. Epicurus, "Principal Doctrines," II, in *The Extant Remains*, trans. Cyril Bailey (Oxford: Oxford University Press, 1926), 95, emphasis added.

14. Immanuel Kant, *Critique of Pure Reason*, trans. Werner S. Pluhar (Indianapolis: Hackett, 1996), Bxxvii-Bxxvii.

15. In this respect I am following Heidegger's idiosyncratic interpretation of Kant's first *Critique* as a work in "fundamental ontology," that is, an exploration of the understanding as the pre-ontological condition which gives rise to a theory of being qua being. This interpretation is given in Martin Heidegger, *Kant and the Problem of Metaphysics*, fifth edition, enlarged, trans. Richard Taft (Bloomington: Indiana University Press, 1997).

16. Immanuel Kant, *Critique of Judgment*, trans. Werner S. Pluhar (Indianapolis: Hackett, 1987), 260, 261.

17. Kant, *Critique of Judgment*, 261-262.

18. Kant, *Critique of Judgment*, 266-267.

19. Paul Guyer, *Kant and the Experience of Freedom* (Cambridge: Cambridge University Press, 1996), 37.

20. Guyer, *Kant and the Experience of Freedom*, 37.

21. The naturalistic fallacy is committed when a person tries to derive an "ought" from an "is," or when they deduce a moral claim from a natural (or ontological) fact. It is commonly acknowledged that G.E. Moore identifies the naturalistic fallacy in *Principia Ethica*.

22. See, for example, Gilles Deleuze's explication of the "Active and Reactive" in *Nietzsche and Philosophy*, trans. Hugh Tomlinson (New York: Columbia University Press, 1983), 39-72.

23. Lawrence Hass, *Merleau-Ponty's Philosophy* (Bloomington: Indiana University Press, 2008), 111, contends that we cannot regard Merleau-Ponty as a monist because there is always a *distance* between the behaving body and the self, as well as between the perceiver and the sensible. But Merleau-Ponty maintains that we *are* our bodies; this identification is one of the most innovative moments in his philosophy. Moreover, it is not enough to cite this distance, as Hass does; it must also be explained. Otherwise, we preclude monism a priori and introduce a mystery at the heart of the flesh. So what are we to make of this self? There is either a new dualism or a new monism at play in Merleau-Ponty and it seems we are given a choice: either continue to speak of a mysterious self that operates "in" or "as" the body, or speak of the body as a thing that senses and perceives (or a "subject-object"), as Merleau-Ponty does in "The Philosopher and His Shadow," in *Signs*, trans. Richard C. McCleary (Evanston: Northwestern University Press, 1964), 166/210. The latter is the more radical and preferable choice. It puts the burden of accounting for the non-physical subject on Merleau-Ponty's readers. The language is what is difficult here, but it is better to attempt to speak of the body's subjectivity as a sensing thing, rather than distinguish between the lived body and the physical body, a distinction that runs the risk of instituting a new dualism or perpetuating a theological element in Merleau-Ponty's philosophy.

24. Renaud Barbaras, *The Being of the Phenomenon: Merleau-Ponty's Ontology*, trans. Ted Toadvine and Leonard Lawlor (Bloomington: Indiana University Press, 2004), xxiv.

25. Throughout the book I use the terms "sensory," "sensitive," "sensuous," and "sensible" synonymously. I employ "sensual" only where there is a libidinal or erotic connotation.

26. See especially the work of Jean-Luc Nancy, for instance, *Corpus*, trans. Richard A. Rand (New York: Fordham University Press, 2008) and Jacques Derrida's *On Touching–Jean-Luc Nancy*, trans. Christine Irizzary (Stanford: Stanford University Press, 2005).

27. A notable exception in the phenomenological tradition to the claim that most philosophers of the body uphold a non-dualist perspective is Michel Henry. Henry provides a helpful contrast in the context of affectivity. Henry's notion of "autoaffection" retains certain personalist elements of dualism, but complicates the picture. Indeed, the problem of embodiment as the problem of incarnation is basically theological and calls for a dualistic solution, and Henry is certainly not the only philosopher who offers a theological phenomenology of incarnation. On this issue in general, see Natalie Depraz, "L'incarnation Phénoménologique, Un Problème Non-théologique?," *Tijdschrift voor Filosofie* 55, no. 3 (1993): 496-518.

28. For Hegel, see John Russon, *The Self and Its Body in Hegel's* Phenomenology of Spirit (Toronto: University of Toronto Press, 2001); for Kant, see Angelica Nuzzo, *Ideal Embodiment: Kant's Theory of Sensibility* (Bloomington: Indiana University Press, 2008); for Husserl, see James Dodd, *Idealism and Corporeity: An Essay on the Problem of the Body in Husserl's Phenomenology* (Dordrecht: Kluwer, 1997); for Heidegger, see Frank Schalow, *The Incarnality of Being: The Earth, Animals, and the Body in Heidegger's Thought* (Albany: State University of New York Press, 2007).

29. George Lakoff and Mark Johnson, *Philosophy in the Flesh: The Embodied Mind and its Challenge to Western Thought* (New York: Basic Books, 1999), xi. Their attention to Dewey and Merleau-Ponty in this text is unfortunately restricted to the Acknowledgements section. It should be noted that their admiration for Dewey and Merleau-Ponty comes from the fact that both thinkers were practitioners of what Lakoff and Johnson call "empirically responsible philosophy," which I interpret to mean that it is their *synthetic* methodology—the attempt to wed first-person and third-person perspectives—that Lakoff and Johnson find laudable about the pragmatist and phenomenologist.

30. Such is the conclusion drawn by the "eliminative materialism" of Paul and Patricia Churchland. See, for example, Patricia Smith Churchland, *Neurophilosophy: Toward a Unified Science of the Mind-Brain* (Cambridge, MA: MIT Press, 1989) and Paul Churchland, *The Neurocomputational Perspective: The Nature of Mind and the Structure of Science* (Cambridge, MA: MIT Press, 1992). For a more modest attempt to close the gap between phenomenology and the brain sciences, see the various attempts to "naturalize" phenomenology which are being met with resistance by phenomenology's orthodox adherents. See, for example, Bryan Smith, "Merleau-Ponty and the 'Naturalization' of Phenomenology," *Philosophy Today* 54 (2010): 153-162.

31. Mark Johnson, *The Meaning of the Body: Aesthetics of Human Understanding* (Chicago: University of Chicago Press, 2007), 175.

32. Johnson, *The Meaning of the Body*, 275-278.

33. Johnson, *The Meaning of the Body*, xi-xii.

34. Johnson points to Dewey's "principle of continuity" as the guiding principle of his naturalistic theory in *The Meaning of the Body*, 10. For a perspective on how phenomenology bridges the internalist/externalist gap, see Shaun Gallagher and Dan Zahavi, *The Phenomenological Mind: An Introduction to Philosophy of Mind and Cognitive Science* (London: Routledge, 2008), 121-126.

35. Lakoff and Johnson, *Philosophy in the Flesh*, 5.

36. Johnson, *The Meaning of the Body*, 103.

37. Yuriko Saito, *Everyday Aesthetics* (Oxford: Oxford University Press, 2007), 9.

38. Johnson, *The Meaning of the Body*, 27.

39. Phenomenological philosophy is at its best when it is "empirically responsible," as Lakoff and Johnson would say. But by the same token, we should not assume that all good philosophy is empirically verifiable. Philosophical critique, as Kant teaches in the first *Critique*, always leaves a bit of room for metaphysics. His principle is even more pertinent given the finite perspective afforded us as embodied minds.

40. To my knowledge, the only text which attempts a thorough philosophical history of the concept of sensation is D.W. Hamlyn's *Sensation and Perception: A History of the Philosophy of Perception* (New York: Humanities Press, 1961). Daniel Heller-Roazen's *The Inner Touch: Archaeology of a Sensation* (New York: Zone, 2007) secondarily serves as a history of sensation, but its focus is on the sense of sensing, not sensation itself.

41. Maurice Merleau-Ponty, *Phenomenology of Perception*, trans. Colin Smith (London: Routledge, 1962), 4/10. Hereafter cited parenthetically as PP with English and French page references.

42. This claim is perhaps a bit unfair in the case of Descartes, who was certainly interested in the senses, but Descartes' interest is more scientific or physicalist in texts like the *Treatise on Light, Optics,* and *Treatise on Man*.

43. Davide Panagia's *The Political Life of Sensation* (Durham: Duke University Press, 2009), 28.

44. See Tom Rockmore, *In Kant's Wake: Philosophy in the Twentieth Century* (Malden, MA: Blackwell, 2006), especially chapter 5, and Lee Braver, *A Thing of This World: A History of Continental Anti-Realism* (Evanston: Northwestern University Press, 2007).

45. This epistemological view, which sees the world of experience as fundamentally constructed by the mind of the observer, opposes the objectivist ontology of empiricism and the representational theory of knowledge it engenders. The world of the empiricist is populated by a multitude of discrete objects which exist in themselves and interact with each other according to causal laws. Humans come to know these objects, their properties, and their laws of interaction by observing their behavior. All of this information, claims the empiricist, is transmitted to our minds by sensations. David Hume, arguably Kant's most provocative predecessor, formulates the empiricist view in the *Enquiry Concerning Human Understanding* (Indianapolis: Hackett, 1993), 10. Hume holds that, corresponding to the discrete objects of the external world, the mind is constituted such that it receives discrete *impressions* from the world. These impressions are simple, disparate perceptual states that only get connected to one another after the fact, by habits of the mind. The classical empiricist's perceptual world is not comprised of a "stream of consciousness" like the kind William James and Husserl speak about. Representationalist interpretations fail to adhere to Kant's claim that we can never access the things in themselves to verify the accuracy of our representations. Thus, the constructivist reading is more persuasive than the representationalist, even if Kant calls the objects of perception representations (*Vorstellungen*).

46. Quentin Meillassoux, *After Finitude: An Essay on the Necessity of Contingency*, trans. Ray Brassier (London: Continuum, 2008), 7.
47. Kant, *Critique of Pure Reason*, Bxvi-xviii, B62.
48. Kant, *Critique of Pure Reason*, A19/B33.
49. Kant, *Critique of Pure Reason*, B1.
50. Kant, *Critique of Pure Reason*, B1-B2.
51. Maurice Merleau-Ponty, "The Primacy of Perception," in *The Primacy of Perception and Other Essays on Phenomenological Psychology, the Philosophy of Art, History and Politics*, ed. James M. Edie (Evanston: Northwestern University Press, 1964), 14. This account of practical synthesis is filled out as "operative intentionality," an update of what Husserl calls "passive synthesis," in *Phenomenology of Perception*.
52. For an extended treatment of the problem of individuation in Kant, see Alberto Toscano, *The Theatre of Production: Philosophy and Individuation between Kant and Deleuze* (New York: Palgrave, 2006).
53. Kant, *Critique of Pure Reason*, B34/A20.
54. For Kant, causality is a category of the understanding and therefore applicable only to phenomena. He cannot claim that the noumenal realm has causal power (such as the power to cause sensations) because that would make causality an extra-subjective law, which is something he rejects. This is originally Maimon's objection.
55. G.W.F. Hegel, *Phenomenology of Spirit*, trans. A.V. Miller (Oxford: Oxford University Press, 1977), 29.
56. Samuel Todes, *Body and World* (Cambridge, MA: MIT Press, 2001).
57. Todes, *Body and World*, 159.
58. Todes, *Body and World*, 174, emphasis added. Levinas extensively argues a similar point in his discussions of separation, habitation/dwelling, and enjoyment in *Totality and Infinity*. These are places where we see most clearly what I am calling Levinas's material ontology. The relevant subsections of *Totality and Infinity*, trans. Alphonso Lingis (Pittsburgh: Duquesne University Press, 1969), "Separation as Life," "Enjoyment and Representation," "I and Dependence," and "The Dwelling" will be studied in chapter 4.
59. Todes, *Body and World*, 161.
60. Todes, *Body and World*, 170.
61. See Erwin Straus, "The Upright Posture," *Psychiatric Quarterly* 26 (1952): 529-561.
62. Todes, *Body and World*, 106, 118.
63. Todes, *Body and World*, 173, emphasis added.
64. Todes, *Body and World*, 174.
65. Angelica Nuzzo, "Kant and Herder on Baumgarten's *Aesthetica*," *Journal of the History of Philosophy* 44, no. 4 (October 2006): 587.
66. "Kant and Herder," 578.

67. Nuzzo, *Ideal Embodiment*, 5.
68. Nuzzo, *Ideal Embodiment*, 10-11.
69. Nuzzo, "Kant and Herder," 577-597.
70. See Charles Taylor, "The Validity of Transcendental Arguments," in *Philosophical Arguments* (Cambridge, MA: Harvard University Press, 1995), where Taylor argues for a continuity between the transcendental approaches of Kant and Merleau-Ponty.
71. Nuzzo, "Kant and Herder," 582.
72. As Nuzzo points out ("Kant and Herder," 596), this is similar to Herder's criticism of Kant. Herder preferred a historicism which sought "to grasp genetically and materially ... the origins of historical human individuality" whereas "Kant's transcendental inquiry into the human cognitive faculty is an investigation of the *a priori* sources and validity of our judgments" (597).
73. Nuzzo, "Kant and Herder," 584.
74. Nuzzo, "Kant and Herder," 587.
75. This is the consequence of overcoming the subject-object duality retained by Kant. The implications for Merleau-Ponty, along with Husserl, Heidegger, and others who reject the essential distinction of subject and object are apparent. See Tom Rockmore, *Cognition: An Introduction to Hegel's* Phenomenology of Spirit (Berkeley: University of California Press, 1997), 23, passim.
76. Hegel, *Phenomenology of Spirit*, 60. Regarding the possibility of immediate acquaintance, Hegel also writes: "In *ap*prehending [an object], we must refrain from trying to *com*prehend it," 58.
77. Hegel, *Phenomenology of Spirit*, 59.
78. See Hegel, *Phenomenology of Spirit*, 56-57.
79. Irmgard Scherer, "The Problem of the A Priori in Sensibility: Revisiting Kant's and Hegel's Theories of the Senses," *The Review of Metaphysics* 52, no. 2 (December 1998), 362.
80. This is a reference, of course, to Hegel's criticism of Kant (echoed by Todes) from *The Encyclopedia Logic*, trans. T.F. Geraets et al. (Indianapolis: Hackett, 1991), §11: "But to want to have cognition *before* we have any is as absurd as the wise resolve of Scholasticus to learn to *swim before he ventured into the water.*"
81. Husserl remains close to Hegel when he writes: "*An object that has being in itself (an sich seiender) is never such as to be out of relation to consciousness and its Ego.* The thing is thing of *the world about me*, even the thing that is not seen and the really possible thing, not experienced...." Edmund Husserl, *Ideas: General Introduction to Pure Phenomenology*, trans. W.R. Boyce Gibson (New York: Collier, 1962), 134. Hereafter cited as *Ideas* I.
82. On the one hand, like Merleau-Ponty, Husserl maintains that the object of consciousness evidently transcends consciousness; the evidence of this lies in its perspectival presentation (§43 of *Ideas* I points out that even God could not perceive non-perspectivally). On the other hand, although he admits that objects are given to us "in one blow" (see the sixth Logical Investigation), Husserl says that we must build up the unity of objects "with increasing completeness through perceptual continua harmoniously developed, and through certain methodic

thought-forms grounded in experience" (*Ideas* I, 138). This last remark seems to align Husserl with Hegel and against Kant, and to replace the actuality of the thing in itself with the intuition of an essential appearance.

83. Scherer, "The Problem of the A Priori in Sensibility," 364. "Form is the Concept which, fully developed, is the I or pure self-consciousness."

84. This is why I treat twentieth-century phenomenology—occasionally reinscribing it in older terms and categories—as a moment in the history of philosophy and not as a movement that radically breaks with this history, which is a common way to regard the effect of the various "reductions" performed by phenomenologists.

85. Tom Rockmore, *Kant and Phenomenology* (Chicago: University of Chicago Press, 2011), 101. To a great extent I follow Rockmore's characterization of phenomenology as an extension of German idealism, which is why I insist that phenomenology, even in its corporeal form, cannot provide us with a metaphysical realism.

86. Edmund Husserl, *Logical Investigations*, trans. J.N. Findlay, vol. 2 (New York: Humanity Books, 1970), Introduction, §7; *Ideas* I, §24.

87. Mark Rowlands, *Externalism: Putting Mind and World Back Together Again* (Montreal: McGill-Queen's University Press, 2003), 61.

88. As the "principle of all principles" states (*Ideas* I, 83, emphasis omitted): "every primordial dator Intuition is a source of authority (*Rechtsquelle*) for knowledge ... whatever presents itself in 'intuition' in primordial form (as it were in its bodily reality), is simply to be accepted as it gives itself out to be, though only within the limits in which it then presents itself."

89. Rockmore, *Kant and Phenomenology*, 120.

90. There is a long tradition in philosophy of mind that sees sensation as internal to the subject. Now, it is one thing to make sensation internal to the body and another thing to make it internal to consciousness. I take Husserl to be doing the latter, but not necessarily the former. In fact, he explicitly contests the view that sensations (*Empfindungen*) are internal to the body in Edmund Husserl, *Ideas Pertaining to a Pure Phenomenology and to a Phenomenological Philosophy*, Second Book, trans. Richard Rojcewicz and Andre Schuwer (Dordrecht: Kluwer, 1989).

91. Husserl, *Ideas* I, 227.

92. Dodd, *Idealism and Corporeity*, 46.

93. Husserl, *Logical Investigations*, vol. 2, 814, 815.

94. Husserl, *Ideas* I, 226.

95. See Alia Al-Saji, "Rhythms of the Body: A Study of Sensation, Time and Intercorporeity in the Phenomenology of Edmund Husserl" (PhD dissertation, Emory University, 2002), 1.

96. See Husserl, *Ideas* I, §85.

97. Husserl, *Ideas* I, 227: "Whether ... sensile experiences in the stream of experience are of necessity everywhere the subjects of some kind of 'animating synthesis' which informs them ... or, as we also say, whether they ever take their part in *intentional functions*, does not here call for decision."

98. Dodd, *Idealism and Corporeity*, 46.

99. Husserl, *Ideas* I, 45. He goes on to specify that "to have something real primordially given, and to 'become aware' of it and 'perceive' it in simple intuition, are one and the same thing." Yet, in *The Crisis of the European Sciences and Transcendental Phenomenology*, trans. David Carr (Evanston: Northwestern University Press, 1970), 164, Husserl admits that each of our perceptions is simply an "appearance" of an object that transcends each of its perspectives. That is, he admits the "thing in itself" into his ontology—but on what grounds? Is he not in the same position as Kant, forced only to speculate on the givenness of the thing in itself and thus break from the phenomenological attitude?

100. Husserl, *Ideas* I, §§128-129.

101. Rowlands, *Externalism*, 60. Rowlands calls Husserl's position "methodological" or "logical" idealism and argues (see chapter 4 of his book) that it is actually Sartre who effects a "radical reversal" of Husserl's idealism by insisting that consciousness has *no content, is nothing at all*. Thus, content must come from somewhere outside consciousness.

102. Husserl, *Ideas* I, 228.

103. Husserl, *Ideas* I, 228.

104. Husserl, *Ideas* I, 228.

105. Husserl, *Ideas* I, 229.

106. Husserl, *Ideas* I, 229, 230; Dodd, *Idealism and Corporeity*, 44-45.

107. Dodd, *Idealism and Corporeity*, 45, writes: "Insofar as the thing is present in perceptual consciousness an apprehension that bears within itself a sense-content is involved; sensation itself, however, is not to be confused with anything thingly-real—which means, within the transcendental perspective, that sensation does not belong to the noematic [object side] correlate of the act of perception."

108. Husserl, *Ideas* I, 233.

109. Al-Saji, "Rhythms of the Body," 2.

110. Al-Saji, "Rhythms of the Body," 4. For a thorough analysis of similar themes in Merleau-Ponty, see David Morris, *The Sense of Space* (Albany: State University of New York Press, 2004).

111. See Alia Al-Saji, "The Site of Affect in Husserl's Phenomenology: Sensations and the Constitution of the Lived Body," *Philosophy Today* 44, SPEP Supplement (2000): 51-59, where she shows how Husserl allows us to "rethink sensation as a creative, differentiating, and dynamic multiplicity, as the way we feel our contact with the world, with others, and with our own life" (52).

112. Bertrand Russell, *The Problems of Philosophy* (New York: Oxford University Press, 1997), 1.

113. Russell, *The Problems of Philosophy*, 12. Russell here echoes Berkeley on sensation (*A Treatise Concerning the Principles of Human Knowledge* [Indianapolis: Hackett, 1982], §87): "Colour, figure, motion, extension and the like, considered only as so many *sensations* in the mind, are perfectly known, there being nothing in them which is not perceived." See Ayer's *The Foundations of Empirical Knowledge* (New York: Macmillan, 1940) and J.L. Austin's reply in *Sense and Sensibilia* (London: Oxford University Press, 1962).

114. The constancy hypothesis is a staple of direct realism, but it problematically situates perception in the mind and therefore sets up a questionable kind of correspondence. Merleau-Ponty summarizes: "Hence we have in principle a point-by-point correspondence and constant connection between the stimulus and the elementary perception" (PP 8/14).

115. "*Externalism*," writes Rowlands, "is the view that not all mental things are exclusively located inside the head of the person or creature that has these things." See *Externalism*, 2.

116. Merleau-Ponty resists such a view when he writes in a working note of *The Visible and the Invisible*, trans. Alphonso Lingis (Evanston: Northwestern University Press, 1968), 250, that "the flesh of the world is not *self-sensing* (*se sentir*) as is my flesh—It is sensible and not sentient—I call it flesh nonetheless ... in order to say that it is a *pregnancy* of possibles...." Even in this later text, which is often thought to overcome the latent dualism of the *Phenomenology of Perception,* Merleau-Ponty retains a dualism which separates being into two spheres, the human and the nonhuman, but this division comes without explanation. Precisely how this division comes to be, if it actually exists, is a metaphysical problem that Merleau-Ponty does not work through.

117. John Locke, *An Essay Concerning Human Understanding*, abridged and edited by Kenneth Winkler (Indianapolis: Hackett, 1996), 49.

118. Berkeley, *Principles of Human Knowledge*, §1. Of course, Berkeley found faith in mind-independent (but not God-independent) objects "repugnant," but his conviction that objects are nothing more than collectives of qualities provides a true model of the theory of objects I am presupposing here and will elaborate in subsequent texts.

119. For objectivity, I follow for the most part the realist theory of objects developed by Graham Harman, principally in his *Tool-Being: Heidegger and the Metaphysics of Objects* (Chicago: Open Court, 2002) and *Guerrilla Metaphysics: Phenomenology and the Carpentry of Things* (Chicago: Open Court, 2005), as well Stephen Mumford's *Dispositions* (Oxford: Oxford University Press, 1998). Consequently, the ethics of things defended by Silvia Benso in her book *The Face of Things: A Different Side of Ethics* (Albany: State University of New York Press, 2000) is allied with my project.

120. The idea that objects possess capacities or "powers," as well as the ontological status of these powers, is the subject of a debate in analytic philosophy, a short overview of which can be found in the introduction to George Molnar, *Powers: A Study in Metaphysics*, ed. Stephen Mumford (Oxford: Oxford University Press, 2003). Occasionally I will distinguish between the ontological and practical sense of "power." The sense of the virtual I intend here is taken from Gilles Deleuze, *Difference and Repetition*, trans. Paul Patton (New York: Columbia University Press, 1994), 208: "The virtual is opposed not to the real but to the actual. *The virtual is fully real in so far as it is virtual.*"

121. See Ernst Mach, *The Analysis of Sensations*, trans. C.M. Williams and Sydney Waterlow (New York: Dover, 1959), 5. Mach allies himself with the "philosophy of immanence" and cites Spinoza as his original predecessor (46), a point we will return to in our discussion of bodies, plasticity, and corporeal integrity.

122. The language and ontology of dispositions I borrow directly from Mumford, *Dispositions*, vi and 5. Mumford's ontology of dispositions appears to have many points of contact with Deleuze's ontology of the actual and virtual, but this book

is not the place to delve into the comparison. See also Molnar's five features of powers—directedness, independence, actuality, intrinsicality, objectivity—in *Powers*, 8-9.

123. Alva Noë, *Action in Perception* (Cambridge, MA: MIT Press, 2004), 143. On the effects of color contrast on the appearance of color, see Josef Albers, *Interaction of Color* (New Haven: Yale University Press, 1963).

124. This formulation is more appropriate for the account of embodiment given in *Phenomenology of Perception*, where the consciousness-object duality is still at play. Merleau-Ponty acknowledges the inadequacy of this model in *The Visible and the Invisible*, 200/253; a reformulation is evident in his searching discussion of the "two leaves" of the body (135-138/178-183). What exactly remains out of step with the world is open for debate, although good candidates are volition, imagination, and emotion.

125. The diacritical nature of perception is affirmed by Merleau-Ponty in *The Visible and the Invisible*, 213/267, and likewise in the chapter on "The Thing and the Natural World" in *Phenomenology*.

126. Timothy Morton, *The Ecological Thought* (Cambridge, MA: Harvard University Press, 2010).

127. Aristotle, *De Anima*, trans. Hippocrates G. Apostle (Grinnell: Peripatetic Press, 1981), 416b34-35.

128. I begin to explore the theme of sensory alimentation and its ethical potential in "Enabling/Disabling Sensation: Toward an Alimentary Imperative in Carnal Phenomenology," *Philosophy Today* 52, no. 2 (Summer 2008): 99-115.

Chapter 2

129. It must always be kept in view that when Merleau-Ponty, or any philosopher at all, speaks about perception, it is always human perception that is denoted. This makes it quite difficult, it seems to me, for an ontology grounded in human perception to escape anthropocentrism.

130. Gary Brent Madison, *The Phenomenology of Merleau-Ponty: A Search for the Limits of Consciousness* (Athens, OH: Ohio University Press, 1981), 7.

131. For an extended critique of the physicalist/neurobiological ("objectivist") account of pain from a Merleau-Pontyan perspective, see Abraham Olivier, *Being in Pain* (Frankfurt: Peter Lang, 2007). Merleau-Ponty's *The Structure of Behavior*, trans. Alden Fisher (Pittsburgh: Duquesne University Press, 1963) is a book which demonstrates that positivistic approaches to psychology fail to adequately explain human behavior because they miss the phenomenon of structure identified and analyzed by Gestalt psychology. Following the Gestalt theorists as well as phenomenology, Merleau-Ponty redefines behavior as a meaning-laden phenomenon that cannot be explained solely by reflex theories, but needs rather a "principle" that accounts for the "relevance" of stimuli (SB 99/109).

132. It is true that Merleau-Ponty calls the body the "third term" in the figure-ground structure specifically in the context of a discussion of spatiality. But if all perception is situated in a spatiotemporal horizon, and perception is the origin of both

determinate objects and objective thought, then we must consider the body as conditioning every horizon of experience.

133. M.C. Dillon, *Merleau-Ponty's Ontology*, second edition (Evanston: Northwestern University Press, 1988), Introduction.

134. On Merleau-Ponty's idealism, see Madison, *The Phenomenology of Merleau-Ponty*, 32; Barbaras, *The Being of the Phenomenon*, 14ff.

135. Since the present chapter is concerned specifically with the ontology of the body, I will forgo discussion of the way in which the primacy of perception thesis cuts across traditional intellectualist/rationalist and empiricist epistemologies and refer the reader to the secondary literature, especially the books by Dillon, Madison, Hass, and de Waelhens.

136. Objects are not simply postulated as transcendent in order to account for the content of perception, their transcendence is evinced in the way they resist appropriation and only ever present themselves to us incompletely or perspectivally. This is doubly true of other persons. See Merleau-Ponty, PrP 18/53; PP 322-323/372.

137. John Sallis, *Phenomenology and the Return to Beginnings* (New York: Humanities Press, 1973), 30.

138. Sallis, *Phenomenology and the Return to Beginnings*, 31. Merleau-Ponty maintains that the object, rather than the subject, remains "aloof" from perception, that it "remains self-sufficient" (PP 322/372). See also Merleau-Ponty's discussion of Stratton's experiment in PP 248-251/287-291. For an alternative reading of the Kantian subject as transcendentally embodied and therefore rooted in the world and capable of distinguishing "up" from "down," see Nuzzo, *Ideal Embodiment*.

139. Sallis, *Phenomenology and the Return to Beginnings*, 30.

140. Sallis, *Phenomenology and the Return to Beginnings*, 34.

141. Merleau-Ponty also says, and this we will take up below to determine the priority of sensation, that sense experience "is the intentional tissue" that makes the world "present as a familiar setting of our life" (PP 52-53/64-65).

142. Sallis, *Phenomenology and the Return to Beginnings*, 35, 36.

143. Sallis, *Phenomenology and the Return to Beginnings*, 36.

144. Merleau-Ponty refers to the "silent knowing" and "pre-meaning" and "sedimented meaning" of these "existentials" [*existentiaux*] numerous times in the Working Notes of *The Visible and the Invisible*. They are the "unconscious" "articulations of our field" (VI 180/233-234) and seem to be analogous to what Heidegger intends by *existentialia*, or the ontological structures of Dasein, in *Being and Time*. See Martin Heidegger, *Being and Time*, trans. John Macquarrie and Edward Robinson (San Francisco: HarperCollins, 1962), §9.

145. Lakoff and Johnson, *Philosophy in the Flesh*, xi.

146. "Her corporeal schema is for itself—for the other—It is the *hinge* of the for itself and the for the other" (VI 189/243).

147. Consider Merleau-Ponty's remark that "we are given over to the object and we merge into this body which is better informed than we are about the world, and about the motives we have and the means at our disposal for synthesizing it" (PP 238/276).

148. It is well known that Colin Smith's translation of *Phenomenology of Perception* translates *schéma corporel* sometimes as "body image" and other times as "body schema," which is problematic because these two terms signify disparate phenomena. Shaun Gallagher, *How the Body Shapes the Mind* (Oxford: Oxford University Press, 2005), has sifted through the plentiful literature on the body image and body schema in order to clarify their difference and standardize their reference. He proposes the following: "A *body image* consists of a system of perceptions, attitudes and beliefs pertaining to one's own body. In contrast, a *body schema* is a system of sensory-motor capacities that function without awareness or the necessity of perceptual monitoring" (24). Gallagher further notes that when Merleau-Ponty writes of the *schéma corporel* he intends "a system of dynamic motor equivalents that belong to the realm of habit rather than conscious choice" (20). Part 1 of Morris's *The Sense of Space* unpacks Merleau-Ponty's understanding of the body schema as an "ensemble" of habituated styles (39) and further insists that *schéma corporel* always be rendered as body schema when translating Merleau-Ponty. This is the best way to avoid mistaking the *schéma corporel* for something representational, personal, or explicitly intentional.

149. "Body-subject and world are ultimately mutually constituting despite all the emphasis placed just on the subjective constitution of the world in *Phénoménologie de la Perception*. Neither would be what it is without the other." Stephen Priest, *Merleau-Ponty* (London: Routledge, 1998), 74.

150. Priest (*Merleau-Ponty*, 57) notes that "Merleau-Ponty's originality lies in the idea that subjectivity is physical." Neither materialism, idealism, nor dualism "includes the thesis that I am my body; that I am a subjective object or a physical subject."

151. Dillon, *Merleau-Ponty's Ontology*, 146.

152. Dillon, *Merleau-Ponty's Ontology*, 146.

153. Dillon, *Merleau-Ponty's Ontology*, 147.

154. When I speak of Merleau-Ponty's phenomenology of perception as a "transcendental philosophy," it must be kept in mind that the transcendental in Merleau-Ponty is never a pure a priori, but as M.C. Dillon has shown ("Apriority in Kant and Merleau-Ponty," *Kant-Studien* 17, no. 3 [1987]: 403-423), neither a priori nor a posteriori. This neither/nor once again supports Barbaras's claim that Merleau-Ponty remains caught up in old dualisms and can only situate himself negatively in the tradition he seeks to overcome. In any case, Merleau-Ponty's transcendental is a *historical transcendental*, a concept we will come to grips with later. The historical transcendental will be reconstituted in terms of plasticity, with specific reference to Deleuze, DeLanda, and Spinoza, in chapter 5.

155. Merleau-Ponty's view of time is undoubtedly intersubjective, as when he says that "'events' are shapes cut out by a finite observer from the spatio-temporal totality of the objective world" (PP 411/470). By "objective" here, he means intersubjective: time is the totality of events carved out of being by the totality of observers. Nearly the entire temporality chapter of the *Phenomenology* supports this subjectivist view of time, which is problematic from the realist perspective I am advocating here.

156. "This unconscious is to be sought not at the bottom of ourselves, behind the back of our 'consciousness', but in front of us, as articulations of our field" (VI 180/234).

157. This is not to suggest that the *Phenomenology* does not contain an ontology. Indeed, after Dillon and others I am trying to bring out some of the ontological dimensions of the theory of embodiment put forth in the *Phenomenology*. I do feel, however, that this ontology is hindered (if not contradicted) by the privilege afforded to the first-person perspective deployed in this early text. The reader may refer to Tom Sparrow, *The End of Phenomenology: Metaphysics and the New Realism* (Edinburgh: Edinburgh University Press, 2014), for my critique of phenomenology as a method for doing ontology.

158. See Heidegger, *Being and Time*, §16. For the ontological implications of this breakdown, see Harman, *Tool-Being*. See also Karl Jaspers, *General Psychopathology*, trans. J. Hoenig and Marian W. Hamilton (Chicago: University of Chicago Press, 1963), 88.

159. Shaun Gallagher, "Lived Body and Environment," *Research in Phenomenology* 16 (1986): 152.

160. Dillon, *Merleau-Ponty's Ontology*, 139-150, dispels this notion by contrasting Merleau-Ponty's account of the lived body with Sartre's ontological analysis of the body.

161. For the thesis that the "experiential absence" of the body is more fundamental than the "ambiguous presence" of the body, see Gallagher, "Lived Body and Environment."

162. Madison, *The Phenomenology of Merleau-Ponty*, 26.

163. David Morris, "The Logic of the Body in Bergson's Motor Schemes and Merleau-Ponty's Body Schema," *Philosophy Today* 44, SPEP Supplement (2000): 65, shows that "The logic of the body in Merleau-Ponty would have to be a cultural-historical logic, a logic of a body already infected with 'exterior' meaning, not just a logic of internal translations, repetitions, parts and wholes."

164. Madison, *The Phenomenology of Merleau-Ponty*, 26.

165. Morris, "The Logic of the Body," 64.

166. We again see Merleau-Ponty inserting a certain distance between the physical and lived bodies, and thus imposing a duality of embodiment. This allows him to denote the habit body as the "mediator of a world" (PP 145/169). The metaphysical problem that lingers here is that of how the lived body originally separates itself from its envelopment with the physical environment, or how an impersonal organism becomes the personal subject of perception. This problem is dodged by Merleau-Ponty when he posits that "by an imperceptible twist an organic process issues into human behavior" (PP 88/104). The problem is ramified in *The Visible and the Invisible* because Merleau-Ponty's switch to a monist ontology puts him in the position of explaining the emergence and particularization of perceptual agents. Such a problem is sidestepped from a phenomenological viewpoint because the phenomenologist takes his or her point of departure from the facticity of existence and therefore begins his or her analyses from the perspective of an always already individuated subject. It is, however, in the courses published as *Nature*, trans. Robert Vallier (Evanston: Northwestern University Press, 2003) that Merleau-Ponty takes on the question of the emergence of "spirit," which he tells us "is not what descends into the body in order to organize it, but is what emerges from it" (140/188).

167. William James, *The Principles of Psychology*, vol. 1 (New York: Dover, 1918), 114.

168. James, *Principles*, vol. 1, 116-119. Proprioception describes the tacit ecological awareness that enables the body to maintain its postural equilibrium.

169. James, *Principles*, vol. 1, 105, emphasis omitted.

170. Edward S. Casey, "Habitual Body and Memory in Merleau-Ponty," *Man and World* 17, no. 3/4 (1984): 285.

171. Casey, "Habitual Body and Memory in Merleau-Ponty," 285.

172. On the freeing of perception and movement by the sedimentation of habit, see Félix Ravaisson, *Of Habit*, trans. Clare Carlisle and Mark Sinclair (London: Continuum, 2008), 49.

173. Casey distinguishes between the kinds of habits that can be cultivated "spontaneously" and the habits which are sedimented in the form of customs ("Habitual Body and Memory in Merleau-Ponty," 286-287). His notion of customary habits is comparable to the social habits that tie us to an economic class, as James identifies (*Principles*, vol. 1, 121). Customary and class habits have an effect of contraction and should be contrasted with the "dilating" habits that Merleau-Ponty elaborates.

174. Clare Carlisle, "Creatures of Habit: The Problem and the Practice of Liberation," *Continental Philosophy Review* 38 (2006): 23.

175. Casey, "Habitual Body and Memory in Merleau-Ponty," 290.

176. Alphonso Lingis, *Sensation: Intelligibility in Sensibility* (Atlantic Highlands: Humanities Press, 1996), 1. For Dewey's account of how our originally "plastic" impulses get channeled into social forms of conduct, see John Dewey, *Human Nature and Conduct* (Carbondale and Edwardsville: Southern Illinois University Press, 1988), 69-75.

177. Alphonso Lingis, *Body Transformations: Evolutions and Atavisms in Culture* (London: Routledge, 2005), 57.

178. For the way affective circuits economize our actions and thereby give rise to the identities of our bodies, see Tom Sparrow, "Bodies in Transit: The Plastic Subject of Alphonso Lingis," *Janus Head* 10, no. 1 (Summer/Fall 2007): 114-116.

179. For an ontology of mood, see Heidegger, *Being and Time*, §29.

180. Hass, *Merleau-Ponty's Philosophy*, 78.

181. I detect in Merleau-Ponty's discussion of the physiognomy of color the seeds of a phenomenology of race, some elements of which I will raise throughout this essay but will not pursue at length.

182. Cited by Merleau-Ponty in EM 188/87.

183. Gail Weiss, *Refiguring the Ordinary* (Bloomington: Indiana University Press, 2008), 79. Weiss points out that it is his loss of an intentional arc that disables the patient Schneider's capacity to order his world into a coherent, meaningful whole. The more general point that Merleau-Ponty wants to stress with Schneider's case is that his pathology cannot be fully explained by appealing to the physical disablement of a particular brain function.

184. In "Merleau-Ponty's Critique of Mental Representation," Hubert Dreyfus makes it clear that the intentional arc is *not* a representation of the world, but must be understood as the "feedback loop" of learning that is established as bodies interact with other bodies, things, etc. "The idea of an intentional arc is meant to

capture the idea that all past experience is projected back into the world. The best representation of the world is thus the world itself." Dreyfus's paper is available at: <http://www.class.uh.edu/cogsci/dreyfus.html>

185. Johnson, *The Meaning of the Body*, 68.

186. This is perhaps most apparent in "The Child's Relations with Others" (cf. 108-113/17-23).

187. Shannon Sullivan, *Living Across and Through Skins: Transactional Bodies, Pragmatism, and Feminism* (Bloomington: Indiana University Press, 2001), 68.

188. "A situation becomes neutral when the immediate environment arouses no concern. An environment void of importance is something that also exists, and in such an environment, too, 'stimuli' are active," writes Straus in *The Primary World of Senses*, 81.

189. See Michel Foucault, *Remarks on Marx*, trans. R. James Goldstein and James Cascaito (New York: Semiotext(e), 1991), 31-32.

190. Sullivan, *Living Across and Through Skins*, 68.

191. Sullivan, *Living Across and Through Skins*, 67, 68-69.

192. Alphonso Lingis, *Libido: The French Existential Theories* (Bloomington: Indiana University Press, 1985), 55-56. Lingis challenges Merleau-Ponty's interpretation of Schneider's sexual incompetence as a loss of the capacity to order his erotic world, via the intentional arc, into a meaningful whole. The libido, argues Lingis, is not a force that is ordered by perceptual structures; nor is it organized teleologically like body motility.

193. George Yancy, *Black Bodies, White Gazes: The Continuing Significance of Race* (Lanham: Rowman and Littlefield, 2008), 5. For the full account of whiteness as ambush, see chapter 7.

194. *Black Bodies, White Gazes*, 4, 5. Yancy writes: "Her body language signifies, 'Look, *the* Black!' On this score, though short of a performative locution, her body language functions as an insult." He goes on to say that, "The point here is that deep-seated racist emotive responses may form part of the white *bodily* repertoire, which has become calcified through quotidian modes of bodily transaction in a racial and racist world."

195. Frantz Fanon, *Black Skin, White Masks* (New York: Grove Press, 1967), 111.

196. Fanon, *Black Skin, White Masks*, 113.

197. Fanon, *Black Skin, White Masks*, 112.

198. Fanon, *Black Skin, White Masks*, 112.

199. Fanon, *Black Skin, White Masks*, 111. Fanon is drawing upon Jean-Paul Sartre's analysis of "the look" in *Being and Nothingness*. Yancy shows how the historico-racial schema operates as part of what Foucault calls the "positive unconscious," explaining that "My darkness is a signifier of negative values grounded within a racist social and historical matrix that *predates* my existential emergence" (*Black Bodies, White Gazes*, 3). Cf. Michel Foucault, *The Order of Things* (New York: Vintage, 1970), xi.

200. Fanon, *Black Skin, White Masks*, 112-113. For a fuller account of how the black body is "hailed" by the white gaze, see Yancy, *Black Bodies, White Gazes*, 71-75. For an account of interpellation as a material practice, see Louis Althusser,

"Ideology and the Ideological State Apparatus," in *Lenin and Philosophy and Other Essays*, trans. Ben Brewster (New York: Monthly Review Press, 2001).

201. Citing Iris Marion Young, Cathryn Vasseleu makes this point in *Textures of Light: Vision and Touch in Irigaray, Levinas, and Merleau-Ponty* (London: Routledge, 1998), 57.

202. Sara Ahmed, "A Phenomenology of Whiteness," *Feminist Theory* 8, no. 2 (2007): 150.

203. Ahmed, "A Phenomenology of Whiteness," 153.

204. Ahmed, "A Phenomenology of Whiteness," 154.

205. Saito's *Everyday Aesthetics* is devoted to instilling in the reader an appreciation for the kind of aesthetic (non-theoretical) attitude that can help uncover the sensuous. While I affirm the cultivation of everyday aesthetics, I will also argue that even a detailed appreciation of the sensuous remains incapable of fully accessing the sensuous environment.

206. We will examine the motor physiognomy of sensations in the following chapter.

207. This is why Merleau-Ponty insists that "it is impossible completely to describe the colour of the carpet without saying that it *is* a carpet, made of wool, and without implying in this colour a certain tactile value, a certain weight and a certain resistance to sound" (PP 323/373).

208. "The Earth is the matrix of our time as it is of our space. Every constructed notion of time presupposes our proto-history as carnal beings compresent to a single world," Merleau-Ponty writes in "The Philosopher and His Shadow," in *Signs*, 180/227.

209. Dillon, "Apriority in Kant and Merleau-Ponty," 420.

210. Harman, *Guerrilla Metaphysics*, 56.

211. Harman, *Guerrilla Metaphysics*, 58.

212. Merleau-Ponty insists that expression and existence are "reciprocal," that "the body expresses total existence, not because it is an external accompaniment to that existence, but because existence comes into its own in the body" (PP 166/193). This statement must always be tempered by Merleau-Ponty's quasi-transcendentalism, which holds that we always already find ourselves within a sedimented, linguistic *Lebenswelt* that limits the range of available styles, and his claim that our behavior emerges from an animal *Umwelt* (Nature 208/269). The ontology of the body must be situated between "wild" and "sedimented" being (Nature 220/282).

213. Bernhard Waldenfels, "The Paradox of Expression," trans. Chris Nagel, in *Chiasms: Merleau-Ponty's Notion of Flesh*, eds. Fred Evans and Leonard Lawlor (Albany: State University of New York Press, 2000), 98.

214. Harman, *Guerrilla Metaphysics*, 55.

215. Such a conception of identity becomes visible in the paintings of Cézanne as well as in those of the Impressionists, insofar as these artists exploit the thresholds of form. We have the feeling, for instance, when viewing a Cézanne landscape that its contours are on the cusp of dissolution and chaos, but that a reconfiguration of those contours could express the "same" landscape on the verge of a completely different dissolution. Such is the fluidity of the sensory content which makes up the form of Cézanne's subjects and, for Merleau-Ponty, our world.

216. René Descartes, *Meditations on First Philosophy*, in *Philosophical Essays and Correspondence*, ed. Roger Ariew (Indianapolis: Hackett, 2000), 110-112.

217. Linda Singer, "Merleau-Ponty on the Concept of Style," in *The Merleau-Ponty Aesthetics Reader: Philosophy and Painting*, ed. Galen A. Johnson (Evanston: Northwestern University Press, 1993), 242.

218. Singer, "Merleau-Ponty on the Concept of Style," 242.

219. Singer, "Merleau-Ponty on the Concept of Style," 242.

220. Gallagher, "Lived Body and Environment," 157.

221. Gallagher, "Lived Body and Environment," 157.

222. Elizabeth Grosz, *Volatile Bodies: Toward a Corporeal Feminism* (Bloomington: Indiana University Press, 1994), 83-84.

223. Sullivan, *Living Across and Through Skins*, 65, 66.

224. Grosz, *Volatile Bodies*, 108. See also Iris Marion Young, *Throwing Like a Girl and Other Essays in Feminist Philosophy and Social Theory* (Bloomington: Indiana University Press, 1990).

225. Weiss, *Refiguring the Ordinary*, 4.

226. Emmanuel Levinas, "Sensibility," in *Ontology and Alterity in Merleau-Ponty*, eds. Galen A. Johnson and Michael B. Smith (Evanston: Northwestern University Press, 1990), 65.

227. In his discussion of "levels" (PP 253-254/293-294), Merleau-Ponty acknowledges a certain contingency and instability at the heart of experience, but does not explain where this instability comes from. By positing sensation as non-subjective and below perception, we can account for this instability. For more on levels, see Alphonso Lingis, *The Imperative* (Bloomington: Indiana University Press, 1994), 25-38.

228. Nietzsche writes in *The Will to Power* (quoted in Deleuze, *Nietzsche and Philosophy*, 204, note 5), "In the chemical world the sharpest perception of the difference between forces reigns. But a protoplasm, which is a multiplicity of chemical forces, has only a vague and uncertain perception of a strange reality." This sentiment summarizes the general perspective taken up in Nietzsche's philosophy of the body: when he thinks the body he attempts to think it not at the level of consciousness or perception, but at the level of the material and physiological. I do not feel that we should privilege this level, but we cannot neglect it or give it a derivative status. Indeed, the challenge is to reconcile the identity of the transcendental and material. For Merleau-Ponty's relation to Spinoza and a defense of his "fundamental kinship with Spinoza's monistic metaphysics," see Henry Pietersma, "La place de Spinoza dans le pensée de Merleau-Ponty: convergence, entre les deux penseurs," *International Studies in Philosophy* 20, no. 3 (1988): 89-93.

229. I prefer the term "materialist" to "naturalist" because of the latter's biological and anti-metaphysical connotation. I do not see Merleau-Ponty as ultimately a philosopher concerned with the workings of the natural world of science (in part because he is not concerned with body as physical object), but with giving a non-reductive account of situations whose "subjective" and "objective" features are explicable in corporeal terms.

230. For an extended discussion of these points, and an account of why realist commitments are difficult for phenomenologists, see Tom Sparrow, *The End of Phenomenology*.

Chapter 3

231. See Daniel Guerrière, "Table of Contents of '*Phenomenology of Perception*:' Translation and Pagination," *Journal of the British Society for Phenomenology* 10, no. 1 (1979): 65-69.

232. On the transcendental status of the lifeworld, see Husserl, *The Crisis of the European Sciences and Transcendental Phenomenology*, 139-141. On the anonymity of the lifeworld, see §29.

233. Sullivan, *Living Across and Through Skins*, 71, 74.

234. Johanna Oksala, "Female Freedom: Can the Lived Body Be Emancipated?," in *Feminist Interpretations of Maurice Merleau-Ponty*, ed. Dorothea Olkowski and Gail Weiss (University Park: Penn State University Press, 2006), 212.

235. Judith Butler, "Sexual Ideology and Phenomenological Description: A Feminist Critique of Merleau-Ponty's *Phenomenology of Perception*," in *The Thinking Muse: Feminism and Modern French Philosophy*, eds. Jeffner Allen and Iris Marion Young (Bloomington: Indiana University Press, 1989), 95.

236. *Sentir* denotes at once "to sense" and "to feel" and thus contains, like *sens* (sense, direction), an affective and detective valence. It is synonymous with *percevoir*, which means "to detect," hence the trouble with trying to discriminate the two phenomena.

237. Taylor Carman, "Sensation, Judgment, and the Phenomenal Field," in *The Cambridge Companion to Merleau-Ponty*, eds. Taylor Carman and Mark B.N. Hansen (New York: Cambridge University Press, 2005), 52.

238. Carman, "Sensation, Judgment, and the Phenomenal Field," 54.

239. Al-Saji, "The Site of Affect in Husserl's Phenomenology," 52.

240. Al-Saji, "The Site of Affect in Husserl's Phenomenology," 53.

241. Erwin Straus, *The Primary World of Senses*, 7.

242. Straus, *The Primary World of Senses*, 18.

243. Straus, *The Primary World of Senses*, 101.

244. Straus, *The Primary World of Senses*, 200.

245. Straus, *The Primary World of Senses*, 208.

246. Renaud Barbaras, "Affectivity and Movement: The Sense of Sensing in Erwin Straus," trans. Elizabeth A. Behnke, *Phenomenology and the Cognitive Sciences* 3 (2004): 218-219.

247. See Merleau-Ponty's discussions of the *Umwelt* and Uexküll in *Nature*, 167ff./220ff.

248. Barbaras, "Affectivity and Movement," 219. Cf. Straus, *The Primary World of Senses*, 211ff.

249. Barbaras, "Affectivity and Movement," 220.
250. Alphonso Lingis, "The Sensitive Flesh," in *The Collegium Phaenomenologicum: The First Ten Years*, eds J.C. Sallis, G. Moneta, and J. Taminiaux (Dordrecht: Kluwer, 1989), 234.
251. Lingis, "The Sensitive Flesh," 239.
252. Merleau-Ponty only apparently contradicts this statement later on in the *Phenomenology* (PP 317/367), when he writes, "Hardness and softness, roughness and smoothness, moonlight and sunlight, present themselves in our recollection, not pre-eminently as sensory contents, but as certain kinds of symbiosis, certain ways the outside has of invading us and certain ways we have of meeting this invasion...." The qualification of sensing as a "symbiosis" tempers his use of "invasion" in this passage.
253. Michael B. Smith, "Merleau-Ponty's Aesthetics," in *The Merleau-Ponty Aesthetics Reader*, 209.
254. Smith, "Merleau-Ponty's Aesthetics," 208.
255. Alphonse de Waehlens, "Merleau-Ponty: Philosopher of Painting," in *The Merleau-Ponty Aesthetics Reader*, 178.
256. Maurice Merleau-Ponty, "Indirect Language and the Voices of Silence," in *Signs*. Hereafter ILVS.
257. de Waehlens, "Merleau-Ponty: Philosopher of Painting," 187.
258. "It is necessary that meaning and signs, the form and matter of perception, be related from the beginning and that, as we say, the matter of perception be 'pregnant with its form'" (PrP 15/48).
259. Alia Al-Saji, "'A Past Which Has Never Been Present': Bergsonian Dimensions in Merleau-Ponty's Theory of the Prepersonal," *Research in Phenomenology* 38 (2008): 63.
260. Al-Saji, "'A Past Which Has Never Been Present'," 47.
261. Al-Saji, "'A Past Which Has Never Been Present'," 55.
262. Al-Saji, "'A Past Which Has Never Been Present'," 58.
263. Al-Saji, "'A Past Which Has Never Been Present'," 67.
264. This is not an act of judgment, but the work of operative intentionality, or what Husserl calls "passive synthesis." Speaking of this synthesis, Merleau-Ponty writes: "What is called passivity is not the acceptance by us of an alien reality, or a causal action exerted upon us from the outside: it is being encompassed, being in a situation—prior to which we do not exist—which we are perpetually resuming and which is constitutive of us" (PP 427/488).
265. Timothy Morton, *Ecology without Nature: Rethinking Environmental Aesthetics* (Cambridge, MA: Harvard University Press, 2007), 69.
266. Vasseleu, *Textures of Light*, 56, points out that Merleau-Ponty's choice of the hand as the paradigm of reversibility neglects other forms of tactility proper to the body. As she puts it, "not all tactile surfaces of the body can be felt as both self and other self-reflexively, and the mucous membranes of the eyelids, lips and labia can touch each other together but cannot be differentiated as a body feeling or being felt, that is, a body reversible at will."

267. Merleau-Ponty defends this point in VI 142/187: "The handshake too is reversible; I can feel myself touched as well and at the same time as touching."

268. Beata Stawarska, "From the Body Proper to the Flesh: Merleau-Ponty on Intersubjectivity," in *Feminist Interpretations of Maurice Merleau-Ponty*, 92.

269. Diana Coole, *Merleau-Ponty and Modern Politics After Anti-Humanism* (Lanham: Rowman and Littlefield, 2007), 246.

270. Coole, *Merleau-Ponty and Modern Politics*, 247.

271. Stawarska, "From Body Proper to the Flesh," 99.

272. Elie Wiesel illustrates this point in a passage from *Night*, trans. Marion Wiesel (New York: Hill and Wang, 2006), 53, which recounts his experience in a WWII concentration camp: "One day when Idek was venting his fury, I happened to cross his path. He threw himself on me like a wild beast, beating me in the chest, on my head, throwing me to the ground and picking me up again, crushing me with ever more violent blows, until I was covered in blood. As I bit my lips in order not to howl with pain, he must have mistaken my silence for defiance and so he continued to hit me harder and harder. Abruptly, he calmed down and sent me back to work as if nothing had happened. As if he had taken part in a game in which both roles were of equal importance."

273. Ahmed, "A Phenomenology of Whiteness," 161.

274. Coole, *Merleau-Ponty and Modern Politics*, 141.

275. Hass, *Merleau-Ponty's Philosophy*, 129.

276. The idea that the flesh is "narcissistic" does not help explain the individuation of bodies, which seems to me to be a major shortcoming of *The Visible and the Invisible*'s metaphysics. To explain individuation and intercorporeal conflict, we would need a story about how and why the narcissistic flesh turns against itself in the case of violence and, ultimately, destroys the bodies that emerge out of it.

277. As Fred Evans, "'Solar love': Nietzsche, Merleau-Ponty, and the Fortunes of Perception," *Continental Philosophy Review* 31 (1998): 178, points out, this is not a typical teleology. "The 'imminent coincidence' that haunts the chiasms of the flesh is less restrictive than the teleological form of convergence [from PP]; it acknowledges only that flesh tends (though without success) to rejoin itself and does not specify more particular horizons that must be fulfilled. But imminent coincidence still serves to ensure stability and the community suggested by the idea of a common flesh."

278. Levinas, "Sensibility," 66/171.

279. Irigaray, commenting on the privilege of the seer and visibility in Merleau-Ponty, writes the following: "A carnal look, which becomes that which gives perspective to 'things': shelters them, gives birth to them, wraps them in the touch of a visibility that is one with them, keeps them from ever being naked, envelops them in a conjunctive tissue of visibility, an exterior-interior horizon in which, henceforth, they appear without being able to be distinguished, separated, or torn away from it." The privileging of vision effects a "reduction of the tactile to the visible" and fulfills a form of "idealism, under its material, carnal aspects." Luce Irigaray, *An Ethics of Sexual Difference*, trans. Carolyn Burke and Gillian C. Gill (Ithaca: Cornell University Press, 1993), 153-154; 175.

280. "Sensory experience [*l'expérience sensorielle*] is unstable, and alien to natural perception, which we achieve with our whole body all at once, and which opens on a world of inter-acting senses [*un monde intersensoriel*]" (PP 225/260-261).

281. I am thinking here of the function of our autonomic nervous system, which for the most part regulates organ function and controls the body's homeostasis. It is possible to see proprioception as a form of autonomic regulation and to consider the sensory life of the body as predominantly an autonomic system.

282. On the carnal form of the imperative, its practical and ethical force, see Lingis, *The Imperative*. I will expand on this theme below.

283. For further critique of convergence, cf. Evans, "'Solar Love'," section 4.

284. Gilles Deleuze, *Pure Immanence: Essays on a Life*, trans. Anne Boyman (New York: Zone, 2001), 26.

285. In Leibniz's philosophy of mind, *petites perceptions* are perceptions which are not apperceived, that is, are in a sense "unconscious." Macroperception, or perception of things, is said to arise from aggregates of these microperceptions. See the Preface to G.W. Leibniz, *New Essays on Human Understanding*, eds. Peter Remnant and Jonathan Bennett (Cambridge: Cambridge University Press, 1996). On a certain Leibnizianism in Merleau-Ponty, see Barbaras, who does not introduce the notion of *petites perceptions* or Leibniz's perception-apperception distinction (*The Being of the Phenomenon*, chapter 13). See also C.S. Peirce, as well as Joseph Jastrow, "On Small Differences of Sensation" for a discussion of "sensations so faint that we are not fairly aware of having them...." <http://psychclassics.yorku.ca//Peirce/small-diffs.htm>

286. Proprioception is the body's means of maintaining its posture and keeping aware of its ecological positioning. Gallagher distinguishes proprioceptive awareness, a conscious process, from proprioceptive information, a non-conscious process. The latter is denoted as "the result of physiological stimuli activating certain proprioceptors, but not consciously experienced by the subject. On this view, proprioceptive information, generated at peripheral proprioceptors and registered at strategic sites in the brain, but below the threshold of consciousness, operates as part of the system that constitutes the body schema. This aspect of proprioception is not something we can be directly aware of." *How the Body Shapes the Mind*, 46.

Chapter 4

287. Following convention, when I capitalize "Other," I am referring to the human other. Otherwise, "other" refers to otherness generally, whatever is not-I.

288. When I speak of Levinas's "materialism" I mean that his descriptions of embodiment display a marked concern for the matter of subjectivity. But, of course, he is not endorsing properly physicalist or mechanistic accounts of bodily action. Instead, he offers us a phenomenology of physiological concepts like nourishment, effort, and labor. If his approach on this score is close to another materialist, it is perhaps Marx, as well as (surprisingly) Nietzsche.

289. Emmanuel Levinas, "Is Ontology Fundamental?," in *Entre Nous: Thinking-of-the-Other*, trans. Michael B. Smith and Barbara Harshav (New York: Columbia University Press, 1998), 7-9.

290. For instance, see Robert John Sheffler Manning, *Interpreting Otherwise than Heidegger: Emmanuel Levinas's Ethics as First Philosophy* (Pittsburgh: Duquesne University Press, 1993), 95ff.

291. David Wood, "Some Questions for My Levinasian Friends," in *Addressing Levinas*, eds. Eric Sean Nelson, Antje Kapust, and Kent Still (Evanston: Northwestern University Press, 2005), argues that "we cannot separate ontology from ethics" (156). He also helpfully displays some of Levinas's basic ontological prejudices, including his Cartesian notion of substance (158).

292. For an account of Levinas's affinity with Kantian ethical theory, see Catherine Chalier, *What Ought I to Do? Morality in Kant and Levinas*, trans. Jane Marie Todd (Ithaca: Cornell University Press, 2002).

293. Emmanuel Levinas, "From Consciousness to Wakefulness," in *Discovering Existence with Husserl*, trans. Richard A. Cohen and Michael B. Smith (Evanston: Northwestern University Press, 1998), 154.

294. On the primacy of the practical/equipmental, see Heidegger, *Being and Time*, §15.

295. John Sallis, "Levinas and the Elemental," *Research in Phenomenology* 28 (1998): 156.

296. On the productivity of desire, see TI 33-35/3-5.

297. On the alimentary aspects of Levinas's ethics, and the phenomenology of alimentation generally, see Sparrow, "Enabling/Disabling Sensation."

298. For an alternative discussion of individuation, which compares Levinas and Heidegger and focuses on the individuating function of death, see Michael Lewis, "Individuation in Levinas and Heidegger: The One and the Incompleteness of Beings," *Philosophy Today* 51, no. 2 (Summer 2007): 198-215.

299. It may be asked what the subject could possibly be prior to its taking up of a position. I think an answer could be sought in Levinas's view that we, as embodied creatures, live a life prior to reflection which is characterized by a nearly pure, almost infantile, affective life. Fatigue and indolence, for instance, first and foremost belong to the affective realm before they become cognitive objects (EE 11/30). They belong to a pre-reflective sphere which, if it does not precede, it at least takes priority over, consciousness. And insofar as, for the phenomenologist, subjectivity requires conscious reflection, a pre-conscious event would have to be granted a certain anonymity, and thus belong to no subject in particular—or, it belongs forever to the subject's past. What is perhaps needed here is an analysis of maternity (Levinas provides content for this in OB) and the prenatal life of the infant. Intrauterine existence seems a good contender for anonymity from the perspective of conscious reflection, but of course it is beyond the reach of the phenomenologist.

300. John E. Drabinski, "From Representation to Materiality," *International Studies in Philosophy* 30, no. 4 (1998): 30.

301. Emmanuel Levinas, "The Ruin of Representation," in *Discovering Existence with Husserl*, 112/127.

302. Levinas, "The Ruin of Representation," 115/129.

303. Levinas, "The Ruin of Representation," 116/130-131.

304. Levinas, "The Ruin of Representation," 116/131.

305. Sallis, "Levinas and the Elemental," 157.
306. Vasseleu (*Textures of Light*, 46), however, attempts to bring to the fore the importance of the elemental in Merleau-Ponty when she writes: "Lighting is the lining of what it is that we see, the assumed intermediary directing or supporting our gaze. *We* do not see. We perceive in conformity with a carnal light that already knows and sees, because it is not detachable from the things we see. Lighting supports our gaze as a background of sensibility."
307. Levinas, "The Ruin of Representation," 119/134.
308. Emmanuel Levinas, "Intentionality and Sensation," in *Discovering Existence with Husserl*, 139/149 (translation modified).
309. Levinas, "Intentionality and Sensation," 139/150.
310. Levinas, "Intentionality and Sensation," 145/156.
311. I am somewhat skeptical that there is a continuity between Husserl's and Levinas's conceptions of the sensible. I have noted a few of my concerns with Husserl's theory of sensation in chapter 1. Because I cannot here explore the merit of Levinas's interpretation of Husserl, I point the reader to John E. Drabinski, *Sensibility and Singularity: The Problem of Phenomenology in Levinas* (Albany: State University of New York Press, 2001).
312. Bernard Andrieu, "Brains in the Flesh: Prospects for a Neurophenomenology," *Janus Head* 9, no. 1 (2006): 138.
313. I retrieve this concept in the following chapter, drawing out its implications for a plastic conception of embodiment.
314. In TI 167/141 Levinas speaks of the action of a body which would seek to escape its entrenchment in being as unfolding according to a "final" causality guided by the hand. "The end is a term the hand searches for in the risk of missing it. The body as possibility of a hand—and its whole corporeity can be substituted for the hand—exists in the virtuality of this movement betaking itself toward the tool." The critical edge of these remarks is certainly aimed at Heidegger's ontology (with its primacy of the ready-to-hand), but it applies as well to the privilege of the grasp or hold (*prise*) in Merleau-Ponty, as does Levinas's examination of "the caress."
315. Silvia Benso, "The Breathing of the Air: Presocratic Echoes in Levinas," in *Levinas and the Ancients*, eds. Brian Schroeder and Silvia Benso (Bloomington: Indiana University Press, 2008), 20.
316. Benso, "The Breathing of the Air," 20.
317. The anarchic and unrepresentable source of the elemental belongs to an unstable future that brings with it the disintegration of what has been done in the past. It is the promise of insecurity, the constant threat of the end of enjoyment, "menace and destruction." We combat this insecurity with work and labor (TI 141-142, 146/115, 120).
318. Levinas is drawing here upon a tradition in French philosophy concerned with thinking the autoaffection of the body as the initiation of subjectivity. This tradition includes modern figures like Maine de Biran and Ravaisson, and is best represented contemporarily by Michel Henry. Ravaisson notes how effort is suspended between action and passion, and how effort comprises "not only the primary condition, but also the archetype and essence, of consciousness." It is evident that he, like Levinas, is trying to conceive the birth of consciousness in the

voluntary initiation of a position against the resistance of the material world. See Ravaisson, *Of Habit*, 43.

319. Jean-Jacques Rousseau, *Discourse on the Origin of Inequality*, trans. Donald A. Cress (Indianapolis: Hackett, 1992), 45.

320. Jean Starobinski, *Jean-Jacques Rousseau: Transparency and Obstruction*, trans. Arthur Goldhammer (Chicago: University of Chicago Press, 1988), 26, 27.

321. Vigilance is the condition of the ego "riveted" to being, that is, unable to *not* exist. "The ego is swept away by the fatality of being," says Levinas (EE 61/110). Whereas consciousness would be an escape from existence, vigilance is an encounter with existence that lacks intuition, illumination, and attention. Indeed, it is an event wherein the ego given over to the existence as though existence, rather than the ego, were consciousness. In the vigilance of insomnia the ego becomes the object of the night which subjects it (EE 62-63/EE; TO 48-51/27-30).

322. Levinas suggests that a direct encounter with the *il y a* is perhaps possible through a thought experiment wherein we imagine the total destruction of everything, but such a feat of the imagination seems dubious. See Levinas, EE 31, 35, 44, 51/60-61, 66, 80, 91-92.

323. From a methodological perspective, it is important to note that Levinas sees his descriptions of vigilance, insomnia, and so on as going beyond the limits of phenomenological description. They are beyond intuition and argued for analogically (see EE 8/26, where Levinas writes that our relationship with being "is called a relationship only by analogy"). The subject is cast as an object, the ego is suspended, and the phenomena under examination are supposed to take place *before* the advent of consciousness. Thus, Levinas writes: "Our affirmation of an anonymous vigilance goes beyond the *phenomena*, which already presupposes an ego, and thus eludes descriptive phenomenology" (EE 63/112). The direct experience of insomnia allows us to *infer* a possible relationship with being in which we are rendered anonymous beings.

324. Merleau-Ponty likes to speak of the matter of perception as "pregnant with its form" (PrP 15/48) so as to avoid the notion that it is perception or consciousness that informs matter. Levinas, by contrast, holds that matter lies in the depths of things, but is *concealed* by the light of intentionality which shrouds it with forms (TI 192-193/167). Against the tradition, the interpretation of light at work in Levinas's texts opposes the idea that light illuminates and unconceals. Matter, he says, is the "dark background of existence." It is this materiality that "makes things appear to us in a night, like the monotonous presence that bears down on us in insomnia" (EE 55/98).

325. On the human-centered nature of Levinas's take on things, see Harman, *Guerrilla Metaphysics*, chapter 3 and Graham Harman, "Levinas and the Triple Critique of Heidegger," *Philosophy Today* 53 (Winter 2009): 407-413. On the negative implications of Levinas's position for environmental philosophy, see Christian Diehm, "Facing Nature: Levinas Beyond the Human," *Philosophy Today* 44, no. 1 (Spring 2000): 51-59.

326. Friedrich Nietzsche, *On the Genealogy of Morality*, trans. Maudemarie Clark and Alan J. Swensen (Indianapolis: Hackett, 1998), Second Treatise, §16.

327. If it is conceded that sensing for Levinas is analogous to what Merleau-Ponty calls operative intentionality, then the pre-reflective content of the latter must be stressed in contrast with its complicity with intentionality of act. That is, the

anonymous dimension of sensing must be regarded as discontinuous with the content of perception. The difference is subtle, but important: it results in the decentering of the lived body, which in turn implies a decentering of the primacy of perception.

328. The resistance/deferral of possession inherent in the caress suggests an ethical interpretation which would oppose the apprehensiveness of the caress to the ability of the grasp. This notion is at play in Irigaray, "The Fecundity of the Caress: A Reading of Levinas, *Totality and Infinity*, 'Phenomenology of Eros'," in *An Ethics of Sexual Difference*.

329. As Levinas says, "our consenting to [rhythm] is inverted into a participation." Emmanuel Levinas, "Reality and Its Shadow," in *Collected Philosophical Papers*, 4.

330. I take it that this is what Levinas is implying when he says, "An image is interesting, without the slightest utility, interesting in the sense of *involving*, in the etymological sense—to be *among* things which should have had only the status of objects" ("Reality and Its Shadow," 3-4). Contained in the Latin for "involve," *involvere*, is the sense of folding into or enveloping, as one would fold together the ingredients of a recipe.

331. Levinas, "Reality and Its Shadow," 5.

332. Levinas, "Reality and Its Shadow," 5.

333. On the problem of diachronicity, see Meillassoux, *After Finitude*, 112-113, who goes even further than Levinas in thinking the metaphysical consequences of the diachronic.

334. See Levinas's remarks on "the meanwhile" in "Reality and Its Shadow," 8-11, and "Diachrony and Representation," in *Entre Nous*, 159-177/177-197.

335. Levinas, "Reality and Its Shadow," 5. For further investigation of this point and others in this chapter, see Tom Sparrow, *Levinas Unhinged* (Winchester, UK: Zero Books, 2013).

336. Gilles Deleuze, *Francis Bacon: The Logic of Sensation*, trans. Daniel W. Smith (Minneapolis: University of Minnesota Press, 2004), 37.

337. Deleuze, *Francis Bacon*, 39.

338. Deleuze, *Francis Bacon*, 31.

339. Deleuze, *Francis Bacon*, 32.

340. Panagia, *The Political Life of Sensation*, 108.

341. Deleuze, *Francis Bacon*, 33-35.

342. Levinas writes in TI 188-189/162: "A phenomenology of sensation as enjoyment, a study of what we could call its transcendental function, which does not necessarily issue in the object nor in the qualitative specification of an object ... would be required." Also: "A transcendental phenomenology of sensation would justify the return to the term sensation to characterize the transcendental function of the quality corresponding to it."

343. Deleuze, *Francis Bacon*, 35.

344. See Levinas, "Sensibility," 65/170.

345. See the section entitled "The Glory of the Infinite," especially the remarks on infinity and *illeity*, in OB 140-153/179-195. Radical passivity is proper to the human

Other for Levinas, because the human Other is elevated to a quasi-divine status which renders its vulnerability unique, even sacred, and my responsibility for it infinite.

346. Given this remark, I think a fruitful exchange over the question of identity can take place between Levinas and architecture theorist Michael Benedikt, who writes in *For An Architecture of Reality* (New York: Lumen, 1987), 4, that "we build our best and necessary sense of an independent yet meaningful reality" when we take part in *"direct esthetic experiences of the real."* If our direct aesthetic experiences are sensuous and constitutive of our subjectivity, as Levinas suggests, then the aesthetics of built space takes on an ethical quality. I explore this possibility further in my conclusion.

347. Lingis writes in *Foreign Bodies* (London: Routledge. 1994), 210, of "the imperative that our sensibility expose itself to the *element* in which sensory patterns and forces take form: the earth, the flux, the air, the light."

348. Lingis, *The Imperative*, 67-68. For a further exploration of sensation, see the collection of essays published as *Sensation: Intelligibility in Sensibility*.

349. Levinas, "Diachrony and Representation," 171/190. For another discussion of the ethical implications of this a priori subjection and the role of sensibility in it, see Chalier, *What Ought I to Do?*, 87, 93.

350. Vivian Sobchack, *Carnal Thoughts: Embodiment and Moving Image Culture* (Berkeley: University of California Press, 2004), 312. For an alternative view of interobjectivity as a replacement for intersubjectivity, see Morton, *Ecology without Nature*, 106.

351. Sobchack, *Carnal Thoughts*, 288, 290. Italics in original.

352. On the dark side of ecology, see Morton, *The Ecological Thought*, chapter 2.

353. Stella Sandford, "Levinas in the Realm of the Senses: Transcendence and Intelligibility," *Angelaki* 4, no. 3 (1999): 66.

354. If in *Totality and Infinity* the autoaffection of enjoyment holds a certain priority, in *Otherwise than Being* heteroaffection takes precedence. This shift contrasts the trajectory of Michel Henry, one of Levinas's allies in the theological turn in French phenomenology. For Henry, immanence means autoaffection; for Levinas, immanence comes to involve a constitutive heteronomy. See Michel Henry, *The Essence of Manifestation*, trans. Girard Etzkorn (Dordrecht: Springer, 2008) and *Philosophy and Phenomenology of the Body*, trans. Girard Etzkorn (The Hague: Martinus Nijhoff, 1975).

355. Sensation is the divergence of temporality, whereas sensing reveals the temporality of being (OB 34, 63/43, 79-80).

356. Dennis King Keenan, *Death and Responsibility: The "Work" of Levinas* (Albany: State University of New York Press, 1999), 43.

357. The relation between self and other is never reversible for Levinas, but always a matter of irreversibility. As he writes in TI 35-36/5-6: "The metaphysician and the other do not constitute a simple correlation, which would be reversible. The reversibility of a relation where the terms are indifferently read from left to right and from right to left would couple them the *one* to the *other*. ... The intended transcendence would be thus reabsorbed into the unity of the system, destroying the radical alterity of the other."

358. Sandford, "Levinas in the Realm of the Senses," 67.

359. Rudolf Bernet, "The Encounter with the Stranger: Two Interpretations of the Vulnerability of the Skin," in *The Face of the Other and the Trace of God*, ed. Jeffrey Bloechl (New York: Fordham University Press, 2000), 45-46.

360. Bernet, "The Encounter with the Stranger," 46.

361. Graham Harman argues this same point, albeit for different reasons and with different metaphysical concerns, in "Aesthetics as First Philosophy: Levinas and the Non-Human," *Naked Punch* 9 (Summer/Fall 2007): 21-30.

362. Sandford, "Levinas in the Realm of the Senses," 69-70.

363. David Michael Levin, "The Embodiment of the Categorical Imperative: Kafka, Foucault, Benjamin, Adorno and Levinas," *Philosophy and Social Criticism* 27, no. 4 (2001): 13.

364. Emmanuel Levinas, "No Identity," in *Collected Philosophical Papers*, 146/92-93 (emphasis added).

365. Levinas, "No Identity," 146/93.

366. More succinctly put in Levinas, TO, 75/63: "In death the existing of the existent is alienated."

367. Dan Zahavi, "Alterity in Self," in *Ipseity and Alterity: Interdisciplinary Approaches to Intersubjectivity*, ed. Shaun Gallagher et al. (Rouen: Presses Universitaires de Rouen, 2004), 145.

368. For a non-anthropocentric engagement with Levinasian ethics that extends ethical consideration to inanimate things, see Benso, *The Face of Things*.

369. It is tempting to call this privileging a humanism, but not without qualification. Levinas places such an emphasis on the passivity, responsibility, and subjection of human beings that it seems as though he could be called an anti-humanist. Indeed, I am arguing here that the material/sensuous world, for Levinas, enacts a certain displacement of human sovereignty. But this is from an ontological perspective that he does not identify with. Given Levinas's explicit ethical commitments, it is clear that humans remain central, as both moral agents and as objects of moral consideration.

Chapter 5

370. John Mullarkey notes a "conflict of attitudes" between thinkers like Merleau-Ponty, Sartre, and David Levin, on the one hand, and Bataille, Deleuze, and Foucault, on the other. While I agree that this divergence of attitude is palpable, it cannot be taken to indicate two fundamentally opposed philosophies of the body. Mullarkey concurs that the two positions are not incompatible. See John C. Mullarkey, "Duplicity in the Flesh: Bergson and Current Philosophy of the Body," *Philosophy Today* 38, no. 4 (Winter 1994): 340.

371. James, *Principles*, vol. 1, 105.

372. Ronald Bruzina, "Method and Materiality in the Phenomenology of Intersubjectivity," *Philosophy Today* 41, SPEP Supplement (1997): 131. Bruzina enumerates four primary modes of powerlessness derived from our finite

relationship to nature: object independence; exposure to accident; sleep and fainting; dependence on temporality.

373. Bruzina writes in "Method and Materiality" (131) that the "independence of nature, and the correlative powerlessness human being feels regarding it, is internal to human being precisely in its bodiliness." It is in this "materially functioning feeling that the interaction of human persons in a bond of community must be explicated...."

374. See chapter 4 of *After Finitude* for the suggestion that lurking behind the stability of natural laws is a chaos that could break through at any time.

375. On the malleability of form and the primacy of power over purpose, see Nietzsche, *On the Genealogy of Morality*, Second Treatise, §12.

376. See Mumford, *Dispositions*, 5-6.

377. Mach, *The Analysis of Sensations*, 4.

378. On dying without becoming a corpse, or the body as a system of relations, see Martial Gueroit, *Spinoza II—L'âme* (Paris: Aubier, 1997), 559-560 and Daniel Selcer, "Singular Things and Spanish Poets: Spinoza on Corporeal Individuation" (paper presented at Spinoza and Bodies conference, University of Dundee, September 10-11, 2009).

379. See the "brief preface concerning the nature of bodies" in Part II (72-76) of Baruch Spinoza, *Ethics*, trans. Samuel Shirley (Indianapolis: Hackett, 1992).

380. Spinoza, *Ethics*, Part II, Definition 7.

381. Spinoza, *Ethics*, Part II, Proposition 13, Lemma 3, Definition.

382. As Spinoza puts it in Part II, Proposition 13, Lemma 4: "If from a body, or an individual thing composed of a number of bodies, certain bodies are separated, and at the same time a like number of other bodies of the same nature take their place, the individual thing will retain its nature as before, without any change in its form."

383. Gilles Deleuze, *Spinoza: Practical Philosophy*, trans. Robert Hurley (San Francisco: City Lights, 1988), 123. Deleuze draws here an analogy between kinetics and musical form, particularly how the latter is determined by the relations of speed and slowness between the sound particles of a given piece. What Deleuze is calling musical form is here quite close to what Merleau-Ponty calls style. It is possible to think of painting in this way too, especially that of Cézanne, with all its visual mobility.

384. Deleuze, *Spinoza: Practical Philosophy*, 125; Gilles Deleuze and Félix Guattari, *A Thousand Plateaus*, trans. Brian Massumi (Minneapolis: University of Minnesota Press, 1987), 241.

385. Deleuze, *Spinoza: Practical Philosophy*, 123.

386. "You will define an animal, or a human being, not by its form, its organs, and its functions, and not as a subject either; you will define it by the affects of which it is capable. Affective capacity, with a maximum threshold and a minimum threshold, is a constant in Spinoza." Deleuze, *Spinoza: Practical Philosophy*, 124. For more on this new taxonomy, see Manuel DeLanda, *A New Philosophy of Society: Assemblage Theory and Social Complexity* (London: Continuum, 2006), chapter 2.

387. For a remarkably clear exposition of this idea, see Manuel DeLanda, "Immanence and Transcendence in the Genesis of Form," *The South Atlantic Quarterly* 96, no. 3 (Summer 1997): 499-514.

388. Toscano, *The Theatre of Production*, 122.

389. John Dewey, *Art As Experience* (New York: Penguin, 1934), 137, italics omitted.

390. Dewey, *Art As Experience*, 147, 150, 154.

391. Deleuze, *Spinoza: Practical Philosophy*, 125-126.

392. On how flat ontology democratizes existence, see Levi Bryant, *The Democracy of Objects* (Ann Arbor: Open Humanities Press, 2011).

393. Grosz, *Volatile Bodies*, 164-165.

394. Andy Clark, *Being There: Putting Brain, Body, and World Together Again* (Cambridge, MA: MIT Press, 1997), 179.

395. Noë, *Action in Perception*, 50. By allowing networks like the Internet to process and store data for us, we free ourselves to concentrate on other tasks.

396. See Clark, *Being There*, 45-47. I must tip my hat to Levi Bryant for pointing out the affinity between my work and Clark's.

397. Clark, *Being There*, 191. On society as a dynamic system, see DeLanda, *A New Philosophy of Society*.

398. Jane Bennett, *Vibrant Matter: A Political Ecology of Things* (Durham: Duke University Press, 2010), 23.

399. On difference-making as the mark of reality, see Levi Bryant, "The Ontic Principle," in *The Speculative Turn: Continental Materialism and Realism*, eds. Levi Bryant, Nick Srnicek, and Graham Harman (Melbourne: re.press, 2011), 261-278.

400. Bennett, *Vibrant Matter*, 32.

401. Grosz, *Volatile Bodies*, 167.

402. Deleuze and Guattari, *A Thousand Plateaus*, 33.

403. Brian Massumi, *Parables for the Virtual: Movement, Affect, Sensation* (Durham: Duke University Press, 2002), 15. See Deleuze, *Difference and Repetition*, 246.

404. Deleuze and Guattari, *A Thousand Plateaus*, 253.

405. Deleuze and Guattari, *A Thousand Plateaus*, 260.

406. DeLanda, *A New Philosophy of Society*, 28.

407. Gilles Deleuze and Félix Guattari, *Anti-Oedipus*, trans. Robert Hurley, Mark Seem, and Helen R. Lane (Minneapolis: University of Minnesota Press, 1983), 36.

408. Andy Clark, "Re-Inventing Ourselves: The Plasticity of Embodiment, Sensing, and Mind," *Journal of Medicine and Philosophy* 32 (2007): 264.

409. DeLanda, *A New Philosophy of Society*, 50.

410. On masochism as machinism, see Deleuze and Guattari, *A Thousand Plateaus*, 155-156.

411. Deleuze and Guattari, *A Thousand Plateaus*, 344-347.

266 Notes

412. For other accounts of the machinic, the work of Donna Haraway and N. Katherine Hayles are good resources. For a phenomenological perspective, see Don Ihde, *Bodies in Technology* (Minneapolis: University of Minnesota Press, 2002); for commentary on Deleuze's concept of machine, see Slavoj Žižek, *Organs Without Bodies: On Deleuze and Consequences* (New York: Routledge, 2004), 15-19.

413. I borrow this facile distinction from Mullarkey, "Duplicity in the Flesh," 340, who argues that Bergson fits in neither the modern nor postmodern era when it comes to thinking of the body.

414. I mean to suggest here that when Merleau-Ponty writes of "the body," he often has in mind the average able body, complete with its ability to circumnavigate objects, explore them unceasingly, and move itself about the world with relative freedom. This does not entail that Merleau-Ponty neglects to analyze the disabled body (see his analysis of Schneider, for example), but that one cannot help but see Schneider as somehow deficient when compared to the body which *Phenomenology of Perception* generally speaks about. There is something "special" about Schneider.

415. See Panagia, *The Political Life of Sensation*, particularly the discussion of Caravaggio and Bacon in chapter 4. In effect, Panagia's entire book is an exploration of the political valence of the zone of indistinction, or what I am here calling the anonymity of the aesthetic.

416. Catherine Malabou, *What Should We Do with Our Brain?*, trans. Sebastian Rand (New York: Fordham University Press, 2008), 5.

417. Malabou, *What Should We Do with Our Brain?*, 12.

418. Malabou, *What Should We Do with Our Brain?*, 6, 8. See also Andrieu, "Brains in the Flesh," 148.

419. For the "open" and "closed" senses of plasticity discussed by Malabou, see *What Should We Do with Our Brain?*, 15-16.

420. Malabou, *What Should We Do with Our Brain?*, 24.

421. Malabou, *What Should We Do with Our Brain?*, 30, 38.

422. Michel Foucault, *Discipline and Punish*, trans. Alan Sheridan (New York: Vintage, 1977), 135.

423. Johanna Oksala, *Foucault on Freedom* (Cambridge: Cambridge University Press, 2005), 126ff.

424. Foucault, *Discipline and Punish*, 138.

425. Michel Foucault, "Nietzsche, Genealogy, History," in *The Foucault Reader*, ed. Paul Rabinow (New York: Pantheon, 1984), 87 (emphasis added). Judith Butler has argued that, despite his proclamations to the contrary, Foucault's body does display certain constants. This is evident in his employment, in "Nietzsche, Genealogy, History," of metaphors and figures of inscription, and his description of the body as a "surface." Moreover, it is present in *Discipline and Punish*, wherein Foucault argues that, for disciplined prisoners, the "law is not literally internalized, but incorporated on [their] bodies." Butler is worried that Foucault is retaining a notion of the body as a pre-cultural material medium upon which historical significations are inscribed, a notion she completely rejects because of its complicity with naturalized gender norms. Butler's critique is right to target this complicity, but if what we have said about brain plasticity is correct, then we have some reason to imagine the brain (or the body) as a surface of inscription, albeit a

surface which is less like a blank slate and more like a rolled out piece of dough. It could be argued that the neuronal determination of the brain is culturally formed, but this does not mean that its form is indiscriminately malleable or without certain biological necessities. See Judith Butler, "Foucault and the Paradox of Bodily Inscriptions," *The Journal of Philosophy* 86, no. 11 (November 1989): 603, 605.

426. I am relying to some extent on Mumford's refutation of event ontology in *Dispositions*, chapter 3.

427. Catherine Malabou, *Ontology of the Accident: An Essay on Destructive Plasticity*, trans. Carolyn Shread (Malden: Polity, 2012).

428. Andrieu, "Brains in the Flesh," 137.

429. Andrieu, "Brains in the Flesh," 137.

430. Carlisle suggests that there are "four basic conditions of habit, which may be regarded as modifications of action: retention, synthesis, affectivity, and plasticity." See "Creatures of Habit," 26.

431. Edward Casey, *Getting Back into Place* (Bloomington: Indiana University Press, 1993), 293.

432. James, *Principles*, vol. 1, 104-105.

433. James, *Principles*, vol. 1, 107-108.

434. Clark, "Re-Inventing Ourselves," 272.

435. For an updated version of how neural maps are built up from an organism's interaction with the topology of its environment, see Johnson, *The Meaning of the Body*, 126-134. Johnson makes the connection between neural maps and behavior in terms of plasticity, and argues the non-reductionist point I am establishing here: "we must always be clear that an organism never actually experiences its neural maps as internal mental structures. We do not experience the *maps*, but rather *through them* we experience a structured world full of patterns and qualities" (132).

436. Carlisle, "Creatures of Habit," 33.

437. Carlisle, "Creatures of Habit," 33.

438. James, *Principles*, vol. 1, 115. Emphasis in original.

439. James, *Principles*, vol. 1, 118.

440. James, *Principles*, vol. 1, 120.

441. Cited in James, *Principles*, vol. 1, 118.

442. Massumi, *Parables for the Virtual*, 179-180.

443. See, for example, Henri Bergson, *Two Sources of Morality and Religion*, trans. R. Ashley Audra and Cloudesley Brereton (Notre Dame: University of Notre Dame Press, 1977).

444. I am following a line of argument that is found in Bernard Williams, Simon Blackburn, and Alphonso Lingis. It holds that, although our ethical commitments may include cognitive processes and the rational weighing of maxims, we really only act on what we value, that is, what we *feel* is important. Nothing is important in itself; importance derives from passionate attachment. See Bernard Williams, *Ethics and the Limits of Philosophy* (Cambridge, MA: Harvard University Press,

1985), 182; Simon Blackburn, *Ruling Passions* (Oxford: Oxford University Press, 1998), especially chapter 5; Alphonso Lingis, *The First Person Singular* (Evanston: Northwestern University Press, 2007), chapter 7.

445. This term is of course one of the key concepts of *Phenomenology of Perception* and I will return to it in the following chapter to explicate Merleau-Ponty's idea of power. For a detailed study, see Aron Gurwitsch, *The Field of Consciousness* (Pittsburgh: Duquesne University Press, 1964).

446. DeLanda, *A New Philosophy of Society*, 13, 15.

447. Brian Massumi, *A User's Guide to Capitalism and Schizophrenia: Deviations from Deleuze and Guattari* (Cambridge, MA: MIT Press, 1992), 135.

448. John Protevi, *Political Affect: Connecting the Social and the Somatic* (Minneapolis: University of Minnesota Press, 2009), 50.

449. Deleuze and Guattari, *A Thousand Plateaus*, 314-315. Fuller analyses of performativity can be found in *A Thousand Plateaus*, but also in the work of Foucault, Butler, and Althusser in the continental tradition; Austin and Searle, in the analytic tradition.

450. Deleuze and Guattari, *A Thousand Plateaus*, 312.

451. Deleuze and Guattari, *A Thousand Plateaus*, 311.

452. Deleuze and Guattari, *A Thousand Plateaus*, 314.

453. Rhythm gives us an immanent conception of form or code, as discussed earlier. Consider what Massumi, *A User's Guide*, 51, writes: "A pattern or repeated act is a 'code'. A code is always of a 'milieu', or relatively stable, often statistical, mixing of elements.... A code is the same as a 'form' in the sense discussed above (an order and organization of functions)."

454. Deleuze and Guattari, *A Thousand Plateaus*, 314.

455. Deleuze and Guattari, *A Thousand Plateaus*, 317 (emphasis in original).

456. Hans Jonas's *The Phenomenon of Life: Toward a Philosophical Biology* (Evanston: Northwestern University Press, 1966) is a notable exception to the claim that phenomenology generally neglects the natural and material aspects of our dependence on the environment. It is true that Merleau-Ponty thematizes maturation in "The Child's Relations with Others," but I would contend that his concern is fundamentally psychological, and does not consider the growth of the body qua material entity.

457. Dewey, *Human Nature and Conduct*, 70, 77.

458. Dewey, *Human Nature and Conduct*, 47.

459. Dewey, *Human Nature and Conduct*, 38.

460. John Dewey, *Democracy and Education* (New York: The Free Press, 1944), 44.

461. Alva Noë, *Out of Our Heads* (New York: Hill and Wang, 2009), 51.

462. James, *Principles*, vol. 1, 122. Italics in original.

463. John Dewey, *Experience and Nature* (Mineola: Dover, 1958), 281. Malabou discusses the "explosive" connotation of plasticity and links this explosiveness to vitality as such (*What Should We Do with Our Brain?*, 5, 72), a point I contest in the following chapter.

464. Johnson, *The Meaning of the Body*, 75.
465. Johnson, *The Meaning of the Body*, 75.
466. Johnson, *The Meaning of the Body*, 76.
467. Johnson, *The Meaning of the Body*, 83.
468. Casey, *Getting Back into Place*, 223.
469. Casey, *Getting Back into Place*, 224.
470. I am indebted to Patrick Craig for alerting me to this point in Casey's work and for much helpful discussion of the problems of Casey's phenomenological method. The problems in Casey's early work seem to be overcome in *The World At a Glance* (Bloomington: Indiana University Press, 2007), although I have not yet worked through this text.
471. Immanuel Kant, *Grounding for the Metaphysics of Morals*, third edition, trans. James W. Ellington (Indianapolis: Hackett, 1993), 25.
472. Lingis, *The Imperative*, 3.
473. Lingis, *The Imperative*, 4.
474. Lingis, *Sensation*, 33.
475. Lingis, *Sensation*, 33.
476. Lingis, *Sensation*, 33, 35, 36-37.
477. Jonas, *The Phenomenon of Life*, 75.
478. Jonas, *The Phenomenon of Life*, 75, 76, note 13.
479. Andrieu, "Brains in the Flesh," 137.
480. Jonas, *The Phenomenon of Life*, 78.
481. Jonas, *The Phenomenon of Life*, 79.
482. Bennett, *Vibrant Matter*, 50.
483. Henri Bergson, *The Creative Mind*, trans. Mabelle L. Andison (New York: Citadel, 1974), 231. For an ethnographic study of some of the themes under discussion, see Nick Crossley, "The Circuit Trainer's Habitus: Reflexive Body Techniques and the Sociality of the Workout," *Body & Society* 10, no. 1 (2004): 37-69.
484. Yukio Mishima, *Sun and Steel*, trans. John Bester (New York: Kodansha, 1970), 24-25.
485. Mishima, *Sun and Steel*, 25-26.
486. Lingis, *Foreign Bodies*, 82.
487. Mishima, *Sun and Steel*, 28, 32. "Just as muscles slowly increase their resemblance to steel, so we are gradually fashioned by the world...."
488. Mishima, *Sun and Steel*, 26.
489. Metabolism is a key concept in Marx as well. For instance, in *Capital*, vol. 1, trans. Ben Fowkes (London: Penguin, 1992), 133, he calls labor "the eternal natural necessity which mediates the metabolism between man and nature...." The term appears several more times in his text.

490. Peter Zumthor, *Atmospheres* (Basel: Birkhäuser, 2006), 13. On this point, see also Teresa Brennan, *The Transmission of Affect* (Durham: Duke University Press, 2002).

491. Zumthor, *Atmospheres*, 23.

492. Zumthor, *Atmospheres*, 33. See also Joy Monice Malnar and Frank Vodvarka, *Sensory Design* (Minneapolis: University of Minnesota Press, 2004).

493. See Juhani Pallasmaa, "An Architecture of the Seven Senses," in Steven Holl et al. (eds.), *Questions of Perception* (San Francisco: William Stout, 2008), 36-37.

494. Pallasmaa, "An Architecture of the Seven Senses," 30.

495. Pallasmaa, "An Architecture of the Seven Senses," 31. The "Sounds" chapter of Thoreau's *Walden* illustrates the aural identity of its namesake. The birdsongs, train whistles and cars, bells, etc., that Thoreau records get coded as "Walden." From the standpoint of the ear, Walden just is this aggregate of sounds.

496. Pallasmaa, "An Architecture of the Seven Senses," 36. Pallasmaa sees the skin as central to this process. He explores this further in *The Eyes of the Skin: Architecture and the Senses*, second edition (Academy Press, 2005).

497. Pallasmaa, "An Architecture of the Seven Senses," 41.

498. Impressions are here taken in Hume's non-representational sense to connote the *force* they exert on us, whether physical (scraping, pinching, cutting) or affective (distress, somberness, elation). Hume, *An Enquiry Concerning Human Understanding*, 10.

499. Deleuze, *Spinoza: Practical Philosophy*, 127-128.

500. Dewey, *Art As Experience*, 37.

501. On the production of subjectivity from an empiricist standpoint, with an emphasis on the function of habit, see Gilles Deleuze, *Empiricism and Subjectivity: An Essay on Hume's Theory of Human Nature*, trans. Constantin V. Boundas (New York: Columbia University Press, 1991), especially chapter 5. See also Martin Jay, *Songs of Experience: Modern American and European Variations on a Universal Theme* (Berkeley: University of California Press, 2005), chapter 4, which stages, between Kant and Dewey, a confrontation over the body's place in aesthetic experience.

502. Mach, *The Analysis of Sensations*, 6-7.

503. William James, *The Principles of Psychology*, vol. 2 (New York: Dover, 1918), 35.

504. James, *Principles*, vol. 2, 8.

505. See chapter 1 for an alternate exposition of these points.

506. See what he says about the "law of contrast" in *Principles*, vol. 2, 13-31.

507. Heller-Roazen, *The Inner Touch*, 23.

508. Aristotle, *De Anima*, 415b25, says that "no thing without soul can have sensations." As Heller-Roazen puts it, "On the scale of increasing vital complexity and diversification, a threshold separates those beings with a nutritive faculty, but not more [i.e., plants], from those living things with more able souls. It is *aisthēsis*." *The Inner Touch*, 25.

509. On this point, see Fred Evans, "'Unnatural Participations': Merleau-Ponty, Deleuze, and Environmental Ethics," *Philosophy Today* 54, SPEP Supplement (2010): 142-152.

Conclusion

510. Elizabeth Grosz, *Architecture from the Outside: Essays on Virtual and Real Space* (Cambridge, MA: MIT Press, 2001), 32.

511. Aira, *An Episode in the Life of a Landscape Painter*, 32-33. See the opening scene of chapter 1 above.

512. Spinoza, *Ethics*, Part III, Proposition 7; Part IV, Definition 8; Part 1, Proposition 11, Scholium (translation modified). In *Spinoza and Politics*, trans. Peter Snowdon (London: Verso, 2008), Étienne Balibar demonstrates the several ways in which Spinoza's metaphysics is identical to his practical philosophy. As he says, "His work is not divided into a metaphysics (or an ontology) on the one hand and a politics or an ethics, which are seen as 'secondary' applications of 'first' philosophy, on the other. From the very beginning, his metaphysics is a philosophy of praxis, of activity; and his politics is a philosophy, for it constitutes the field of experience in which human nature acts and strives to achieve liberation" (102).

513. "Much of what is the 'individualism' of the early nineteenth century has in truth little to do with the nature of individuals. It goes back to a metaphysics which held that harmony between man and nature can be taken for granted, if once certain artificial restrictions upon man are removed." *Human Nature and Conduct*, 210.

514. For a critique of this view, see Elaine P. Miller, "Bodies and the Power of Vulnerability: Thinking Democracy and Subjectivity Outside the Logic of Confrontation," *Philosophy Today* 46 (2002): 102-112.

515. Michel Foucault, *Ethics: Subjectivity and Truth*, ed. Paul Rabinow (New York: The New Press, 1997), 261.

516. Bennett, *Vibrant Matter*, 23, 31-32.

517. Spinoza, *Ethics*, Part II, Proposition 13, Scholium; Part II, Definition 7 reads: "By singular things (res singulares) I mean things that are finite and have a determinate existence. If several singular things concur in one act in such a way as to be all together the simultaneous cause of one effect, I consider them all, in that respect, as one singular thing" (translation modified).

518. Gilles Deleuze and Félix Guattari, *What is Philosophy?*, trans. Hugh Tomlinson and Graham Burchell (New York: Columbia University Press, 1994), 164.

519. Malabou, *What Should We Do with Our Brain?*, 70.

520. Malabou, *What Should We Do with Our Brain?*, 71.

521. Malabou, *What Should We Do with Our Brain?*, 72.

522. Malabou, *What Should We Do with Our Brain?*, 71.

523. This gap is embodied in the distance that exists between neurons and is emblematic of the aleatory aspect of self-creation. *What Should We Do with Our Brain?*, 36.

272 Notes

524. See Catherine Malabou, *The New Wounded: From Neurosis to Brain Damage*, trans. Steven Miller (New York: Fordham University Press, 2012).

525. Catherine Malabou, *Plasticity At the Dusk of Writing: Dialectic, Destruction, Deconstruction*, trans. Carolyn Shread (New York: Columbia University Press, 2010), 61.

526. Friedrich Nietzsche, "Why I Am a Destiny," §1, in *On the Genealogy of Morals* and *Ecce Homo*, trans. Walter Kaufmann (New York: Vintage, 1967).

527. Weiss, *Refiguring the Ordinary*, 87.

528. Weiss, *Refiguring the Ordinary*, 81, 87. Her solution is to show that Merleau-Ponty's habit body affords us new possibilities for recreating our habits and, as a result, "dilating our being in the world."

529. Michel Serres, *The Five Senses: A Philosophy of Mingled Bodies*, trans. Margaret Sankey and Peter Cowley (London: Continuum, 2008), 29.

530. James, *Principles*, vol. 1, 104: "The laws of Nature are nothing but the immutable habits which the different elementary sorts of matter follow in their actions and reactions upon each other."

531. Spinoza denies, on metaphysical grounds, that contingency (and, in a sense, possibility) exists. The illusion of contingency and freedom is a product of our ignorance of efficient causes (Ethics, Part I, Proposition 33, Scholium). See also Michael LeBuffe, *From Bondage to Freedom: Spinoza on Human Excellence* (Oxford: Oxford University Press, 2010), 34. Dewey's defense of freedom puts a positive spin on this ignorance to save the phenomenon, writing that "if objective uncertainty is the stimulus to reflection, then variation in action, novelty and experiment, have a true meaning." *Human Nature and Conduct*, 213. It seems to me that Dewey's view is close to Merleau-Ponty's in its treatment of freedom as a positive phenomenon, but this definition evades the ontological question of freedom.

532. Discussing the nature of freedom, Dewey highlights how organization tends toward rigidity because there is "no effective or objective freedom without organization." *Human Nature and Conduct*, 211, 212.

533. Pleasurable affects transition us to a greater degree of perfection, as Spinoza says at *Ethics*, Part III, Proposition 11, Scholium.

534. Noë, *Out of Our Heads*, 49-50.

535. Dewey, *Democracy and Education*, 42, 44.

536. This idea, which follows Jacques Rancière's analyses of how the sensible realm is politically and aesthetically partitioned, is given clear explication in the Prologue to Panagia, *The Political Life of Sensation*. See also Jacques Rancière, *The Politics of Aesthetics*, trans. Gabriel Rockhill (London: Continuum, 2004).

537. Malabou, *Plasticity At the Dusk of Writing*, 67, italics omitted. I am following here the "dark" political ecology of Timothy Morton's *The Ecological Thought* and the ecological conception of politics advanced by Jane Bennett, particularly in chapter 7 of *Vibrant Matter*.

538. Deleuze, *Nietzsche and Philosophy*, 17.

539. For more on how identity is done and undone, see Judith Butler, *Undoing Gender* (London: Routledge, 2004).

540. Levinas, "Reality and Its Shadow," 4.

541. Panagia, *The Political Life of Sensation*, 108.

542. Many environmental aestheticians and architectural theorists, often inspired by phenomenology, have already caught onto this. The work of Arakawa and Gins is especially instructive, and I must thank Bobby George for leading me to it. Foucault, too, was onto this, as is evidenced in his remarks on the relation between technologies of domination and technologies of the self, and the possibility of reconstructing oneself by reconstructing the technologies of civilization. See, for instance, "About the Beginnings of the Hermeneutics of the Self: Two Lectures at Dartmouth," *Political Theory* 21, no. 2 (1993): 198-227.

543. Paul Duncum, "A Case for an Art Education of Everyday Aesthetic Experiences," *Studies in Art Education* 40, no. 4 (Summer 1999): 295-311. Cited in Saito, *Everyday Aesthetics*, 14.

544. Dewey, *Human Nature and Conduct*, 47, 211; *Democracy and Education*, chapter 4.

545. Spinoza, *Ethics*, Part III, Propositions 6-8; Part IV, Proposition 44, Scholium. Compare Levinas on enjoyment.

546. Deleuze and Guattari, *What is Philosophy?*, 164.

547. Serres, *The Five Senses*, 28-29.

548. Spinoza, *Ethics*, Part I, Definition 7; Part IV, Definition 8; Proposition 18, Scholium.

549. Balibar, *Spinoza and Politics*, 59, italics omitted.

550. Deleuze, *Spinoza: Practical Philosophy*, 127-128; Deleuze and Guattari, *A Thousand Plateaus*, 256-257.

551. Deleuze and Guattari, *A Thousand Plateaus*, 257.

552. Spinoza, *Ethics*, Part II, Proposition 49, Scholium; Part V, Proposition 10, Scholium; Proposition 42, Scholium. This is a principle Spinoza adopts from the Stoics. See Susan James, "Spinoza the Stoic," in *The Rise of Modern Philosophy*, ed. Tom Sorrell (Oxford: Clarendon, 1993), 289-316. See also LeBuffe, *From Bondage to Freedom*, 34.

553. Spinoza, *Ethics*, Part III, Proposition 2, Scholium.

554. Michel Foucault, "What is Enlightenment?" in *The Foucault Reader*, 50.

Works Cited

All citations of Levinas and Merleau-Ponty (excepting Levinas's "Reality and Its Shadow") include English and French pagination, respectively.

By Emmanuel Levinas

Collected Philosophical Papers. Edited by Alphonso Lingis. Pittsburgh: Duquesne University Press, 1987.

"Diachrony and Representation." In *Entre Nous*.

Discovering Existence with Husserl. Translated by Richard A. Cohen and Michael B. Smith. Evanston: Northwestern University Press, 1998. Translation of *En découvrant l'existence avec Husserl et Heidegger*. Paris: Vrin, 1967.

Entre Nous: Thinking-of-the-Other. Translated by Michael B. Smith and Barbara Harshav. New York: Columbia University Press, 1998. Translation of *Entre nous: essais sur le penser-à-l'autre*. Paris: Grasset, 1991.

Existence and Existents. Translated by Alphonso Lingis. Pittsburgh: Duquesne University Press, 1988. Translation of *De l'existence a l'existant*. Paris: Vrin, 1978.

"From Consciousness to Wakefulness." In *Discovering Existence with Husserl*.

"Intentionality and Sensation." In *Discovering Existence with Husserl*.

"Is Ontology Fundamental?" In *Entre Nous*.

"No Identity." In *Collected Philosophical Papers*. Translation of "Sans identité." In *Humanisme de l'autre homme*. Montpellier: Fata Morgana, 1972.

Otherwise than Being, or Beyond Essence. Translated by Alphonso Lingis. Pittsburgh: Duquesne University Press, 1997. Translation of *Autrement qu'être ou au-delà de l'essence*. La Haye: Nijhoff, 1974.

"Reality and Its Shadow." In *Collected Philosophical Papers*. Translation of "La réalité et son ombre." *Les Temps Modernes* 38 (1948): 771-789.

"The Ruin of Representation." In *Discovering Existence with Husserl*.

"Sensibility." In *Ontology and Alterity in Merleau-Ponty*, edited by Galen A. Johnson and Michael B. Smith. Translation of "De la sensibilité." In *Hors Sujet*. Montpellier: Fata Morgana, 1987.

Time and the Other. Translated by Richard A. Cohen. Pittsburgh: Duquesne University Press, 1987. Translation of *Le temps et l'autre*. Montpellier: Fata Morgana, 1979.

Totality and Infinity: An Essay on Exteriority. Translated by Alphonso Lingis. Pittsburgh: Duquesne University Press, 1969. Translation of *Totalité et infini: essai sur l'extériorité*. The Hague: Nijhoff, 1961.

By Maurice Merleau-Ponty

"Cézanne's Doubt." In *Sense and Non-Sense*. Translation of "Le doute de Cézanne." In *Sens et non-sense*. Paris: Les Editions de Nagel, 1948.

"The Child's Relations With Others." In *The Primacy of Perception*. Translation of *Les relations avec autrui chez l'enfant*. Paris: Centre de Documentation Universitaire, 1975.

"Eye and Mind." In *The Primacy of Perception*. Translation of *L'oeil et l'esprit*. Paris: Gallimard, 1964.

"Indirect Language and the Voices of Silence." In *Signs*.

Nature. Translated by Robert Vallier. Evanston: Northwestern University Press, 2003. Translation of *La nature, cours du Collège de France*. Paris: Éditions du Seuil, 1994.

Phenomenology of Perception. Translated by Colin Smith (London: Routledge and Kegan Paul, 1962). Translation of *Phénoménologie de la perception*. Paris: Gallimard, 1945.

The Visible and the Invisible. Translated by Alphonso Lingis. Evanston: Northwestern University Press, 1968. Translation of *Le visible et l'invisible*. Paris: Gallimard, 1964.

"The Philosopher and His Shadow." In *Signs*.

"The Primacy of Perception and its Philosophical Consequences." In *The Primacy of Perception*. Translation of *Le Primat de la perception et ses conséquences philosophiques*. Grenoble: Cynara, 1989.

The Primacy of Perception and Other Essays on Phenomenological Psychology, the Philosophy of Art, History and Politics. Edited by James M. Edie. Evanston: Northwestern University Press, 1964.

Signs. Translated by Richard C. McCleary. Evanston: Northwestern University Press, 1964. Translation of *Signes*. Paris: Gallimard, 1960.

The Structure of Behavior. Translated by Alden Fisher. Pittsburgh: Duquesne University Press, 1963. Translation of *Le structure de comportement*. Paris: Presses Universitaires de France, 1953.

Other Texts

Ahmed, Sara. "A Phenomenology of Whiteness." *Feminist Theory* 8, no. 2 (2007): 149-168.

Aira, César. *An Episode in the Life of a Landscape Painter*. Translated by Chris Andrews. New York: New Directions, 2006.

Al-Saji, Alia. "'A Past Which Has Never Been Present': Bergsonian Dimensions in Merleau-Ponty's Theory of the Prepersonal." *Research in Phenomenology* 38 (2008): 41-71.

----------. "Rhythms of the Body: A Study of Sensation, Time and Intercorporeity in the Phenomenology of Edmund Husserl." PhD diss., Emory University, 2002.

----------. "The Site of Affect in Husserl's Phenomenology: Sensations and the Constitution of the Lived Body." *Philosophy Today* 44, SPEP Supplement (2000): 51-59.

Althusser, Louis. "Ideology and the Ideological State Apparatus." In *Lenin and Philosophy and Other Essays*. Translated by Ben Brewster. New York: Monthly Review Press, 2001.

Andrieu, Bernard. "Brains in the Flesh: Prospects for a Neurophenomenology." *Janus Head* 9, no. 1 (2006): 135-155.

Aristotle. *De Anima*. Translated by Hippocrates G. Apostle. Grinnell: Peripatetic Press, 1981.

Austin, J.L. *Sense and Sensibilia*. London: Oxford University Press, 1962.

Ayer, A.J. *The Foundations of Empirical Knowledge*. New York: Macmillan, 1940.

Balibar, Étienne. *Spinoza and Politics*. Translated by Peter Snowdon. London: Verso, 2008.

Barbaras, Renaud. "Affectivity and Movement: The Sense of Sensing in Erwin Straus." Translated by Elizabeth A. Behnke. *Phenomenology and the Cognitive Sciences* 3 (2004): 215-228.

----------. *The Being of the Phenomenon: Merleau-Ponty's Ontology*. Translated by Ted Toadvine and Leonard Lawlor. Bloomington: Indiana University Press, 2004.

Benedikt, Michael. *For An Architecture of Reality*. New York: Lumen, 1987.

Bennett, Jane. *Vibrant Matter: A Political Ecology of Things*. Durham: Duke University Press, 2010.

Benso, Silvia. "The Breathing of the Air: Presocratic Echoes in Levinas." In *Levinas and the Ancients*, edited by Brian Schroeder and Silvia Benso. Bloomington: Indiana University Press, 2008.

----------. *The Face of Things: A Different Side of Ethics*. Albany: State University of New York Press, 2000.

Bergson, Henri. *The Creative Mind*. Translated by Mabelle L. Andison. New York: Citadel, 1974.

----------. *Two Sources of Morality and Religion*. Translated by R. Ashley Audra and Cloudesley Brereton. Notre Dame: University of Notre Dame Press, 1977.

Berkeley, George. *A Treatise Concerning the Principles of Human Knowledge*. Indianapolis: Hackett, 1982.

Bernet, Rudolf. "The Encounter with the Stranger: Two Interpretations of the Vulnerability of the Skin." In *The Face of the Other and the Trace of God*, edited by Jeffrey Bloechl. New York: Fordham University Press, 2000.

Blackburn, Simon. *Ruling Passions*. Oxford: Oxford University Press, 1998.

Braver, Lee. *A Thing of This World: A History of Continental Anti-Realism*. Evanston: Northwestern University Press, 2007.

Brennan, Teresa. *The Transmission of Affect*. Durham: Duke University Press, 2002.

Bruzina, Ronald. "Method and Materiality in the Phenomenology of Intersubjectivity." *Philosophy Today* 41, SPEP Supplement (1997): 127-133.

Bryant, Levi. *The Democracy of Objects*. Ann Arbor: Open Humanities Press, 2011.

---------. "The Ontic Principle: Outline of an Object-Oriented Ontology." In *The Speculative Turn: Continental Materialism and Realism*, edited by Levi Bryant, Nick Srnicek, and Graham Harman. Melbourne: re.press, 2011.

Butler, Judith. "Foucault and the Paradox of Bodily Inscriptions." *The Journal of Philosophy* 86, no. 11 (November 1989): 601-607.

----------. "Sexual Ideology and Phenomenological Description: A Feminist Critique of Merleau-Ponty's *Phenomenology of Perception*." In *The Thinking Muse: Feminism and Modern French Philosophy*, edited by Jeffner Allen and Iris Marion Young. Bloomington: Indiana University Press, 1989.

---------. *Undoing Gender*. London: Routledge, 2004.

Carlisle, Clare. "Creatures of Habit: The Problem and the Practice of Liberation." *Continental Philosophy Review* 38 (2006): 19-39.

Carman, Taylor. "Sensation, Judgment, and the Phenomenal Field." In *The Cambridge Companion to Merleau-Ponty*, edited by Taylor Carman and Mark B.N. Hansen. New York: Cambridge University Press, 2005.

Casey, Edward S. *Getting Back into Place*. Bloomington: Indiana University Press, 1993.

----------. "Habitual Body and Memory in Merleau-Ponty." *Man and World* 17, no. 3/4 (1984): 279-297.

----------. *The World At a Glance*. Bloomington: Indiana University Press, 2007.

Chalier, Catherine. *What Ought I to Do? Morality in Kant and Levinas*. Translated by Jane Marie Todd. Ithaca: Cornell University Press, 2002.

Churchland, Patricia Smith. *Neurophilosophy: Toward a Unified Science of the Mind-Brain*. Cambridge, MA: MIT Press, 1989.

Churchland, Paul. *A Neurocomputational Perspective: The Nature of Mind and the Structure of Science*. Cambridge, MA: MIT Press, 1992.

Clark, Andy. *Being There: Putting Brain, Body, and World Together Again*. Cambridge, MA: MIT Press, 1997.

----------. "Re-inventing Ourselves: The Plasticity of Embodiment, Sensing, and Mind." *Journal of Medicine and Philosophy* 32 (2007): 263-282.

Coole, Diana. *Merleau-Ponty and Modern Politics After Anti-Humanism*. Lanham: Rowman and Littlefield, 2007.

Crossley, Nick. "The Circuit Trainer's Habitus: Reflexive Body Techniques and the Sociality of the Workout." *Body & Society* 10, no. 1 (2004): 37-69.

DeLanda, Manuel. *A New Philosophy of Society: Assemblage Theory and Social Complexity*. London: Continuum, 2006.

----------. "Immanence and Transcendence in the Genesis of Form." *The South Atlantic Quarterly* 96, no. 3 (Summer 1997): 499-514.

Deleuze, Gilles. *Empiricism and Subjectivity: An Essay on Hume's Theory of Human Nature*. Translated by Constantin V. Boundas. New York: Columbia University Press, 1991.

----------. *Difference and Repetition*. Translated by Paul Patton. New York: Columbia University Press, 1995.

----------. *Francis Bacon: The Logic of Sensation*. Translated by Daniel W. Smith. Minneapolis: University of Minnesota Press, 2004.

----------. *Nietzsche and Philosophy.* Translated by Hugh Tomlinson. New York: Columbia University Press, 1983.

----------. *Pure Immanence: Essays on a Life.* Translated by Anne Boyman. New York: Zone, 2001.

----------. *Spinoza: Practical Philosophy.* Translated by Robert Hurley. San Francisco: City Lights, 1988.

Deleuze, Gilles and Félix Guattari. *A Thousand Plateaus.* Translated by Brian Massumi. Minneapolis: University of Minnesota Press, 1987.

----------. *Anti-Oedipus.* Translated by Robert Hurley, Mark Seem, and Helen R. Lane. Minneapolis: University of Minnesota Press, 1983.

----------. *What is Philosophy?* Translated by Hugh Tomlinson and Graham Burchell. New York: Columbia University Press, 1994.

Depraz, Natalie. "L'incarnation phénoménologique, un problème non-théologique?" *Tijdschrift voor Filosofie* 55, no. 3 (1993): 496-518.

Derrida, Jacques. *On Touching—Jean-Luc Nancy.* Translated by Christine Irizarry. Stanford: Stanford University Press, 2005.

Descartes, René. *Meditations on First Philosophy.* In *Philosophical Essays and Correspondence.* Edited by Roger Ariew. Indianapolis: Hackett, 2000.

Dewey, John. *Art As Experience.* New York: Penguin, 1934.

----------. *Democracy and Education.* New York: The Free Press, 1944.

----------. *Experience and Nature.* Mineola: Dover, 1958.

----------. *Human Nature and Conduct.* Carbondale and Edwardsville: Southern Illinois University Press, 1988.

Diehm, Christian. "Facing Nature: Levinas Beyond the Human." *Philosophy Today* 44, no. 1 (Spring 2000): 51-59.

Dillon, M.C. "Apriority in Kant and Merleau-Ponty." *Kant-Studien* 17, no. 3 (1987): 403-423.

----------. *Merleau-Ponty's Ontology*, second edition. Evanston: Northwestern University Press, 1988.

Dodd, James. *Idealism and Corporeity: An Essay on the Problem of the Body in Husserl's Phenomenology*. Dordrecht: Kluwer, 1997.

Drabinski, John. E. "From Representation to Materiality." *International Studies in Philosophy* 30, no. 4 (1998): 23-37.

----------. *Sensibility and Singularity: The Problem of Phenomenology in Levinas*. Albany: State University of New York Press, 2001.

Dreyfus, Hubert. "Merleau-Ponty's Critique of Mental Representation: The Relevance of Phenomenology to Scientific Explanation" (1998), http://www.class.uh.edu/cogsci/dreyfus.html

Duncum, Paul. "A Case for an Art Education of Everyday Aesthetic Experiences." *Studies in Art Education* 40, no. 4 (Summer 1999): 295-311.

Epicurus. *The Extant Remains*. Translated by Cyril Bailey. Oxford: Oxford University Press, 1926.

Evans, Fred. "'Solar love': Nietzsche, Merleau-Ponty, and the Fortunes of Perception." *Continental Philosophy Review* 31 (1998): 171-193.

----------. "'Unnatural Participations': Merleau-Ponty, Deleuze, and Environmental Ethics." *Philosophy Today* 54, SPEP Supplement (2010): 142-152.

Fanon, Frantz. *Black Skin, White Masks*. New York: Grove Press, 1967.

Foucault, Michel. "About the Beginnings of the Hermeneutics of the Self: Two Lectures at Dartmouth." *Political Theory* 21, no. 2 (1993): 198-227.

----------. *Discipline and Punish*. Translated by Alan Sheridan. New York: Vintage, 1977.

----------. *Ethics: Subjectivity and Truth*. Edited by Paul Rabinow. New York: The New Press, 1997.

----------. "Nietzsche, Genealogy, History." In *The Foucault Reader*. Edited by Paul Rabinow. New York: Pantheon, 1984.

----------. *The Order of Things*. Translator not provided. New York: Vintage, 1970.

----------. *Remarks on Marx*. Translated by R. James Goldstein and James Cascaito. New York: Semiotext(e), 1991.

----------. "What is Enlightenment?" In *The Foucault Reader*.

Gallagher, Shaun. *How the Body Shapes the Mind*. Oxford: Oxford University Press, 2005.

----------. "Lived Body and Environment." *Research in Phenomenology* 16 (1986): 139-170.

Gallagher, Shaun and Dan Zahavi. *The Phenomenological Mind: An Introduction to Philosophy of Mind and Cognitive Science*. London: Routledge, 2008.

Grosz, Elizabeth. *Volatile Bodies: Toward a Corporeal Feminism*. Bloomington: Indiana University Press, 1994.

----------. *Architecture from the Outside: Essays on Virtual and Real Space*. Cambridge, MA: MIT Press, 2001.

Gueroult, Martial. *Spinoza II—L'âme*. Paris: Aubier, 1997.

Guerrière, Daniel. "Table of Contents of '*Phenomenology of Perception*:' Translation and Pagination." *Journal of the British Society for Phenomenology* 10, no. 1 (1979): 65-69.

Gurwitsch, Aron. *The Field of Consciousness*. Pittsburgh: Duquesne University Press, 1964.

Hamlyn, D.W. *Sensation and Perception: A History of the Philosophy of Perception*. New York: Humanities Press, 1961.

Harman, Graham. "Aesthetics as First Philosophy: Levinas and the Non-Human." *Naked Punch* 9 (Summer/Fall 2007): 21-30.

----------. *Guerrilla Metaphysics: Phenomenology and the Carpentry of Things*. Chicago and La Salle: Open Court, 2005.

----------. "Levinas and the Triple Critique of Heidegger." *Philosophy Today* 53 (Winter 2009): 407-413.

----------. *Tool-Being: Heidegger and the Metaphysics of Objects*. Chicago and La Salle: Open Court, 2002.

Hass, Lawrence. *Merleau-Ponty's Philosophy*. Bloomington: Indiana University Press, 2008.

Hegel, G.W.F. *Encyclopedia Logic*. Translated by T. F. Geraets et al. Indianapolis: Hackett, 1991.

----------. *Phenomenology of Spirit*. Translated by A.V. Miller. Oxford: Oxford University Press, 1977.

Heidegger, Martin. *Being and Time*. Translated by John Macquarrie and Edward Robinson. San Francisco: Harper Collins, 1962.

----------. *Kant and the Problem of Metaphysics*, fifth edition, enlarged. Translated by Richard Taft. Bloomington: Indiana University Press, 1997.

Heller-Roazen, Daniel. *The Inner Touch: Archaeology of a Sensation*. New York: Zone, 2007.

Henry, Michel. *The Essence of Manifestation*. Translated by Girard Etzkorn. Dordrecht: Springer, 2008.

----------. *Philosophy and Phenomenology of the Body*. Translated by Girard Etzkorn. The Hague: Nijhoff, 1975.

Hume, David. *Enquiry Concerning Human Understanding*, second edition. Indianapolis: Hackett, 1993.

Husserl, Edmund. *The Crisis of the European Sciences and Transcendental Phenomenology*. Translated by David Carr. Evanston: Northwestern University Press, 1970.

----------. *Ideas: General Introduction to Pure Phenomenology*. Translated by W.R. Boyce Gibson. New York: Collier, 1962. Cited as *Ideas* I.

----------. *Ideas Pertaining to a Pure Phenomenology and to a Phenomenological Philosophy*, Second Book. Translated by Richard Rojcewicz and Andre Schuwer. Dordrecht, Kluwer, 1989. Cited as *Ideas* II.

----------. *Logical Investigations*, Two Volumes. Translated by J.N. Findlay. New York: Humanity, 1970.

Ihde, Don. *Bodies in Technology.* Minneapolis: University of Minnesota Press, 2002.

Irigaray, Luce. *An Ethics of Sexual Difference*. Translated by Carolyn Burke and Gillian C. Gill. Ithaca: Cornell University Press, 1993.

James, Susan. "Spinoza the Stoic." In *The Rise of Modern Philosophy*, edited by Tom Sorrell. Oxford: Clarendon Press, 1993.

James, William. *The Principles of Psychology*, volume 1. New York: Dover, 1918.

----------. *The Principles of Psychology*, volume 2. New York: Dover, 1918.

Jaspers, Karl. *General Psychopathology*. Translated by J. Hoenig and Marian W. Hamilton. Chicago: University of Chicago Press, 1963.

Jay, Martin. *Songs of Experience: Modern American and European Variations on a Universal Theme*. Berkeley: University of California Press, 2005.

Johnson, Galen A. (ed.), *The Merleau-Ponty Aesthetics Reader: Philosophy and Painting*. Evanston: Northwestern University Press, 1993.

Johnson, Galen A. and Michael B. Smith (eds.), *Ontology and Alterity in Merleau-Ponty*. Evanston: Northwestern University Press, 1990.

Johnson, Mark. *The Meaning of the Body: Aesthetics of Human Understanding*. Chicago: University of Chicago Press, 2007.

Jonas, Hans. *The Phenomenon of Life: Toward a Philosophical Biology*. Evanston: Northwestern University Press, 1966.

Kant, Immanuel. *Critique of Judgment*. Translated by Werner S. Pluhar. Indianapolis: Hackett, 1987.

----------. *Critique of Pure Reason*. Translated by Werner S. Pluhar. Indianapolis: Hackett, 1996.

----------. *Grounding for the Metaphysics of Morals*, third edition. Translated by James W. Ellington. Indianapolis: Hackett, 1993.

Keenan, Dennis King. *Death and Responsibility: The "Work" of Levinas*. Albany: State University of New York Press, 1999.

Lakoff, George and Mark Johnson. *Philosophy in the Flesh: The Embodied Mind and its Challenge to Western Thought*. New York: Basic Books, 1999.

LeBuffe, Michael. *From Bondage to Freedom: Spinoza on Human Excellence*. Oxford: Oxford University Press, 2010.

Leibniz, G.W. *New Essays on Human Understanding*, edited by Peter Remnant and Jonathan Bennett. Cambridge: Cambridge University Press, 1996.

Levin, David Michael. "The Embodiment of the Categorical Imperative: Kafka, Foucault, Benjamin, Adorno and Levinas." *Philosophy and Social Criticism* 27, no. 4 (2001): 1-20.

Lewis, Michael. "Individuation in Levinas and Heidegger: The One and the Incompleteness of Beings." *Philosophy Today* 51, no. 2 (Summer 2007): 198-215.

Lingis, Alphonso. *Body Transformations: Evolutions and Atavisms in Culture*. London: Routledge, 2005.

----------. *The First Person Singular*. Evanston: Northwestern University Press, 2007.

----------. *Foreign Bodies*. London: Routledge. 1994.

----------. *The Imperative*. Bloomington: Indiana University Press, 1994.

----------. *Libido: The French Existential Theories*. Bloomington: Indiana University Press, 1985.

----------. *Sensation: Intelligibility in Sensibility*. Atlantic Highlands: Humanities Press, 1996.

----------. "The Sensitive Flesh." In *The Collegium Phaenomenologicum: The First Ten Years*, edited by J.C. Sallis, G. Moneta, and Jacques Taminiaux. Dordrecht: Kluwer, 1989.

Locke, John. *An Essay Concerning Human Understanding*. Abridged and edited by Kenneth Winkler. Indianapolis: Hackett, 1996.

Mach, Ernst. *The Analysis of Sensations*. Translated by C.M. Williams and Sydney Waterlow. New York: Dover, 1959.

Madison, Gary Brent. *The Phenomenology of Merleau-Ponty: A Search for the Limits of Consciousness*. Athens, OH: Ohio University Press, 1981.

Malabou, Catherine. *What Should We Do with Our Brain?* Translated by Sebastian Rand. New York: Fordham University Press, 2008.

----------. *The New Wounded: From Neurosis to Brain Damage*. Translated by Steven Miller. New York: Fordham University Press, 2012.

----------. *Ontology of the Accident: An Essay on Destructive Plasticity*. Translated by Carolyn Shread. Malden: Polity, 2012.

----------. *Plasticity At the Dusk of Writing: Dialectic, Destruction, Deconstruction*. Translated by Carolyn Shread. New York: Columbia University Press, 2010.

Malnar, Joy Monice and Frank Vodvarka. *Sensory Design*. Minneapolis: University of Minnesota Press, 2004.

Manning, Robert John Sheffler. *Interpreting Otherwise than Heidegger: Emmanuel Levinas's Ethics as First Philosophy*. Pittsburgh: Duquesne University Press, 1993.

Massumi, Brian. *A User's Guide to Capitalism and Schizophrenia: Deviations from Deleuze and Guattari*. Cambridge, MA: MIT Press, 1992.

----------. *Parables for the Virtual: Movement, Affect, Sensation*. Durham: Duke University Press, 2002.

Marx, Karl. *Capital*, volume 1. Translated by Ben Fowkes. London: Penguin, 1992.

Mazis, Glen A. *Earthbodies: Rediscovering Our Planetary Senses*. Albany: State University of New York Press, 2002.

Meillassoux, Quentin. *After Finitude: An Essay on the Necessity of Contingency*. Translated by Ray Brassier. London: Continuum, 2008.

Miller, Elaine P. "Bodies and the Power of Vulnerability: Thinking Democracy and Subjectivity Outside the Logic of Domination." *Philosophy Today* 46, SPEP Supplement (2002): 102-112.

Mishima, Yukio. *Sun and Steel*. Translated by John Bester. New York: Kodansha, 1970.

Molnar, George. *Powers: A Study in Metaphysics*. Edited by Stephen Mumford. Oxford: Oxford University Press, 2003.

Morris, David. "The Logic of the Body in Bergson's Motor Schemes and Merleau-Ponty's Body Schema." *Philosophy Today* 44, SPEP Supplement (2000): 60-69.

----------. *The Sense of Space.* Albany: State University of New York Press, 2004.

Morton, Timothy. *The Ecological Thought.* Cambridge, MA: Harvard University Press, 2010.

----------. *Ecology without Nature.* Cambridge, MA: Harvard University Press, 2007.

Mullarkey, John C. "Duplicity in the Flesh: Bergson and Current Philosophy of the Body." *Philosophy Today* 38, no. 4 (Winter 1994): 339-355.

Mumford, Stephen. *Dispositions.* Oxford: Oxford University Press, 2003.

Nancy, Jean-Luc. *Corpus.* Translated by Richard A. Rand. New York: Fordham University Press, 2008.

Nietzsche, Friedrich. *On the Genealogy of Morality.* Translated by Maudemarie Clark and Alan J. Swensen. Indianapolis: Hackett, 1998.

----------. "Why I Am a Destiny." In *On the Genealogy of Morals* and *Ecce Homo.* Translated by Walter Kaufmann. New York: Vintage, 1967.

Noë, Alva. *Action in Perception.* Cambridge, MA: MIT Press, 2004.

----------. *Out of Our Heads: Why You Are Not Your Brain, and Other Lessons from the Biology of Consciousness.* New York: Hill and Wang, 2009.

Nuzzo, Angelica. *Ideal Embodiment: Kant's Theory of Sensibility.* Bloomington: Indiana University Press, 2008.

----------. "Kant and Herder on Baumgarten's *Aesthetica.*" *Journal of the History of Philosophy* 44, no. 4 (October 2006): 577-597.

Oksala, Johanna. "Female Freedom: Can the Lived Body Be Emancipated?" In *Feminist Interpretations of Maurice Merleau-Ponty.*

----------. *Foucault on Freedom.* Cambridge: Cambridge University Press, 2005.

Olivier, Abraham. *Being in Pain.* Frankfurt: Peter Lang, 2007.

Olkowski, Dorothea and Gail Weiss (eds.), *Feminist Interpretations of Maurice Merleau-Ponty.* University Park: Penn State University Press, 2006.

Pallasmaa, Juhani. "An Architecture of the Seven Senses." In Steven Holl et al., *Questions of Perception*. San Francisco: William Stout, 2008.

----------. *The Eyes of the Skin: Architecture and the Senses*, second edition. Hoboken: Wiley & Sons, 2005.

Panagia, Davide. *The Political Life of Sensation*. Durham: Duke University Press, 2009.

Peirce, C.S. and Joseph Jastrow. "On Small Differences in Sensation." <http://psychclassics.yorku.ca/Peirce/small-diffs.htm> Retrieved October 14, 2011.

Pietersma, Henry. "La place de Spinoza dans le pensée de Merleau-Ponty: convergence, entre les deux penseurs." *International Studies in Philosophy* 20, no. 3 (1988): 89-93.

Priest, Stephen. *Merleau-Ponty*. London: Routledge, 1998.

Protevi, John. *Political Affect: Connecting the Social and the Somatic*. Minneapolis: University of Minnesota Press, 2009.

Rancière, Jacques. *The Politics of Aesthetics*. Translated by Gabriel Rockhill. London: Continuum, 2004.

Ravaisson, Félix. *Of Habit*. Translated by Clare Carlisle and Mark Sinclair. London: Continuum, 2008.

Rockmore, Tom. *Cognition: An Introduction to Hegel's* Phenomenology of Spirit. Berkeley: University of California Press, 1997.

----------. *In Kant's Wake: Philosophy in the Twentieth Century*. Malden: Blackwell, 2006.

----------. *Kant and Phenomenology*. Chicago: University of Chicago Press, 2011.

Rousseau, Jean-Jacques. *Discourse on the Origin of Inequality*. Translated by Donald A. Cress. Indianapolis: Hackett, 1992.

Rowlands, Mark. *Externalism: Putting Mind and World Back Together Again*. Montreal: McGill-Queen's University Press, 2003.

Russell, Bertrand. *The Problems of Philosophy*. New York: Oxford University Press, 1997.

Russon, John. *The Self and Its Body in Hegel's* Phenomenology of Spirit. Toronto: University of Toronto Press, 2001.

Saito, Yuriko. *Everyday Aesthetics*. Oxford: Oxford University Press, 2007.

Sallis, John. "Levinas and the Elemental." *Research in Phenomenology* 28 (1998): 152-159.

----------. *Phenomenology and the Return to Beginnings*. New York: Humanities Press, 1973.

Sandford, Stella. "Levinas in the Realm of the Senses: Transcendence and Intelligibility." *Angelaki* 4, no. 3 (1999): 61-73.

Sartre, Jean-Paul. *Being and Nothingness*. Translated by Hazel E. Barnes. New York: Washington Square Press, 1993.

Schalow, Frank. *The Incarnality of Being: The Earth, Animals, and the Body in Heidegger's Thought*. Albany: State University of New York Press, 2007.

Scherer, Irmgard. "The Problem of the A Priori in Sensibility: Revisiting Kant's and Hegel's Theories of the Senses." *The Review of Metaphysics* 52, no. 2 (December 1998): 341-367.

Selcer, Daniel. "Singular Things and Spanish Poets: Spinoza on Corporeal Individuation." Paper presented at Spinoza and Bodies conference, University of Dundee, September 10-11, 2009.

Serres, Michel. *The Five Senses: A Philosophy of Mingled Bodies*. Translated by Margaret Sankey and Peter Cowley. London: Continuum, 2008.

Singer, Linda. "Merleau-Ponty on the Concept of Style." In *The Merleau-Ponty Aesthetics Reader*.

Smith, Bryan. "Merleau-Ponty and the 'Naturalization' of Phenomenology." *Philosophy Today* 54, SPEP Supplement (2010): 153-162.

Smith, Michael B. "Merleau-Ponty's Aesthetics." In *The Merleau-Ponty Aesthetics Reader*.

Sobchack, Vivian. *Carnal Thoughts: Embodiment and Moving Image Culture.* Berkeley: University of California Press, 2004.

Sparrow, Tom. "Bodies in Transit: The Plastic Subject of Alphonso Lingis." *Janus Head* 10, no. 1 (Summer/Fall 2007): 99-122.

---------. "Enabling/Disabling Sensation: Toward an Alimentary Imperative in Carnal Phenomenology. *Philosophy Today* 52, no. 2 (Summer 2008): 99-115

---------. *The End of Phenomenology: Metaphysics and the New Realism.* Edinburgh: Edinburgh University Press, 2014.

---------. *Levinas Unhinged.* Winchester, UK: Zero Books, 2013.

Spinoza, Baruch. *Ethics.* Translated by Samuel Shirley. Indianapolis: Hackett, 1992.

Starobinski, Jean. *Jean-Jacques Rousseau: Transparency and Obstruction.* Translated by Arthur Goldhammer. Chicago: University of Chicago Press, 1988.

Stawarska, Beata. "From the Body Proper to the Flesh: Merleau-Ponty on Intersubjectivity." In *Feminist Interpretations of Maurice Merleau-Ponty.*

Straus, Erwin. *The Primary World of Senses: A Vindication of Sensory Experience.* Translated by Jacob Needleman. London: Free Press of Glencoe, 1963.

----------."The Upright Posture." *Psychiatric Quarterly* 26 (1952): 529-561.

Sullivan, Shannon. *Living Across and Through Skins: Transactional Bodies, Pragmatism, and Feminism.* Bloomington: Indiana University Press, 2001.

Taylor, Charles. "The Validity of Transcendental Arguments." In *Philosophical Arguments.* Cambridge, MA: Harvard University Press, 1995.

Thoreau, Henry David. *Walden and Other Writings.* New York: Bantam, 1983.

Todes, Samuel. *Body and World.* Cambridge, MA: MIT Press, 2001.

Toscano, Alberto. *The Theatre of Production: Philosophy and Individuation between Kant and Deleuze.* New York: Palgrave, 2006.

Vasseleu, Cathryn. *Textures of Light: Vision and Touch in Irigaray, Levinas, and Merleau-Ponty.* London: Routledge, 1998.

Waehlens, Alphonse de. "Merleau-Ponty: Philosopher of Painting." In *The Merleau-Ponty Aesthetics Reader*.

Waldenfels, Bernhard. "The Paradox of Expression." Translated by Chris Nagel. In *Chiasms: Merleau-Ponty's Notion of Flesh*, edited by Fred Evans and Leonard Lawlor. Albany: State University of New York Press, 2000.

Weiss, Gail. *Refiguring the Ordinary*. Bloomington: Indiana University Press, 2008.

Wiesel, Elie. *Night*. Translated by Marion Wiesel. New York: Hill and Wang, 2006.

Williams, Bernard. *Ethics and the Limits of Philosophy*. Cambridge, MA: Harvard University Press, 1985.

Wood, David. "Some Questions for My Levinasian Friends." In *Addressing Levinas*, edited by Eric Sean Nelson, Antje Kapust, and Kent Still. Evanston: Northwestern University Press, 2005.

Yancy, George. *Black Bodies, White Gazes: The Continuing Significance of Race*. Lanham: Rowman and Littlefield, 2008.

Young, Iris Marion. *Throwing Like a Girl and Other Essays in Feminist Philosophy and Social Theory*. Bloomington: Indiana University Press, 1990.

Zahavi, Dan. "Alterity in Self." In *Ipseity and Alterity: Interdisciplinary Approaches to Intersubjectivity*, edited by Shaun Gallagher, Stephen Watson, Philippe Brun, and Philippe Romanski. Rouen: Presses Universitaires de Rouen, 2004.

Žižek, Slavoj. *Organs Without Bodies: On Deleuze and Consequences*. New York: Routledge, 2004.

Zumthor, Peter. *Atmospheres*. Basel: Birkhäuser, 2006.

www.ingramcontent.com/pod-product-compliance
Lightning Source LLC
Chambersburg PA
CBHW071807080526
44589CB00012B/721